7. 23.80

Running Healthy

Sidney Alexander, M.D.

RUNNING HEALTHY

A Guide to Cardiovascular Fitness

DRAWINGS BY FRANCIS E. STECKEL

THE STEPHEN GREENE PRESS
BRATTLEBORO, VERMONT

PHOTO CREDITS: Frontispiece, p. ii, courtesy of *The Boston Globe;* p. **24,** courtesy of Trainex Corporation, Garden Grove, Calif.; p. **79,** courtesy of Trainex Corporation, Garden Grove, Calif.; p. **99,** courtesy of Conventures, Inc.; p. **124,** courtesy of Steve Liggett and New England Running; p. **171,** courtesy of Steve Liggett and New England Running; p. **216,** the New York Marathon, 1977, photo by Susan Alexander; p. **224,** courtesy of Steve Liggett and New England Running; p. **239,** courtesy of Conventures, Inc., photo by Jean Duvoisin.

This book has been produced in the United States of America. It is designed by SUSAN D. PRINDLE, and published by THE STEPHEN GREENE PRESS, Fessenden Road, Brattleboro, Vermont, 05301.

Library of Congress Cataloging in Publication Data

ALEXANDER, SIDNEY, 1931–
  Running healthy.

  Bibliography: p.
  Includes index.

  1. Running—Physiological aspects—Miscellanea.
2. Cardiovascular system—Diseases—Prevention—
Miscellanea.   3. Physical fitness—Miscellanea.
I. Title.   [DNLM: 1. Running. 2. Cardiovascular
system—Physiology. 3. Physical fitness. 4. Exer-
tion. 3. Jogging. QT260 A318r (P)]
RC1220.R8A43   613.7'1   80–12387
ISBN 0–8289–0387–5

Contents

Preface

THIS BOOK is written for the millions of people who run, or who are planning to begin a running program, primarily to achieve fitness and good health. It is meant to serve as a guide and a reliable reference source which runners can trust. It will help them to run safely and allow them to increase the intensity and duration of their running programs so that they can achieve fitness and the other important benefits that running provides.

The book is not written for the competitive athlete anxious to maximize his performance. He had best look elsewhere. After all, I am a physician, not a coach, a trainer, or even an exercise physiologist. Nevertheless, I hope that even those involved in competitive running may benefit from reading some parts of this book.

Fitness and good health are best achieved, I believe, by understanding how the body and mind respond to an exercise program. For that reason, the physiology of exercise and training are described in some detail. Since the heart is the crucial link in the development of good health and fitness and the prevention of disease through running, I have defined at some length the so-called "risk factors" which clearly predispose people to heart and other health problems. Finally, I have surveyed the evidence that an effective running program can successfully modify these risk factors and perhaps slow the processes which lead to ill health. In doing this, I have tried always to distinguish carefully between what is sound scientific evidence and what is merely unjustified enthusiasm, particularly in such confusing and controversial areas as proper diet, blood pressure control, and even the potential benefits of exercise itself.

Physicians are increasingly asked by patients how a running program can help them and if they can safely begin to exercise. I am hopeful that doctors will be able to find answers to many of these questions in this book. I am also hopeful that patients with known heart problems who, with the help of their physicians, want to exercise safely, will find this book helpful.

As a cardiologist, I feel that I can speak with some authority about these topics. In describing the prevention and treatment of injuries to the bones, joints, and muscles, I speak not as an expert, but rather as an interested physician–runner who has learned from personal experience in treating his own and many patient's running injuries, from careful review of the important and ever-growing sports medicine literature, and from regularly observing and consulting colleagues who specialize in orthopedics and podiatry. The readers should also consult the experts, when the advice given here for dealing with running-related injuries is not successful.

Throughout the book the question and answer format has been used, because I believe that it is the best way to teach. I have found it far more effective for instructing patients than lecturing to them, and hope that it will be equally useful to readers.

Of course, no book comes to press as the sole effort of an individual, and I am grateful to many people who have helped me. Most important, perhaps, has been the continued stimulation of my patients, whose needs and intelligent questions spur me to learn. My family also deserves special accolades. They have encouraged me when the creative process slowed, gently and constructively criticized my often clumsy attempts to write, and tolerated me as the chore of writing was added to an already full and demanding schedule.

Many friends, patients, and colleagues have read this book at various stages of its preparation. Their suggestions have been most helpful. I especially want to thank Stephen Wasilewski, M.D., orthopedic surgeon and marathoner, who helped me so much with Chapter 7 and Diane Young, M.S., nutritionist, whose help in Chapter 9 was invaluable. The comments of Joseph Viola,

M.D., were also extremely helpful and Mary Lou Carraher was most helpful in arranging for many of the photographs.

Finally, few fledgling writers survive without a good editor, and I am no exception. Continually observant of my sometimes murky prose, unintelligible physician's jargon, and convoluted ideas, yet sensitive to my easily bruised ego, Susan Prindle immeasurably improved this book, cajoling me to rewrite where necessary or making the needed changes herself. I am most grateful to her.

CHAPTER *1*

Introduction

Q. WHY STILL ANOTHER book about running?

A. Runners want and need a reference source they can trust. It has been estimated that between ten and twenty million people in this country are jogging or running regularly. Many of them are doing it chiefly for health reasons. They want to feel better and perhaps live longer. Although a number of books about running have recently been published, none has been authoritative or detailed enough concerning the effects that running or other similar exercise has on health, what real benefits a person who begins a running program might expect, and what precautions should be taken.

While all runners might benefit from reading this book, it is written particularly for two groups of people: those over 30 who plan to begin or have just started an exercise program, and those who may have a minor or even major heart or vascular problem. I feel strongly about the usefulness of regular exercise in the promotion of health and prevention of disease. I would like as many people as possible to exercise wisely and well.

I also believe that running can be more effective and safer if the runner understands the physiology of exercise and what an exercise program can do for the heart, blood vessels, and other parts of the body. The person about to begin a running program must learn how to begin without injury, what diet is likely to be

1

best, and what danger signs of possible injury or ill health to look for. All these questions will be discussed in detail.

This book should be helpful to physicians who treat runners as well as to runners themselves. The runner needs a doctor who understands and is sympathetic to his unique problems, yet at the same time is not so romantically involved with running that he can't offer sound medical advice. So many outrageous statements have been made about the value of running, that I feel the record needs to be set straight. Running *is* beneficial and often fun. But it is rarely transcendental, mystical, or religious. Moreover, runners do become ill, they don't live forever, their sex lives aren't perfect, and they generally have the same problems as most of the rest of the population.

Q. What are your credentials for writing this book?

A. I have been running for a long time, and firmly believe that books which attempt to offer medical or technical advice about running are more likely to be helpful if they are written by runners. I have lived through many of the problems that runners often face in beginning and trying to maintain a running program. I have had to find doctors for myself who understand runner's injuries and who would not tell me to stop running, because that was the only treatment that was unacceptable.

I am a physician, a cardiologist or heart specialist. The cardiologist's job is not only to treat illness, but to promote and preserve good health. A properly maintained exercise program is crucial for this. I am interested in how exercise and fitness influence body function in general, and particularly how fitness might alter the aging process in our arteries, a process we call atherosclerosis.

As my own interest in running and the problems of runners became better known, both beginning and experienced runners have asked my advice about a number of running-related health problems. To provide the best treatment for them, it has been necessary to learn as much as possible about the potential risks and benefits of running and other types of exercise in both the healthy and the sick, the young and the old.

Q. Are you concerned that running has become a fad?

A.   It's certainly true that many people are now running for what the purists might consider the wrong reason: their friends are doing it and it's "in." You can usually spot such people. They appear on the roads or track gaily attired in expensive, color-coordinated jogging outfits. While most will probably not be there next week, enough will be swept into the mainstream of running to derive the benefits that only long-term participation can produce. Perhaps this fad isn't such a bad one.

Q.   Why have you chosen the question and answer method? Why not just write the usual type of book?

A.   Lecturing to people, either in a classroom or in an office, is not usually the best way to help them learn. Over the years I have collected the questions asked by patients interested in running. These questions are probably the same ones the readers would like to ask. They form the basis for a discussion of the important aspects of running and good health.

Q.   Why did you begin to run?

A.   About 20 years ago I began to run a few miles each day because it was the most convenient way to exercise. I felt better when I exercised regularly. Exercise seemed to relieve the pressures of a very busy life. But there was another reason: I was a heavy smoker and weighed far too much. Worse still, my blood pressure was too high. I seemed headed for a certain heart attack, and hoped that exercise would reduce this risk. I needed to exercise alone, because my schedule was too unpredictable. I did not like to row or swim, and cycling seemed too dangerous in the downtown traffic. So I began to run.

  We lived in a working-class neighborhood, and I literally had to sneak out the back door lest the neighbors think I was slightly mad. In 1960 you just did not appear on the streets in shorts, sneakers, and T-shirt, even in summer. You can imagine the neighbors' reaction to someone crazy enough to brave a Boston winter in long underwear, sweat pants, hat, and gloves in the darkness of early morning. I was a "closet" runner.

  For years I ran a few miles, several days each week. This helped keep me fit, relatively relaxed, and thin. But over the last few years a new dimension has been added. As I began to run a little further, three to five miles each day, running became enjoyable for itself, not solely because of what it might do for me. At times running became exhilarating. As I increased my daily mileage, I was delighted to find that running became easier rather than harder. Many runners have noted the same phenomenon.

Usually I ran by myself, and I never considered entering a race. But a couple of years ago I was persuaded to enter one of the benefit races that have now become so popular. To my surprise, I thoroughly enjoyed it. Training for the race was fun, and it made my daily runs less boring since I had something to point toward. Also, in what other sport could a slow, middle-aged, unskilled but determined plodder compete with the world's best? I have run in races with champion marathoners, and while I have never seen them after the first few hundred yards, it has been great fun.

So you might say I run for the same reasons that most people do: running is fun, it makes me feel better, and a regular running program demands that I pursue a healthier life style.

I am often asked if I really believe that my vigorous running program will actually prolong my life. I am not certain about this, but my hunch is that it may. I think we will eventually find that atherosclerosis, or hardening of the arteries, may be slowed a bit by a vigorous running program. I suspect that many people bought this book to find out if a running program will improve their health. I believe it will.

Q. Are other types of exercise as good as running?

A. Cross-country skiing, cycling, rowing, swimming, rope jumping, and aerobic dancing are all examples of equally effective aerobic or dynamic exercise. Running has become the most popular aerobic activity because it's so easy to run at virtually any time of the year, you don't need special facilities or expensive equipment, and you can do it alone or with friends, as the spirit moves you.

Q. Is there a difference between jogging and running?

A. Some people separate them on the basis of speed: runners go faster. No one has precisely defined at what speed a jogger turns into a runner, although some place the dividing line at 7½ min-

utes per mile. Others recommend a more operational definition: a runner is someone who competes in races and who trains to
improve his performance. A runner runs because he loves it. A
jogger plods along at his same slow pace and shows little interest
in improving his performance. He jogs because he thinks it's good
for him. Personally, I believe any fine distinction is arbitrary and
unimportant. Throughout this book the terms are used interchangeably.

CHAPTER 2

What Is Fitness?

Q. WE HEAR so much about the term *fitness,* and we have seen it defined so many different ways that we're confused. What do you mean by fitness?

A. The dictionaries generally define being fit as "being sound physically and mentally," or "healthy, ready, or prepared; qualified or competent." Dr. Roger Bannister, the first runner to break the four minute barrier for the mile run, and himself a physician, describes fitness more broadly. He prefers to think of fitness as mental and physical harmony, enabling someone to carry on to the best of his ability with great happiness. Fitness thus can be variably defined; the fitness required of a weight lifter is totally different from that of a long-distance runner or even a steel worker. When we talk about fitness, we must ask the question "Fitness for what?"

Cardiovascular Fitness and Aerobic Exercise

Q. What kind of fitness, then, are you recommending?

A. When physicians and exercise physiologists describe the beneficial effects of exercise on health and well-being, they are talking about the development of *cardiovascular fitness.* This type of fitness is produced as a predictable result of the regular performance of a certain type of exercise which has been called *dynamic, isotonic,* or, more popularly, *aerobic.*

Aerobic exercise consists of rhythmic or repetitive activity, using large muscle groups such as the legs or arms, which is performed at an intensity well below maximal exercise capacity. This low intensity allows the exercise to be continued for relatively long periods of time. This kind of exercise requires fairly constant increased blood flow through the heart, lungs, and exercising muscles.

Q. Why is it called aerobic?

A. Aerobic literally means living or working with oxygen. Aerobic exercise is performed at an intensity moderate enough to keep the energy requirements of the exercising muscles from exceeding the ability of the lungs, heart, and blood vessels to bring enough oxygen to them. If enough oxygen is present, the energy sources in muscle, carbohydrates, and fats, are burned completely to carbon dioxide and water, which are easily excreted by the body. During more intense exercise, energy requirements may be so high that not enough oxygen is available. Incomplete burning of carbohydrates then occurs. The products of this incomplete burning are toxic and interfere with normal muscle function.

Aerobic exercise is not concerned mainly with developing muscle strength. Nor is it related to learning a skilled act, such as hitting a tennis ball or swinging a golf club. It's the running in tennis and the walking on the golf course that make these activities useful in developing cardiovascular fitness.

ANAEROBIC EXERCISE

Exercise of higher intensity, which requires more energy for muscle work than can be derived from aerobic metabolism, is called *anaerobic exercise.* Fat can't be utilized as an energy source for anaerobic muscle work; only carbohydrates or sugar can be used. Anaerobic metabolism can produce energy for muscular work fairly quickly, but it is very inefficient, and the lactic acid or lactate which is its end product causes muscle pains and cramps and

7

interferes with muscle function. Because of its high intensity and high energy requirements, anaerobic exercise can be performed for only short periods, far too short to produce cardiovascular fitness.

Q. Can you give an example of anaerobic activity?

A. The 440 and 880 yard dashes are good examples. Most runners try to do these as sprints, going at nearly top speed throughout, hoping that their muscles' lactic acid levels do not get so high that effective muscular work becomes impossible. The fastest times are made by runners who not only have speed, but also have learned how to tolerate and adapt to the pain and other problems caused by lactic acid accumulation.

The mile run, in contrast, is too long to run as a sprint. Successful milers run most of the race aerobically. On the last lap, striving to win, they will increase their pace into the anaerobic range. If they properly time their last lap sprint, they will arrive exhausted at the finish line just before muscle function is significantly impaired. A good middle distance runner learns how to tolerate pain. For good reason you see him grimacing at the finish line.

One of the most common errors made by inexperienced runners is starting off their run at too fast a pace. Quickly they exceed their aerobic capacity (which may be extremely limited at the beginning of the fitness program), and they begin to run anaerobically. Lactic acid accumulates and forces them to stop. This is very discouraging; no progress is being made because they are never able to exercise long enough to develop cardiovascular fitness. *It is critically important for all beginning runners to start slowly so they will not exceed their aerobic capacity,* even if it is distressingly low. They must be patient. Progress will eventually be made, though it may take months.

PHOSPHAGENIC ENERGY AND ISOMETRIC EXERCISE

Q. Are there other types of exercise besides aerobic and anaerobic?

A. Very high intensity exercise requires still a different energy source. If you suddenly smelled smoke, or someone in a crowded theater shouted "Fire," you would immediately mobilize yourself to douse the flames, or get away. The sprinter who runs the 100 yard dash also needs an enormous quantity of energy in a very short period. To perform such activities, we need an immediate energy source within the muscles themselves. This emergency supply is stored in the form of _high-energy phosphate bonds,_ commonly referred to as _ATP._ Even untrained muscles contain some energy in this form, but much of the sprinter's or weight lifter's training is directed toward increasing his capacity for storing it. Some call this _phosphagenic energy._ Phosphagenic energy stores are very limited. Even the best trained weight lifters, for example, can store only a few moment's worth of this type of energy.

Compare the bulky muscles of the sprinter to the distance runner's longer, thinner muscles. Distance runners do not require much phosphagenic energy. Their muscles are primed to burn carbohydrates and fats relatively slowly.

Isometric exercises increase the stores of phosphagenic energy. Tighten your arm or leg muscles, but don't move your arm or leg. This is isometric muscle contraction. It produces muscle strength but not cardiovascular fitness. Weight lifters regularly perform isometrics as an important part of their training. Not only are the energy requirements for isometric activity very high, they are immediate. Even anaerobic metabolism is too slow to meet them.

Q. Are high-energy phosphate bonds also required for aerobic and anaerobic exercise?

A. Yes. _All muscular work requires ATP._ During aerobic and anaerobic exercise new high-energy phosphate bonds are produced from the breakdown or metabolism of energy sources.

Fuels for Muscular Work

Scientists sometimes use the term "fuels" to describe these energy sources. The term is a good one, particularly for the nonscientist, because it enables him to relate the process of muscular exercise to one he is more familiar with, such as the function of the typical automobile motor. To perform its work the motor requires an energy source or fuel in the form of gasoline. The gasoline is burned in the motor, a process which also requires oxygen, and which also produces energy and, as a by-product, heat. Heat produced by muscle work is essential for maintaining normal body temperature. That's how we stay warm in cold weather. But in warm weather the amount of heat produced during vigorous muscular work may exceed the body's ability to dissipate it. Dangerously high body temperatures may be produced. Warm weather running can be dangerous, and will be discussed in detail in Chapter 6.

Q.   What fuels do the muscles use?

A.   Almost exclusively carbohydrate and fat. Protein, the other important potential energy source, is burned only when there are severe shortages of the other two, for example during starvation.

   Carbohydrate is a general term which refers to a large number of different substances, all of which are made up of various types of sugars. Sugars are compounds which contain carbon, hydrogen, and oxygen. Starches, for example, are a type of carbohydrate referred to as "complex" because they contain many different sugar molecules connected together in varying forms. After absorption into the body from the intestine, all carbohydrates are broken down into their various types of sugars. All the sugars are then converted in the liver to one type called *glucose,* the prime fuel for muscular work. The body also is able to store glucose as an energy source. This storage form of glucose is called *glycogen.* It is a series of glucose molecules hooked densely together. One of the major effects of a good aerobic training program is to increase the amount of glycogen the trained muscles can store. *The more glycogen they can store, the more exercise they can perform.*

   Exercising muscles can also burn the sugar that comes to them in the blood, but the body prefers to save this energy source, if possible, for the brain. Unlike muscle, the brain cannot store much glucose, and requires a constant supply from the blood to function normally. The liver also stores glycogen, and when the blood sugar starts to fall, glycogen stored in the liver is broken down to glucose to return the blood sugar toward normal.

   The other important source of energy for muscular work is *fat.* Muscle tissue itself contains a lot of fat which can be used as an immediate fuel source. Fat can also be transported from fat tissue elsewhere in the body to the exercising muscle. The kind of fat the muscles use is *fatty acids*. These are stored in fat tissue as part of larger compounds called *triglycerides*. There are enormous potential stores of energy for muscular work in the form of triglycerides. But for some reason, our ability to metabolize fatty acids is seriously impaired once our muscle glycogen stores fall too low. One of the most intriguing questions the exercise scientist is trying to answer is why we cannot make better use of this huge potential fuel supply. If we can solve this riddle, a significant breakthrough might be made in athletic performance.

One of the major benefits of a fitness program is that during aerobic exercise, when the muscle, theoretically at least, has the choice of using glucose or fatty acids for fuel, the trained muscle uses more fatty acids, thereby sparing muscle glycogen. We also have learned recently that when exercise is less intense, fatty acids are preferentially burned. As exercise intensity increases, there is a shift to burning glucose.

Q. What lessons can the beginning runner learn from these facts?

A. First, we can safely state that not only can the well-trained runner store more glycogen in his muscles, but he also preserves his precious glycogen stores better at any given speed or intensity of exercise because he uses fatty acids instead. No wonder he can run farther before he fatigues. Second, the data underscore the need to start our regular daily training run slowly in order to turn on our fatty acid metabolism and conserve glucose.

Q. Women are supposed to have greater fat stores than men. Does this give them the potential to become better long distance runners than men?

A. This claim has been made by a number of people, but I believe it's based more on enthusiasm than on fact. The limiting factor in running is not a lack of fat; there is plenty of it in even the skinniest of us. Rather the problem is getting our muscles to use it. I suspect that the extra fat women carry may be more of a burden than an advantage.

We'll talk more about carbohydrates, fats, and proteins when we discuss the proper diet for runners in Chapter 9.

Measuring Fitness—Maximum Oxygen Consumption

Q. Let's return to the question of fitness. How do you measure cardiovascular fitness? How do we know how fit we are?

A. Exercise scientists learned early that cardiovascular fitness could be defined in terms of the ability of the individual to perform physical work of an aerobic type. They developed methods for measuring the actual work load performed, using specially designed exercise bicycles and, more recently, treadmills. The fitter the subject, the longer and harder he could pedal the bicycle or run on the treadmill. It was soon learned that *the amount of oxygen used up by the body during the performance of the exercise was directly related to the intensity and duration of the work performed.* Oxygen consumption was highest at peak exercise, and the *level of cardiovascular fitness has thus been defined in terms of the amount of oxygen consumed by the body at peak exercise*—that is, just at the point when exhaustion occurs in a standard exercise test. The more fit the subject, the greater the amount of oxygen consumed at peak exercise load.

THE OXYGEN TRANSPORT SYSTEM

Scientists also learned that one of the major determinants of fitness was the efficient operation of the mechanisms necessary for bringing oxygen to the exercising muscles and burning it properly once it arrived there. Collectively this has been called the *oxygen transport system.* It may be helpful to understand how this system functions and is integrated, in order to plan an exercise program more intelligently. One of the major effects of a training program is increased efficiency of the oxygen transport system.

The first component of the system is *the lungs.* Each time we inhale, oxygen in the air is transported deep into the lungs and is brought into contact, across a microscopically thin membrane, with the blood in the lungs. The red blood cells bind oxygen. At the same time, carbon dioxide, one of the body's main waste products, is blown out in the air we exhale. As we develop fitness, the

12

lungs function more efficiently. There is greater oxygen uptake and carbon dioxide removal. We can take deeper breaths and we breathe more efficiently.

Cigarette smoking is the major cause of poor lung function in adults. Smoking severely injures lung tissues, interfering with oxygen uptake and carbon dioxide removal. Aging also reduces lung function. Some believe that a good fitness program may slow this deterioration.

The next component of the oxygen transport system is _the heart,_ which is basically a pump. The oxygen-rich blood from the lungs returns to the heart, which then pumps it to the rest of the body. In the average adult at rest, the heart may pump four or five quarts each minute at a pulse rate of 60 to 80. During intense exercise the pulse may rise to 200 or more. At peak activity the amount of blood the heart pumps each minute, called the _cardiac output,_ may increase to five or six times the resting level. In the unfit person the heart's pumping ability is less, limiting his ability to exercise. With training, each heartbeat or contraction is more vigorous, pumping more blood to the body.

THE MAXIMUM HEART RATE

Q. As fitness increases, does the peak pulse rate increase also?

A. Usually not. For most of us there is a _peak or maximum heart rate we can achieve which is independent of fitness._ Later we'll see that this is an important factor in defining a safe but effective cardiovascular fitness program. Of course early in the training program, before we become very fit, relatively little exercise will markedly increase the pulse rate. Later, as fitness improves, increasing amounts of exercise can be performed at lower heart rates, and maximum heart rate will not be reached until high levels of exercise are achieved.

The peak heart rate, while independent of the fitness level, does fall gradually with increasing age. This is shown in Table 1. As a rule of thumb you can fairly accurately _calculate your maximum expected heart rate by subtracting your age from 220._ For example, the maximum expected heart rate for a 40 year old would be 180; for a 55 year old, 165.

Q. Do you mean that marathon runners' heart rates can go no higher than that of their fat, beer-drinking, cigarette-smoking friends their own age?

A. That's exactly what I mean. *Maximum heart rate is independent of fitness.* But remember that the unfit person may approach his maximum heart rate just by climbing a couple of flights of stairs. His oxygen transport system is inefficient, and even this low level activity approaches his peak aerobic capacity. The marathoner's maximum heart rate will be reached only by much higher levels of exercise.

THE RESTING PULSE RATE

Q. How useful is the resting pulse rate in estimating the level of fitness?

A. It's not particularly helpful. A good fitness program will lower the resting pulse rate; a well-trained runner's pulse may be as low as 30 or 40 when he first awakens. But there are many exceptions. The reason is that the resting pulse depends on many other factors in addition to the fitness level. It is particularly influenced by the *autonomic nervous system,* called "autonomic" because it's the part of the nervous system over which we have no direct control. The autonomic nervous system has two parts, called *sympathetic* and *parasympathetic.* Activation of the sympathetic nervous system speeds up the heart rate and makes the heart contract more

TABLE 1. *Maximum Expected Heart Rate Adjusted to Age**

						AGE						
	20	25	30	35	40	45	50	55	60	65	70	80
Maximum Heart Rate	200	195	190	185	180	175	170	165	160	155	150	145

*To estimate your maximum heart rate, subtract your age from 220. These are approximate values only. Your maximum heart rate may vary as much as 10 percent from the number listed in the table.

forcefully. The parasympathetic nervous system slows and relaxes the heart. One of the major effects of a training program is to reduce the sympathetic and increase the parasympathetic tone of the heart at rest. That's why the athlete's resting pulse is usually slower. But the pulse rate depends on other factors too, including stress or tension, coffee, alcohol, recent ingestion of food, and, of course, smoking. If you have a stimulating dream just before you awaken, your pulse rate will be faster, but your fitness level will not have changed.

It's been said that persistent elevation of the early morning resting pulse in a runner is a sign of overtraining. This is probably correct for the very fit, very fast runner, but it is not as likely to be true for the rest of us. Patients have called me, literally as an emergency, because their resting pulse rates were up a bit. My first question is whether they otherwise feel well. If they do, I tell them to relax about this. Almost certainly the increased pulse is due to some other factor.

Q. What about the return of the pulse rate to normal after exercising? Is this a useful method for determining the level of cardiovascular fitness?

A. This too is not precise enough to be an infallible guideline. It's true that the more quickly the pulse rate returns to normal after exercise, the higher the level of fitness in general. But here, too, many other factors are involved in determining the final pulse rate. You should not be dismayed if yours returns to normal slowly. Instead pay attention to how you feel after you run. If you feel good, your program is probably fine.

THE OTHER COMPONENTS OF THE OXYGEN TRANSPORT SYSTEM

Q. What are the other components of the oxygen transport system?

A. The arteries, veins, red blood cells, and the exercising muscles. The role of the arteries is to transport blood from the heart to the exercising muscle. But arteries are not merely passive conduits for the movement of the blood. Fitness produces changes in arteries, improving their ability to expand and contract. Even more important, fitness may stimulate the growth of tiny new arteries

15

in the exercising muscles to help improve the efficiency of the oxygen transport system.

Another important adaptation occurs during training: a greater percentage of the blood pumped by the heart is directed to the exercising muscle and away from other parts of the body such as the kidneys and stomach. If blood flow to the kidneys is reduced, urine formation stops, which is a useful adaptation for the runner. There usually is no need to stop to urinate during a run, and if it is hot, the body fluids can be used to produce sweat rather than urine. But because blood flow to the stomach and intestine is reduced during the run, recently ingested food may not be digested adequately. Pain, cramps, and heartburn may result. That is why it is not a good idea to eat solid food for several hours before running.

Even the red blood cells of the fit person work more efficiently. They are able to release more of the oxygen they carry to the tissues. But by far the most important training effects occur in the exercising muscles themselves.

Training Effects in Muscles

Aerobic training produces a tremendous increase in the concentration and activity of certain substances called *enzymes* in the exercising muscles. Chemists define enzymes as catalysts; in muscles they speed up the chemical reactions which break down the fatty acids and glucose to produce energy. Trained muscles can produce much more energy for exercise than untrained muscles.

Q. Do all the muscles of the trained person behave this way? Or just the ones used during the exercise?

A. Unfortunately, just the ones actually exercised. The *training effect is quite muscle specific.* This was convincingly demonstrated by Scandinavian physiologists a few years ago. Saltin and his co-workers asked untrained volunteers to begin an exercise program of bicycle riding during which they could use only one leg to pedal. The other leg was not exercised. At the end of the program, the exercise capacity of the trained leg had increased considerably, but the exercise capacity of the untrained leg had changed very little.

This phenomenon was demonstrated to me in a rather striking manner a few days before I ran my first marathon in 1977. I had put in several straight 70-plus mile weeks of running, and was in the best shape of my life. To test my fitness I tried to swim in a local pool. As usual, I was exhausted by the third lap. I was no more fit for swimming than I had ever been.

Remember, however, that while the training effect in muscles is quite specific for the muscles that are exercised, the very important, general effects of aerobic exercise on the heart and the body's metabolism occur regardless of the type of aerobic activity performed. This will be discussed in detail later.

Maximum Aerobic Capacity and Maximum Cardiovascular Fitness

Q. Are there limits to our ability to perform aerobic exercise?

A. Indeed there are. Each of us has his own peak or maximum oxygen capacity. No matter how intensely he trains, he can raise it no further. To a large degree, this seems to be an inherited characteristic. Those with the highest potential aerobic capacity are likely to become our best endurance athletes.

Each of us can achieve our potential maximal aerobic limits, also called our *maximal aerobic power,* with an effective training program. The gradual increase in our oxygen capacity is called the *training effect.* Once this peak capacity has been reached, however, attempts to increase it further not only will be unsuccessful, but may be counterproductive. Instead of becoming more fit, the runner develops chronic fatigue and a variety of aches and pains suggesting overtraining.

We can define maximum cardiovascular fitness as that point in our training program at which each of us can perform such a high level of physical activity that we reach our maximum (peak) oxygen capacity. This can be directly determined in the laboratory by measuring the difference in the oxygen concentrations of the air we breathe in and out during exercise. The difference between the two is the amount of oxygen taken into the body

17

during each breath and used by the muscle cells to produce energy for the physical activity.

But direct measurement of oxygen consumption is tedious, expensive, and only necessary for research purposes. We can estimate it indirectly by measuring the peak exercise load. Many studies have been performed which correlate oxygen consumption at all levels of exercise. By measuring the peak exercise load, which is relatively easy using a treadmill or exercise bicycle, the physician can estimate quite accurately the subject's probable oxygen consumption and hence his fitness.

Muscle Fiber Types

Q. You stated that individual differences in maximum oxygen capacity were genetically determined. Is the reason for this understood?

A. To some degree this difference seems to depend on the type of muscle fibers we inherit. There are two main types: Type I, the red or slow twitch fibers, are particularly suitable for relatively low intensity, aerobic work. Type II, the white or fast twitch muscle fibers, are designed for the performance of higher intensity activity. A preponderance of Type I fibers characterizes the successful distance runner. The sprinter has a larger proportion of Type II. These are inherited characteristics. All the training in the world is not going to change their proportion very much.

The type of body build we inherit also plays a major role. There aren't many short, squat, heavily muscled champion distance runners. They almost universally have long, slim muscles, big chests, and thin arms.

The MET and Development of Fitness

Q. You have talked about the scientific aspects of physical activity and muscular work, but you haven't yet told us how we can actually improve our aerobic capacity and achieve cardiovascular fitness. How much exercise is necessary? How often must we perform it? How long a period of time must we spend doing it?

A. *Any aerobic activity which even mildly stresses the oxygen transport system for more than a few minutes each day will allow gradual increase in maximum oxygen consumption,* which is the way we measure cardiovascular fitness. Faithful performance of this activity will produce gradual increase in exercise capacity.

Exercise scientists have defined the intensity of each type of exercise by comparing the oxygen required to perform it with the body's oxygen requirements at rest. They have coined a term, the *MET*, short for *metabolic equivalent*. One MET is defined as the amount of oxygen used by an individual at rest, corrected for weight. A one MET activity requires about 3.5 milliliters of oxygen per kilogram (2.2 pounds) of body weight each minute. Thus a 70 kilogram (154 pound) subject uses 245 milliliters of oxygen each minute (70 × 3.5), while an 80 kilogram (176 pound) subject uses 280 (80 × 3.5). Activity which requires twice as much oxygen is described as having an energy equivalent of 2 METs. Slow walking is a 2 MET activity. Jogging 5 miles per hour is a 7 to 8 MET activity, running 8 miles per hour about 13 METs. A training effect, or increase in aerobic capacity, begins in most previously untrained individuals *when exercise requiring 3 to 4 METs is performed continuously for 20 to 30 minutes 3 or 4 times each week.* This is the minimum exercise program which will increase aerobic capacity in most people. The MET is a most useful term because it allows accurate comparison of vastly different kinds of aerobic activity. The relative intensity of various types of exercise is shown in Table 2.

Q. Can we increase our aerobic capacity more rapidly?

A. Yes, you can, if you are able to exercise more vigorously for longer periods of time. But this approach is dangerous, particularly for the middle-aged beginner. Trying to increase aerobic capacity more quickly is far more likely to result in injuries that will set back an exercise program. The beginner must curb the initial enthusiasm and not start too quickly.

19

TABLE 2. *Comparison of Common Types of Aerobic Activity in Terms of METs and Calories Required for Their Performance*

ACTIVITY	METs	CALORIES Per Minute	CALORIES Per Hour
Walking 30 min/mile Golf (using cart) Light housework	2–3	3–4	180–240
Walking 20 min/mile Heavier housework Bowling Cycling 12 min/mile	3–4	4–5	240–300
Heavy housework (scrubbing floors) Golf (carrying clubs) Volleyball, ping pong, badminton Tennis doubles	4–5	5–6	300–360
Walking 15 min/mile Cycling 6 min/mile	5–6	6–7	360–420
Walking 12 min/mile Tennis singles	6–7	7–8	420–480
Skating (ice or roller) X-Country skiing 15 min/mile Swimming, moderate speed Jogging 12 min/mile Cycling 5 min/mile Racketball, paddleball	7–8	8–10	480–600
Basketball Squash or handball	8–9	10–11	600–660
Jogging 10 min/mile Swimming, faster	10	11	660
Running 8 min/mile X-country skiing 6 min/mile	12–14	14–16	840–960
Running 6 min/mile	15–17	17–19	1020–1140

Figures will of course vary according to the subject's weight and the intensity with which the exercise is performed.

THE TARGET HEART RATE

More recently we have found there may be a better way to estimate the amount of exercise that must be performed to improve
cardiovascular fitness. At any level of fitness a training effect is
achieved when aerobic exercise produces a pulse that is 70 to 85
percent of the maximum expected heart rate. Thus, instead of
measuring the oxygen consumed, which is difficult, we can measure the pulse rate to determine if the exercise performed is of
sufficient intensity to improve cardiovascular fitness.

This relation has led to the concept of the _target heart rate_,
which is that rate, adjusted for age, which you must achieve to
improve aerobic capacity and develop cardiovascular fitness. Its
change with age is diagramed in Figure 1. Of course, both the
maximum expected heart rate and the target heart rate _decrease_
with age. But this decrease is slow, and the target rate will be
relatively constant during the important early stages of your
fitness program. _As fitness is achieved, higher intensity and duration of exercise will be required to produce the target heart rate._

Q. Does this mean that the simple measure of the pulse rate is really
all that is necessary to define an effective level of physical activity?

A. This is absolutely correct. Not only is the pulse rate a good indicator of a training effect, but it is also a very accurate indicator of
how hard the heart must work during exercise. Measuring the
pulse rate thus becomes an excellent way of preventing excessive
demands on the heart. Most younger, healthy people who want to
begin a running program need not bother measuring the pulse
rate. If they exercise at or just below a pace which makes them
breathless, they are in the target zone in which fitness is
achieved. But pulse counting is the safer method for older people
or those with a possible heart problem.

_If you exercise much below 70 percent of your maximum ex-
pected heart rate, only a limited training effect occurs. Exercising
above 85 percent, may be safe for a younger person, but might be
dangerous for an older individual._

Doctor Kenneth Cooper, in his best-selling book, _Aerobics_,
recommended that a training program should aim toward a

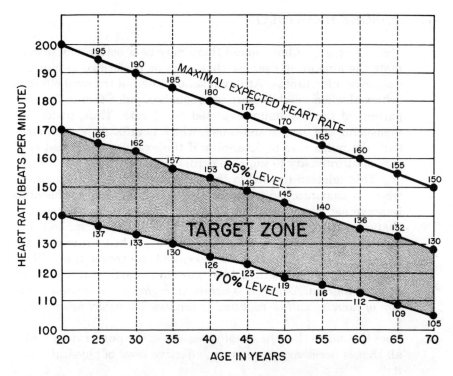

FIGURE 1. *Target heart rates. Note that the target heart rate falls with age just as the maximum heart rate does. The shaded area ranges from a lower level of 70 percent to a higher level of 85 percent of the maximum expected heart rate for a given age.* (Modified from *Exercise Your Way to Fitness and Heart Health* by Lenore R. Zohman, M.D., CPC International, Inc., 1974.)

specific goal. He chose running 1½ miles in 12 minutes or less. He felt that once you were able to do this you had achieved a reasonable fitness level. Many people have followed his program with good results, but I still prefer the target heart rate approach because it is just as effective and perhaps a little safer for older, less fit people.

Q. Could you review again how to calculate the target heart rate?

A. First determine your maximum expected rate by subtracting your age from 220. Then multiply that number by 70 percent. That is a reasonable target rate for you. Thus for a 40-year-old subject the target heart rate would be 70 percent of 180 (220 minus 40), or 126. The relatively well-conditioned 40 year old might aim for a slightly higher rate; the less well-conditioned subject should probably start at a target rate a bit lower.

The aerobic activity you choose should be performed for 20 to 30 minutes 3 or 4 times a week, at an intensity that will produce your target heart rate. If you are able to exercise more frequently, or for longer periods of time, you will become fit more rapidly. But it's a mistake to start too fast. Don't be impatient. Your commitment to fitness should be life-long. A few extra weeks or months getting there is unimportant. I have seen far too many enthusiastic people give up their fitness programs because they developed annoying musculo-skeletal problems. The older you are, the more likely your bones, joints, and muscles will need slow, gradual conditioning.

WARM-UP AND COOL DOWN PERIODS

Q. What other precautions should we take in addition to beginning slowly?

A. Adequate warm-up and cool down periods are very important. The oxygen transport system does not begin to function at 100 percent efficiency right away. Exercise testing of even a normal subject may produce rather worrisome changes in the electrocardiogram if the heart rate is increased too rapidly because the exercise is too intense. _Take at least 5 minutes—longer if you are older—to warm up._ This usually means that you should begin the run at a pace much slower than your steady level for a few minutes. Starting slowly not only allows your cardiovascular system to adjust properly, but also will help prevent injury to your bones, joints, and muscles.

It's almost as important not to stop your physical activity too abruptly. Don't make the all too common, potentially risky mistake of sprinting to the end of your run and finishing exhausted. You may end up in a heap. The return of blood from the legs to the heart depends chiefly on the pumping action of the leg muscles themselves. An enormous amount of blood is contained in these muscles, and it will pool in the legs and not return to the heart if leg exercise abruptly stops. Blood pressure may fall, and dizziness, or even fainting, as well as irregularities of the heart rhythm, may occur.

Body temperature rises considerably during exercise. It is wise to allow it to return to normal before you enter a hot shower. The body rids itself of extra heat through sweating and increased blood flow to the skin, and a hot shower interferes with this heat loss. At least wait until you stop sweating before you shower. You can put these few minutes to good use by performing your post-exercise stretching.

MEASURING THE PULSE

Q. Is it hard to measure the pulse rate?

A. It may be difficult while you are still exercising, but it's usually easy if you count your pulse immediately after you stop. This is fairly accurate because the rate won't fall much for 10 or 20 seconds after the exercise is stopped.

Most of you can easily learn to count your pulse accurately in the neck or at the wrist. The technique is shown in Figure 2. The

pulse should be counted for 10 seconds right after you stop exercising. You can then multiply this number by 6 to obtain the pulse rate per minute, as shown in Table 3 (page 26). A simple, inexpensive, accurate device for measuring pulse rate would be most welcome, and I am hopeful that one will soon become available. Those currently on the market are either inaccurate, cumbersome, or expensive.

Q. Once we have reached a good fitness level, what must we do to maintain it?

A. Loss of fitness occurs at a discouragingly rapid rate if the exercise program is stopped. After just a week or two of inactivity, levels of physical exercise that were previously performed with ease will cause fatigue and breathlessness. However, do not let this rapid deconditioning prevent you from stopping your exercise for a while if you hurt yourself. It may be dangerous to run when you hurt. Rest if you have to. You will quickly regain your previous level of fitness once you start again, and very likely your brief respite from running will prevent a more serious injury.

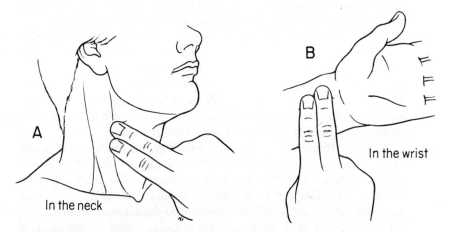

FIGURE 2. _Counting the pulse rate. With a little practice you can learn to count your pulse rate quite accurately. Start immediately after you stop running, because the pulse rate falls soon after exercise is stopped. The most accurate method is to count the pulse for 10 seconds and multiply that number by 6 to obtain the pulse rate or heartbeats per minute. Some of you may need to count for 15 seconds to obtain an accurate result. This figure should be multiplied by 4._

25

TABLE 3. *Pulse Rate per Minute based on a 10-Second Count*

10-Second Count	60-Second Count
40	240
35	210
30	180
25	150
20	120
15	90

Other Aerobic Exercise

Q. Are other kinds of aerobic exercise as effective as running in producing fitness and health?

A. I am sure they are, and they also offer the runner a variety of alternative methods for maintaining hard-won fitness.

Running is probably the chief interest for most of you; otherwise you would not be reading this book. But even the most avid runner may occasionally prefer to participate in other aerobic activities. These can provide welcome relief from the tedium of a year-round running program, or serve as an alternative method of training during inclement weather, or if injuries prevent running. None of these activities will totally substitute for running because of the muscle-specific effects of training, but the muscular requirements of some are close enough to those of running to allow you to maintain most of your training effect.

Table 2 (page 20) compares the energy requirements of many different aerobic activities. Of course, the figures given are at best approximations, and depend on many factors. For example, how fast the activities are performed influences the METs you use, and how much you weigh will determine how many calories you burn. In sports with intermittent activity, such as tennis and racketball, your energy requirements and the calories you burn per minute or hour will also be influenced by how much time you spend between points and how long the ball is in play.

Swimming, cross-country skiing, cycling, skating, rope jumping, aerobic dancing, and rowing all can improve cardiovascular fitness. Although these sports will not be discussed in detail, the runner may find it useful to know something about them.

SWIMMING

In theory at least swimming might be the ideal aerobic activity. No weight bearing is necessary. Therefore musculo-skeletal injuries are less common. Both arms and legs are used vigorously, facilitating conditioning of more muscles. However, few runners choose swimming as an alternative exercise, chiefly because the muscles trained are so different.

Swimming is now frequently recommended as treatment for acute and chronic low back problems. It has been very effective, and I recommend it highly to runners who suffer from back trouble. Swimming may be the only aerobic activity a runner can perform if he has a leg injury, and can certainly be helpful in maintaining some fitness in such a case.

CROSS-COUNTRY SKIING

This sport has become extremely popular the last few years. Champion cross-country skiers have the highest measured oxygen capacity of all athletes, presumably because they must perform vigorous arm as well as leg exercise. Although the muscle movements of a cross-country skier are distinctly different from those of a runner, they are similar enough to maintain some of a runner's fitness. Moreover, a running program does provide some preparation for this type of skiing. Cross-country skiing is often the preferred winter alternative for runners who live in cold climates.

Q. How effective is downhill skiing in promoting cardiovascular fitness?

A. Much less. The exercise is often quite intense, of course, but it is over much too soon. I advise my friends and patients to ski downhill for fun. But if they want to develop cardiovascular fitness and enjoy the outdoors in winter, I suggest cross-country skiing.

27

CYCLING

On days I cannot run, I often use my exercise bicycle. Cycling's muscle requirements are also quite different from those of running, but they are still close enough to produce some training effect for the runner. Cycling strengthens the quadriceps muscle in the front of the thigh. Quadriceps weakness may cause serious problems for some runners and cycling may help this condition (see pages 106–7).

A great advantage of cycling is that it can be performed indoors as well as out. The boredom of indoor cycling can be relieved by watching television, reading, talking, or listening to music.

SKATING

Both ice and roller skating can be excellent aerobic activities if they are performed vigorously enough. I highly recommend them, despite the fact that roller skaters have recently invaded some of my favorite running courses. In fact, I have already had my first collision with a skater, from which we both fortunately emerged unscathed.

ROPE JUMPING

No longer do I believe that rope jumping must be the most boring exercise on earth, rivaled only by running in place. (I am told that rope jumpers have the same opinion about jogging.) I recently witnessed a remarkable exhibition of skillful rope jumping which transformed this activity into a graceful, physically demanding art. To achieve this expertise, however, seems to require a level of coordination which few of us are likely to possess. If you are well coordinated, try rope jumping. You may find it a challenging alternative to running.

AEROBIC DANCING

Its adherents proclaim aerobic dancing's value as both a method of artistic expression and an excellent way to develop cardiovascular fitness. In addition, the improved coordination and muscle skills aerobic dancing produces are reported to be very useful in other sports. There are testimonials, even from huge professional football and basketball players, describing how aerobic dancing has helped them.

ROWING

Rowing is an excellent exercise for developing cardiovascular fitness, training both arm and leg muscles. Runners won't find rowing very helpful, however, because of its vastly different muscle requirements. Vigorous rowing requires isometric activity which also improves muscle strength, but this effect does not detract much from its aerobic value.

RACKET SPORTS

Tennis, squash, racketball, and paddleball are only intermittently aerobic. But significant cardiovascular fitness can be achieved if they are played vigorously for a sufficient length of time. Unfortunately, achieving such a level of intensity in these sports, tennis particularly, requires skills which the novice does not possess. Until the skills are acquired, significant improvement in aerobic capacity may not be possible.

Q. You have ignored a number of other sports, such as basketball, soccer, and football. Will they produce cardiovascular fitness?

A. Yes, they will, if a sufficient amount of running is required. But such competitive team sports are generally played by younger persons. Most of us stopped participating in them when we left school or college.

Recently I have noticed increasing interest in "veteran's" soccer and basketball, which certainly can produce cardiovascular fitness. I recommend them if they are played safely. It is interesting that many participants in these sports have also begun to run. They find that they perform better because they are in much better shape.

CHAPTER 3

Running Can Improve Your Health

Q. RUNNING IS being hailed as a good way to improve health and perhaps lengthen life. Is there any really good evidence for this claim? If it is true, are the mechanisms understood?

A. I firmly believe that a regular exercise program *begun early in life and continued,* will prevent certain medical problems and may lead to a longer life. Whether exercise programs begun much later in life, or after a serious cardiovascular problem has already developed, can significantly lengthen our life spans has not yet been answered.

Exercise may be particularly effective in preventing those diseases caused by the development of atherosclerosis or hardening of the arteries, which is by far the leading health problem in the United States and Europe.

Atherosclerosis and Risk Factors

Q. But isn't hardening of the arteries a natural result of aging?

A. Doctors used to think so, but now we know this need not be true. In other societies—often those we would consider backward, where the life style, diet, and pace of life are so much different from ours—atherosclerosis is uncommon even among the elderly. This finding has made us look at the factors which might predispose some people to atherosclerosis, while others are spared. If these factors can be identified, their early treatment or modification may slow the development of atherosclerosis with age.

Q. Is this what you mean by *"risk factors"*?

A. That is exactly right. "Risk factors" are characteristics or features that have strong predictive value in telling us whether the individual in whom they are found is likely to develop atherosclerosis at a relatively early age and therefore may be "at risk" for death or crippling injury, chiefly from heart attack or stroke. By treating, or in some way modifying the risk factors, it may be possible to reduce the severity and frequency of atherosclerosis. Many believe that exercise may play a key role in accomplishing this end.

Q. Can you tell us what these risk factors are?

A. You already know most of them, I suspect; they have been widely publicized in the last few years. They include:

1. High blood pressure
2. Lack of physical activity
3. Increased level of fats—cholesterol and triglycerides—in the blood and in our diets
4. Stress
5. Personality type
6. Cigarette smoking
7. Diabetes
8. Age
9. Sex
10. Heredity
11. Obesity

Strong proof of the association of these risk factors with atherosclerosis has come from a number of important medical studies in which thousands of apparently healthy, normal people were carefully examined and then closely followed for many years to see what happened to them. In each study, a number of tests were performed to see if any of the test results could predict the subject's medical future.

Perhaps the best known of these studies is being performed in Framingham, Massachusetts. The Framingham Study has followed its participants over many years, carefully recording what has happened to them. We have learned a lot from this study, and hopefully it will continue to provide us with important medical information. Other studies have been differently designed. Some attempt to assess the effects of environment, by studying, for example, Irish or Italians living in the United States compared to those still living in their native countries, or Japanese living in Japan, Hawaii, and the United States. Still other studies compare different groups of people within the same country. For example, there have been studies of sedentary versus physically active college graduates in this country, civil servants with different levels of daily physical activity in Great Britain, and smokers versus nonsmokers in many countries. The results of all these studies have allowed us to define quite precisely the factors associated with atherosclerosis listed above.

Often more than one risk factor is present. For example, an obese person is far more likely to have high blood pressure and lead a sedentary existence. The tense person is more likely to smoke. By definition, of course, the presence of a single risk factor significantly increases the chances for developing atherosclerosis. But when more than one risk factor is present, the outlook may be particularly grim. A middle-aged male with a blood pressure of 160/100 (normal is less than 140/90 for this age group) and a blood cholesterol level over 300 (average is less than 250), who smokes a pack of cigarettes daily, is perhaps ten to twenty times more likely to have a heart attack than a male of the same age who does not smoke and whose blood pressure and cholesterol levels are normal.

Can changing these risk factors significantly alter the risk of hardening of the arteries? Early evidence seems favorable, although systematic studies have been going on for so short a period that results which would satisfy a good scientist are not yet available. I would not recommend waiting until the medical evidence is overwhelming, it may be too late for many of us.

Obviously we can't change our heredity, or perhaps even alter our personalities very much, but we can certainly change some of the other risk factors. None of the methods we use to reduce risk factors are likely to do any harm and very possibly they may have a dramatic impact. Exercise can play a vital role in this approach.

HIGH BLOOD PRESSURE (HYPERTENSION)

Q. Give us an example of modifying risk factors.

A. Hypertension is a good example. Nearly 25 million Americans have high blood pressure. Excellent treatment is readily available, but amazingly, the majority of people afflicted either don't know that they have high blood pressure, or are not being treated adequately. When they finally seek medical attention, it is often tragically too late; they have already sustained a heart attack or stroke. Earlier I mentioned that the development of significant atherosclerosis, even when hastened by high blood pressure, will take decades. For a long period the process of atherosclerosis is potentially reversible, or at least can be prevented from advancing, by adequate treatment of high blood pressure. We know now, beyond any doubt, that lowering blood pressure will prolong life and prevent crippling injury from heart attack and stroke.

In my own practice I am increasingly turning to methods not involving drugs to lower the blood pressure. In many patients we have successfully lowered pressure with an exercise program alone. In others we have combined exercise with one of the various relaxation or meditation techniques. If these don't work, we add medication.

Q. Isn't it dangerous for people with high blood pressure to exercise?

A. Usually not, but several precautions should be taken. In normal subjects, blood pressure rises during the exercise period. Since this rise may be much exaggerated in patients with high blood pressure, we first make sure that exercise is safe by measuring the pressure during exercise. If it goes too high, we may want to start drugs. Once blood pressure is better controlled, an exercise program may be more safely started.

High blood pressure is an important medical problem, and there are many misconceptions about it that should be cleared up.

33

One is that a high pressure reading is not worth becoming concerned about as long as the pressure returns to normal after the subject rests a few minutes, or if a normal pressure reading is obtained the next time it is measured. Indeed, several recently published books about running have promulgated this concept. Just the opposite is true.

Reporting at a recent meeting of the American College of Cardiology, William B. Kannel M.D., for years Director of the Framingham Heart Study, produced data which finally laid this notion to rest. He showed conclusively that subjects whose pressures were abnormal only part of the time (doctors call this "labile hypertension") were no less likely to develop cardiovascular disease than those whose pressures were persistently elevated. The lesson to be learned is that if the pressure is even occasionally high, a definite added risk is present which should not be ignored.

I suspect that early treatment of this type of blood pressure elevation might improve the nation's health more than any other measure, with the possible exception of banning tobacco.

Dr. Kannel also laid to rest another misconception about blood pressure. For years it was thought that the lower blood pressure reading, *the diastolic pressure,* was more important in defining the seriousness of the blood pressure problem than the upper reading, *the systolic pressure.* The Framingham Study has shown that the systolic pressure is an equally important indicator of a potentially serious medical problem.

Millions of people in this country have mild elevation of systolic pressure. Life insurance statistics show clearly that such people do have an added risk for later development of heart disease, stroke, and other cardiovascular problems. Many physicians, perhaps rightly, have felt that drug treatment, because of potentially serious side-effects, should not be recommended for such patients. But *running may be the treatment of choice for many of these people.* Such a cardiovascular fitness program may produce stunning results.

Let me give you a personal example. At age 30, before I started running regularly, I weighed 215 pounds and my blood pressure was consistently 150/90. Over the last 10 years my pressure has rarely been above 110/70. I have never taken a pill for it. Running has done it. Of course, I lost a lot of weight as well, and whether weight loss without running might have produced a similar result is uncertain. I do know this: I never would have lost the weight without the running.

Sometimes I literally want to shake my overweight, middle-aged patients whose blood pressure is a little too high or somewhat labile. They have the ability in a very simple, safe fashion, to rid themselves of this distressing risk factor, which very probably will shorten their lives. Most are unwilling even to begin an exercise program no matter how patiently I explain, cajole, or threaten them. Many don't even seem to care. All they want is a pill. I suspect my success in motivating such people is higher than average, but it remains distressingly low.

Q. Isn't your blood pressure of 110/70 too low? Isn't 120/80 supposed to be normal? 2112308

A. This is still another misconception about blood pressure: 120/80 isn't "normal," nor is it optimal. It is merely an average reading in healthy young people. The insurance company statistics now clearly demonstrate that the lower the blood pressure the better, at least as far as longevity and freedom from future cardiovascular disease are concerned. All other things being equal, pressure of 110/70 is "better" than 120/80. And 100/60 is even "better" still.

We used to think that low blood pressure was a disease; pressures much less than 120/80 were worrisome and should be treated. This is nonsense. Of course, very low blood pressure may result from some disease processes, but it is a good finding in otherwise well people. A few days before a marathon, when I am in peak condition, my blood pressure will often be around 90/60. I may even become a bit lightheaded when I first get out of bed in the morning. But this low resting pressure will rise very nicely when the demands for extra heart work occur during exercise. I welcome my low blood pressure; it means I am very fit.

Another misconception is that blood pressure must rise as we grow older. In the United States and other affluent countries, blood pressure does rise in most people until the fifth or sixth decade and then tends to level off. But in societies in which physical activity continues throughout life, and older people do not grow fat, blood pressure does not rise much with age. _In societies in which long life is common, you will generally find low blood pressure and high levels of daily physical activity in older people._

35

Q. Does a running program always lower high blood pressure?

A. Absolutely not. Some people will have high blood pressure no matter how many miles they run each day. They will probably require drug treatment. The response to running also depends on when the running program is begun. If hypertension has been present for many years, it is less likely to respond to an exercise program. Treatment begun early is likely to be more effective.

LACK OF PHYSICAL ACTIVITY

Q. High on your list of risk factors you include lack of physical activity. Do you mean that even in the absence of all the other risk factors, reduced physical activity may cause atherosclerosis?

A. There is increasing evidence that this may be true. Stevedores performing heavy physical labor daily develop heart disease less frequently than stevedores with less physically demanding jobs. A British study has shown that even moderate weekend activity, such as gardening or walking, offers some protective effect. There seems to be some hope for even the often-scorned weekend athlete.

The likelihood of heart disease developing in college athletes after graduation has recently been studied. The heart attack rate was lowest in the athletes who continued to exercise regularly and highest in those who stopped exercising after graduation. The heart attack rate for this latter group was even higher than that of their fellow graduates who had never exercised at all, either in college or after.

Much higher levels of daily physical activity provide even more protection. An often quoted example is that of the Masai Tribesmen of Africa. These nomadic shepherds, who walk many miles each day, rarely have heart attacks or strokes, even though their diets contain a relatively high percentage of fat. In our sedentary society, such high fat intake would almost certainly constitute an important risk factor.

The protective effect of exercise is also seen in our own Eskimo population, where an interesting sociological event has provided us with important medical information. Adult Eskimos traditionally perform heavy physical work. They also consume a

very high fat diet. As long as they continue their high daily physical activity, they seem relatively immune to atherosclerosis, and
their blood cholesterol levels remain normal. But some Eskimo
societies have become more Westernized. The elderly receive the
dubious privilege of early retirement. Their vigorous daily activity stops, but their high fat intake continues. Both blood cholesterol level and the frequency of heart attacks rise sharply.

CHOLESTEROL AND OTHER FATS

Q. Does cholesterol actually cause atherosclerosis?

A. There is still considerable disagreement among experts about
cholesterol's role in atherosclerosis, and particularly whether low
cholesterol, low fat diets really make much difference.
    One fact is indisputable: *the actual level of cholesterol in the
blood is an excellent predictor of future heart attacks and other
kinds of vascular disease.* Subjects with low cholesterol levels
have only a fraction of the risk of those whose levels are very
high. What we call a "normal" cholesterol in this country—about
220 to 240—isn't really normal at all. Rather, it is an average
value for adult Americans, who have a high heart attack rate. In
societies with low heart attack rates, cholesterol levels in the
blood are low, usually well below 200, and they do not rise with
age.
    These findings have encouraged us to try to lower cholesterol
levels, and our early experience does indeed suggest that we have
some control over them. Whether this effort will eventually lower
our heart attack rate is not yet established.

Q. Can the risk of heart attack be lowered by following a low fat
diet?

A. Many authorities believe that such a diet is crucial for reducing
this risk. They correctly point out that in most countries in which
heart attacks are common, fats usually constitute a major portion
of the diet. Others place less emphasis on how much fat we actually eat every day, but rather believe that other aspects of our
way of life, such as obesity, lack of exercise, and stress, are more
important in producing high blood cholesterol levels. These ex-

perts urge us to pay more attention to exercise and weight control as a way to lower the cholesterol blood levels.

Q. Which theory do you support?

A. There seems to be an element of truth in both. A low fat diet seems to me to be a prudent one. There is certainly no evidence that it might be harmful and there is considerable evidence that a high fat intake, particularly if associated with obesity, can raise the blood cholesterol. Moderate reduction of fat in the diet can lower the blood cholesterol levels 10 or 15 percent in many individuals. A low fat diet is usually a lower calorie diet as well. (I will discuss diet in greater detail in Chapter 9.)

But the other point of view also has considerable merit. There is strong evidence that, if we stay thin and exercise vigorously, cholesterol blood levels will stay low no matter what we eat. For example, a recent medical study showed that long distance runners have significantly lower cholesterol levels than nonexercising subjects of the same weight and age. This difference was independent of diet, since the diets of the two groups were essentially the same, the only difference being that the runners had to eat more to maintain their weights because they burned so many calories running. Perhaps even more important, more of the runners' cholesterol was contained in high density lipoproteins, which have recently received considerable publicity because they may protect against heart attacks.

HIGH DENSITY LIPOPROTEINS (HDL)

Q. Is this what has been called the "good" cholesterol?

A. Yes it is. But this is not really an accurate name. Cholesterol is transported in the blood by several different chemical compounds called lipoproteins. One type, the high density lipoproteins, also called HDL, serve the very important function of taking excessive cholesterol away from tissues, including the arteries, thereby lowering their cholesterol content and retarding the development of atherosclerosis. Subjects with high levels of HDL in the blood seem less likely to develop atherosclerosis.

The ideal cholesterol reading would be a low total blood

cholesterol, with a high percentage carried in the HDL. This is precisely what happened to the long distance runners studied. Whether the same process occurs in older people who exercise intensively has not yet been carefully examined, but early indications suggest that it may. Some authorities now feel that the major effect exercise has in retarding atherosclerosis may be the rise in HDL that exercise produces.

ALCOHOL AND HDL

Q. We have recently read that alcohol raises the levels of high density lipoproteins and that moderate amounts of alcohol may be good for us.

A. It's true, at least according to one study. But a more recent one disputes this finding. I am always reluctant to recommend alcohol to anyone, since it is so easy to abuse it. But I am fairly confident that alcohol in moderation, less than 2 or 3 ounces daily, will not harm the otherwise healthy individual.

In some individuals, alcohol in larger amounts may actually raise some of the blood fat levels, particularly triglycerides. Also alcohol has a strong depressant effect on the nervous system and on the heart muscle itself. I strongly advise people to avoid running soon after significant alcohol intake. Save your drinking for after you run, and, if you must drink, drink beer.

Q. Why beer?

A. Because not only will beer help replenish your fluid loss, but it contains enough minerals and complex carbohydrates to help return your nutritional state to normal after running.

THE COMPLICATED PROCESS OF ATHEROSCLEROSIS

Q. Let's return to atherosclerosis. Can you explain what really happens?

A. This is currently one of the most exciting areas of medical research and we are still only beginning to unravel the mysteries of this process.

The end result of atherosclerosis is the blockage of an artery. The blocking material contains a high proportion of cholesterol and other fatty substances, as well as other blood elements including platelets and proteins, all of which are involved in the normal blood clotting process.

We've known this for a long time, but only recently have we begun to understand how the process actually begins. In humans at least we now are fairly certain that atherosclerosis begins when we are young and takes decades to develop. It probably starts with damage to the very thin layer of cells which form the important inner wall of the artery called the *endothelium*. Normal endothelium is shown in Figure 3. Like most of our body tissues, the endothelium does weaken with age and is more prone to damage. In addition to age, endothelial damage is caused by high blood pressure and high cholesterol levels. When we are young the endothelium retains the capacity to repair itself, but with time this capacity is lost and permanent damage can occur.

Then a series of complex events happen. First, the smooth muscle cells in the wall of the artery, which underlie the damaged area, are stimulated to grow and multiply. At the same time they accumulate large amounts of cholesterol and other fats. The growth of a number of other tissue elements is stimulated, and the involved area enlarges. If it becomes large enough, it may interfere with the flow of blood within the artery. This situation is pictured in Figure 4. No signs or symptoms of this obstruction will be evident for a considerable period, because the flow of blood

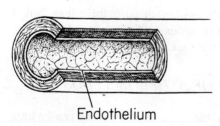

Endothelium

FIGURE 3. *A normal artery free from atherosclerosis. Note the smooth inner lining of the artery, called the endothelium.*

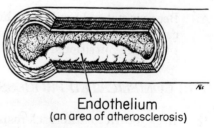

Endothelium
(an area of atherosclerosis)

FIGURE 4. *Atherosclerosis in an artery. This condition reduces the inner area of the artery and can interfere with blood flow.*

through the artery is not significantly impaired until the cross-sectional area of the artery is reduced by more than half.

This is what happens in angina patients with atherosclerosis of the coronary arteries. When the blood requirements of the heart muscle are low, at rest for example, no symptoms are present. During exercise, when the heart works harder, adequate flow of blood may not be possible in the partially blocked artery, the heart muscle is starved for blood, and symptoms begin.

Q. You have stated repeatedly that this process takes years to develop. Yet heart attacks or strokes appear rather abruptly. Why?

A. The acute event apparently is caused by sudden complete blockage of the artery, either by a clot that forms in the area already involved by the atherosclerosis, by a hemorrhage in the wall of the artery which expands the size of the involved area, or by a spasm of the artery itself. When complete blockage occurs, the results are disastrous: the death and destruction of the tissues supplied by the blocked artery. If this occurs in the heart, we call it a coronary, heart attack, or myocardial infarction. In the brain, we call it a stroke.

Therefore, *it is crucial to prevent the atherosclerotic process from beginning and progressing.* We believe that this can be done. But the earlier such a program is started, the more likely is success. That's why it is so important to begin a healthy life style before some severe illness such as a heart attack or stroke occurs. For many, the key to this healthy life style is a running program.

How Much Exercise Is Needed for Protection?

Q. Could you be a bit more specific about how much activity is necessary and what levels of exercise might provide maximum protection from atherosclerosis?

A. At the most extreme end of the exercise spectrum is the widely publicized contention, most eloquently and loudly proclaimed by Dr. Thomas Bassler, a pathologist from California who is prominent in the American Medical Joggers Association, that a

41

marathoner's life style affords absolute protection against heart attacks. What he means is that the high level of regular physical activity required to train for and successfully complete a marathon, prevents the development and progression of athero-sclerosis. Many argue that this statement is much too strong, and offer specific examples of marathoners who have died of heart attacks. I am sure there have been and will continue to be marathoners who die of heart attacks. I am equally convinced that regular training of the intensity and duration required to complete a marathon, if begun early enough, offers considerable, though not complete, protection from future heart attacks.

Q. But it is unrealistic to expect most of us to devote such enormous time and effort to exercise. How much exercise must we perform to obtain considerable if not maximal protection from future heart attacks?

A. Dr. Ralph Paffenbarger, an epidemiologist–physician from California, whose studies on stevedores and former college athletes we have already discussed, has carefully evaluated this problem. He has found that considerable, although perhaps not optimal, protection from heart attacks occurs when there is an exercise program of high enough intensity to burn about 2500 to 3000 calories per week. Less intense exercise provides less protection.

Q. How much running does this mean we actually must perform?

A. This translates to about 18 to 21 miles of running each week at a pace of about 9 to 10 minutes per mile. The exact amount will depend on the individual's weight. Heavier runners do not have to run as far as thin ones.

I think it is reasonable to point a fitness program toward reaching this weekly exercise level. This mileage can conveniently be divided into a 3-mile run six or seven days each week, or perhaps a 4-mile run five times each week. The beginning runner, of course, cannot hope to achieve this level immediately. We will discuss how to do so safely and sensibly in Chapter 5.

Q. Can the exercise level be achieved by running longer distances less frequently?

A. Yes, it can, but I do not advise it until long after you have reached this weekly level with shorter, more frequent runs. Longer runs increase the risks of musculo-skeletal injury. This risk seems to increase with runs of more than 30 or 40 minutes.

Q. Can lower-intensity exercise performed for longer periods afford the same protection? For example, can long periods of brisk walking, so long as they consume the required 2500 to 3000 calories a week, produce the same protective effect?

A. I suspect that walking can, but here too the evidence is uncertain. Walking is probably the optimal exercise to protect us from the development of atherosclerosis, even though it will not produce maximal cardiovascular fitness. The problem is that most of us do not have the time to walk long enough to burn the necessary calories. The example of the African Bushmen strongly supports this assumption.

WHAT WE CAN LEARN FROM THE BUSHMEN

The Bushmen of Africa, long isolated from the rest of the world, live essentially as man did 20,000 years ago, before he learned to grow crops and raise livestock. The Bushmen must spend most of their time searching for food, since they do not grow their own. They walk prodigious distances, but rarely perform any more vigorous activity. Their diets consist of what they can kill with primitive weapons or what grows wild. Their cholesterol levels are closer to 100 than 200 and do not rise with age. They die of a variety of causes, but almost never of atherosclerosis.

The creatures we know today as man, both the Bushmen and the sedentary citizens of our society, are products of an evolutionary process which has operated over millions of years. An important result of this evolutionary process has been the development of a very efficient musculo-skeletal system designed to perform the physical activity necessary to find food at a very low energy or calorie cost. The well-conditioned Bushman, walking

43

his usual 15 to 20 miles each day, burns only an extra 1500 or 1600 calories. This obviously was a most helpful evolutionary process. If higher energy expenditures had been necessary, the Bushman's survival would have been imperiled, since food was scarce.

Primitive man also required an efficient method for storing the energy contained in the food he ate. He was not presented with three meals daily plus the luxury of snacking in between. He had no good methods for food preservation or storage, so he immediately ate what he found, consuming as much food as possible. Thus evolved over these millions of years the ability to store extra calories as fat, by far our most efficient storage form of energy.

Like the Bushmen, we have inherited the results of these millions of years of evolution. We have the same efficient mechanisms for performing muscular work and we maintain our ability to store energy efficiently in fat tissue. But our problems are just the opposite. *Having an efficient musculo-skeletal system means that we must perform prodigious amounts of physical activity to burn the calories we consume.* Now that we suffer from an abundance rather than a lack of calories, we store too much fat, often overwhelming the ability of our bodies to handle this excess.

Modern living has robbed us of the need to be physically active. Our marvelously efficient and complex musculo-skeletal system has grown soft from disuse. Our metabolism and digestive systems, ingeniously designed to store extra calories in our fat tissue, now become the vehicles for overloading our bodies with the excess calories we consume each day. Our appetites seem to be controlled more by custom and habit than hunger. No wonder our arteries are clogged with fatty deposits!

Our nervous systems were also once exquisitely tuned to allow us to respond quickly and violently if our safety was threatened. Scientists called this the "fight or flight reaction." Now our threats and stresses are more subtle. We can't hit the driver who cuts us off in traffic or the boss who screams at us without reason. Instead our reaction to stress is directed inward. We become short-tempered and ill-humored; blood pressure and pulse rate rise.

Recently a variety of meditation and relaxation techniques have been shown to be useful in reducing stress. In some patients, vigorous physical activity may be equally effective. Exercise can be a marvelous tranquilizer.

Stress, Depression, and Middle-Aged Melancholy

Q. Are you implying that exercise can help us cope with stress and help depression?

A. I am very definitely. Even if physical fitness through exercise did not help us live a moment longer, it would still be worth achieving. Often its single most important effect is the feeling of well-being it produces. We become aware of and begin to enjoy our bodies. Our self-image improves. We are less likely to overindulge in food and drink, and better able to break the cigarette habit. In short, an exercise program often serves as the foundation for a major commitment to preserving health.

CAN RUNNING HELP YOUR SEX LIFE?

Q. Among the many claims made for running is that it can improve your sex life. Is there any good evidence this is really true?

A. This claim is very difficult to verify scientifically, but I am sure it is true for some. Physically fit people, runners among them, seem less likely to become depressed, and depression is a major cause of an unsatisfactory sex life. Runners often have more energy, take pride in their bodies, and may be more physically attractive. All these factors are likely to benefit an individual's sex life.

But if you become addicted to running, or are training intensively for a race, so much of your psychological as well as physical energy is devoted to your training that there is often little energy and time for anything else, including sex. Male runners' wives confirm that during intense training, their husbands' interest in sex declines significantly. I am not sure whether the same is true of women runners, but I suspect that it is.

While we are discussing sex, I would like to dispel one myth. Sexual activity does not reduce athletic performance. I suppose a boxer or wrestler might be made more savage if he were sexually deprived before a match, but there is not a shred of evidence that sexual relations, even just before athletic activity, have any adverse effects.

45

MIDDLE-AGED MELANCHOLY

Exercise may be particularly helpful for those who, although not excessively tense or depressed, may be sinking slowly into the pattern of what some have called "middle-aged melancholy." Most of us have presumed that, as we enter middle age, we must inexorably gain weight, reduce our physical activity, and develop a flatness of thought and action. Chronic, mild fatigue becomes accepted. At an age when life could be most rewarding, before the infirmities of old age and after the uncertainties and groping of youth, we lapse into comfortable, flat, unexciting middle age. I have seen exercise reverse this process in so many people that I am convinced that it may be the best medicine for middle-aged melancholy. Psychiatrists are now finding that exercise may be equally effective in helping moderate depression when more traditional treatment has failed.

A recent medical study, presented at the 1977 meeting of the American Psychiatric Association has provided strong confirmation of this theory. Physicians at the University of Wisconsin compared the benefits of running with those of traditional psychiatric treatment in two groups of depressed college students. Every student who ran felt better, and careful testing showed that depression was reduced in all the runners. The runners as a group did at least as well, and sometimes better, than the others, and most of them continued to run after the formal study was finished because they felt that the running definitely helped them.

I am not surprised. I have witnessed similar results in some of my mildly depressed patients, who were able to sustain a running program. Whether older or sicker patients will similarly benefit is less certain. I have found them much more resistant to all types of treatment and I doubt that most of them could continue an adequate running program.

Even more impressive may be the results in treating people who have just the opposite problem, who, instead of being depressed, are tense and overreact to life's stresses.

The Type A Personality

Q. Is this type of person what is called a "Type A personality"?

A.   Not everyone who is tense or "uptight" has the same type of personality, but in a recent best-selling book, *Type A Personality and Your Heart,* Doctors Meyer Friedman and Raymond Rosenman describe a common personality characteristic which they consider to be the most important risk factor of all for developing heart disease. They call this the "Type A personality." Such people are usually not difficult to recognize. They are hard-driving, tense, ambitious, punctual, and demanding. Type A people are often considered successful by the usual criteria. They are very time-oriented. You can pick them out in a crowd because they are continually glancing at their watches, anxious to get on to the next order of business. They seem unable to relax and are compulsive workers. If they read at all, they read to enhance their skills rather than to relax.

I question the authors' conclusion that the Type A personality is the *most important* risk factor, but I certainly agree it's an important one. In discussing the possible management of such patients, the authors scoff at exercise as an effective therapy. In fact, they consider exercise to be down-right dangerous. I strongly disagree with this conclusion. In my experience, Type A persons often benefit most from an exercise program, particularly if they begin the program early in life before any heart problem has developed. Such patients must be carefully watched lest in their typical, enthusiastic fashion they overdo a good thing. But they are often the ones who will be most faithful to the program. Exercise often becomes an absolutely vital safety valve for their aggressions, tensions, and exuberance.

The effects of exercise in relieving tension are not limited to those with Type A personalities. Vigorous exercise may help anyone who has trouble relaxing. It is often better than Valium and as effective as Yoga and meditation. Some, in fact, combine exercise with one of the accepted meditation techniques with excellent results. Exercise also has the very useful added benefits of producing physical fitness and burning excess calories.

Smoking

Q.   Cigarette smoking is high on your list of risk factors. It is clear how smoking might damage the lungs, but how does it affect the heart?

A.   No one is certain why smokers are far more likely to have heart attacks and die suddenly from them, but the evidence is quite clear that this is indeed the fact. Recent evidence suggests that smoking actually accelerates the atherosclerotic process itself. Some suspect that the nicotine in tobacco overstimulates the heart. Another possibility is that cigarette smokers develop such high concentrations of carbon monoxide in their blood that the oxygen-carrying capacity of their red blood cells is interfered with. Or perhaps the major risk from cigarette smoking comes from the production of potentially serious irregularities of the heartbeat due to the excessive adrenalin production that smoking causes.

   The risks of cigarette smoking are evident when we look at the incidence of heart disease in women. While the frequency of heart disease seems to be falling slightly in men, it is rising in women. The major factor seems to be the greater number of young and middle-aged women who smoke.

   Cigarettes are particularly dangerous to people who possess other risk factors or who have already sustained a heart attack. The frequency of sudden death in heart patients who smoke is twice that of those who do not smoke. I feel so strongly about smoking that I will not continue to see heart patients who still smoke or who make no effort to stop. They are wasting my time and their money. This firm stand against smoking is sometimes the one thing that makes a patient stop.

Q.   Isn't it dangerous for smokers to exercise vigorously? Shouldn't they stop smoking before they begin their exercise program?

A.   Let me answer the second question first: This approach is unrealistic and unlikely to succeed. In almost every case an exercise program can safely begin before smoking is stopped. Often this makes it easier for the patient to cut down tobacco consumption gradually as exercise capacity increases. If the exercise program can be sustained, so strong a distaste for smoking often occurs that it becomes relatively easy to stop completely. The aching lungs, breathlessness, and general feeling of self-contempt that running often produces in smokers are potent forces to help kick the habit.

   The possible benefits of this approach considerably outweigh the slight risk of exercise in patients who smoke. Of course those who have severe lung disease because of smoking are not likely to be able to exercise very vigorously. Nevertheless, there is some evidence that regular exercise can help even such patients.

Q. Are pipe and cigar smoking as dangerous as cigarette smoking?

A. Usually not, since pipe and cigar smokers usually don't inhale. If they do, then their smoking can become dangerous.

Diabetes

Q. Is it safe for diabetics to exercise? Does exercise help to control the diabetes?

A. Most diabetics can be divided into two groups. The first are the so-called juvenile diabetics who develop the disease in childhood and usually require insulin. The second group, by far the majority, includes those who develop diabetes during or after middle age. Most of them will not require insulin. Many are overweight and "lose" their diabetes if they reduce. In both groups the risk of atherosclerosis is increased. A careful exercise program may improve diabetic control and also the quality of life. I suspect that it may also slow down atherosclerosis, but as yet this is unproved. Exercise can be safe for the juvenile diabetic, but since it may significantly alter his insulin requirements, it should be supervised and regulated by a physician.

Q. What about the other risk factors?

A. _Age,_ of course, is an important risk factor. The older one grows the greater the chance of dying from almost anything, heart attacks included. It's no tragedy to have a heart attack at 85 and die suddenly; most of us would settle for that. It is a tragedy, however, to suffer a heart attack, fatal or not, at age 45. This is when a great many heart attacks happen, particularly in men.

49

The "Weaker" Sex

Why males are so much more likely to develop atherosclerosis is unclear. Some suggest that the stress and strain of life more severely affects males, but many believe that women are protected by the female hormones, which seem to slow the development of hardening of the arteries. If both ovaries which manufacture the hormones are surgically removed from a woman before the menopause, she may lose her resistance to atherosclerosis. After natural menopause, women also become more likely to develop atherosclerosis.

Q. Then why not give female hormones to all women after the menopause? Could men also be protected this way?

A. This seems like a logical approach, and not surprisingly it has been extensively tried in both men and women. In men the side effects of the female hormones are usually unacceptable: the men become feminized. This is no problem for women, but there are other bad effects to consider, such as a slightly higher frequency of breast and uterine cancer. I do not routinely recommend hormones to women after the menopause, but I have little hesitation in prescribing them for younger women whose ovaries have been removed. I usually recommend that they take the hormones at least until the time they would have sustained a normal menopause.

"THE PILL"

While we're on the subject of female hormones, we should briefly discuss birth control pills. From what has just been said you might expect that these drugs, which contain female hormones in various combinations, might offer protection against atherosclerosis. But just the opposite seems to be true. Heart attacks, strokes, and other vascular problems are more common in young women who take them. Fortunately we can predict fairly accurately which women are most likely to experience serious reactions to them. If there is a strong family history of heart or blood pressure problems, or if the woman herself has these illnesses, if she smokes heavily or has a high cholesterol, I advise her not to take birth control pills.

Are We the Prisoners of Our Genes?

Q. Is heredity an important risk factor?

A. Heredity seems to operate chiefly through the development of the risk factors we have been discussing. We inherit the tendency to high cholesterol, diabetes, and in some instances high blood pressure. In this sense heredity is a very important risk factor. But in the absence of these factors, heredity alone seems not to be so important. Before those of you whose parents died of heart attacks at an early age lose hope, remember that even if you have inherited some of these risk tendencies, they often can be modified. They are not indelibly stamped on you like the color of your eyes or the shape of your nose. If you have a strong family history of heart disease, check with your doctor to find out if you possess any risk factors, so that they can be treated as early in life as possible.

Obesity

Q. You have said little about obesity as a risk factor. Is it as important as the others?

A. Obesity is extremely important, but like heredity it seems to operate by making the obese patient more likely to develop other risk factors, particularly high blood pressure, diabetes, and high blood cholesterol levels. Obesity may be the single most important cause of high blood pressure. High blood pressure in turn is probably the single most important cause of coronary and other types of heart disease and stroke. When obesity is unaccompanied by any of the other risk factors, the chances for developing atherosclerosis are not increased much.

Unfortunately even a moderate amount of obesity, no more than 10 or 20 pounds, may stimulate the other risk factors. Strict

51

attention to keeping the susceptible person's weight normal is extremely important in avoiding risk factors. Exercise, combined with correct eating, can play an important role in weight control, thereby reducing risk factors.

EXERCISE AND WEIGHT LOSS

Q. A lot of people are interested in how an exercise program can help them lose weight. Can exercise really do this? If it can, does it make dieting easier?

A. My answer to both these questions is a very strong *Yes.*

Most people would like to be thin. Our youth-oriented culture rewards being thin and scorns people who are fat. Exercise is currently being touted as the easy way to control weight. The exercise bandwagon has formed. All you have to do is jump on and the pounds will start melting off.

It is true that exercise can help you lose weight. It can make dieting easier. The combination of exercise and moderate dietary calorie restriction is perhaps the best way to lose weight. But it still isn't easy.

Q. How does exercise actually work in a weight loss program?

A. Exercise helps with weight loss in at least three ways:

1. *By burning calories during the performance of the exercise.*
2. *By giving psychological support.* People who exercise regularly seem less likely to cheat on their diets. They realize that the extra trip to the refrigerator can quickly reverse the good effects of their hard work. They become more calorie conscious.
3. *By suppressing the appetite.* We think of exercise as stimulating the appetite; a long walk in the woods on a crisp autumn day, or chopping wood for the fire, is supposed to make us ravenous. But in some people the opposite effect occurs, particularly if the exercise is of high intensity and performed regularly. It's often most useful for a person to exercise just before that time of day when he is most likely to overeat. For many this may mean exercising late in the afternoon or early evening before dinner, which is usually the biggest meal.

Q. Some people have a chronic problem with weight even though they don't seem to overeat. Others seem to be able to eat anything and never gain an ounce. Do they have different metabolism? Or are they really eating fewer calories?

A. *Calories do count,* but they are not the whole story by a long shot. If we sweep away all the nonsense and half-truths about diet, we are left with one basic fact about calories: *our weights are the direct result of the balance between our energy intake (the calorie content of the food we eat) and our energy expenditure (the calories we burn up).* We gain weight if we eat more calories than we burn. Conversely, we lose weight if our daily physical activity requires more calories than are present in the food we eat. Regardless of how much or little each of us eats, let me repeat this basic fact: we gain weight when we eat more than we burn, and lose it when we burn more than we eat.

But there is another factor to consider: Until quite recently doctors presumed that people were fat because they ate a lot more calories than they should. Traditional treatment emphasized decreased calorie intake. Many patients unfortunately bear witness to the futility of this approach. Protests that they really did not eat a lot provoked only looks of scorn or disbelief. They received a low calorie diet and were ushered out of the doctor's office with a pat on the back.

Some were able to follow the low calorie diet for a few weeks or months and lose weight. Others tried crash diets, perhaps with some initial success. But old eating habits and patterns generally returned. Pounds lost with great difficulty reappeared with astounding rapidity. Group therapy helped some for a while; witness the success of Weight Watchers and Diet Workshop. But even these props failed most people.

Now we know that at least some fat people were telling the truth. They really didn't eat a lot, and their calorie intake was low. *But even at their low calorie intake they gained weight because their daily physical activity was even lower.*

Q. It always seemed to us that fat people do move about less, but we thought this was only because they were fat. Are you implying that they may be fat because they don't move around much?

A. This is absolutely correct. It is perhaps most strikingly illustrated

53

by studies of overweight children. Most fat children do not eat more than their skinny friends. Instead, they perform much less physical activity. It would be illogical to think that further calorie restriction would help in such cases. Almost certainly this same pattern of decreased physical activity is the cause of obesity in many adults.

Reflect for a moment. Was your weight once normal? Has it gradually crept up as you passed through your 30s and 40s? Are you really eating more than you used to? Probably you are not. Are you less active physically? Very probably you are.

Q.   Does this imply that exercise alone without dietary changes can produce significant weight loss?

A.   This fact was convincingly demonstrated in a study recently performed in California. Writing in the May, 1975, issue of the *Archives of Internal Medicine,* Dr. Grant Gwinup described the effects of exercise on eleven obese women who had consulted him for weight control. All had given up dieting and had shown no particular weight change for three months preceding their entry into the study. The women were advised not to diet or change their eating pattern in any way.

Each was then allowed to select a type of exercise which she could perform on a daily basis. All chose walking. They were also instructed not to change established occupational or recreational routines. Exercise was performed daily, and all eleven women eventually were walking steadily for 30 minutes or more each day. They all continued this program for at least one year. All lost weight, the average being about 22 pounds. One woman lost 38 pounds.

The amount of weight lost generally paralleled the amount of walking and did not begin until walking exceeded 30 minutes daily. Weight tended to stabilize, and further weight loss could be accomplished only if the duration or frequency of the walking increased. In two patients who temporarily discontinued exercise due to illness, rapid weight gain followed. When the exercise was resumed, weight loss once more started.

Equally important, most of the subjects noted that their weight loss through exercise, unlike that previously achieved through dieting, was not associated with weakness, nervousness, and the other uncomfortable feelings that so often made them discontinue previous diets. Not everyone liked the exercise program, but none found it intolerable. All of them planned to continue because they were happy with the results. Measurements of skin fold thickness, an accurate way of estimating body fat content, showed that most of the weight loss, unlike that achieved by crash dieting, resulted from the loss of fat, not muscle.

This study deserves more publicity because it shows without question that significant weight loss can be achieved by moderate physical activity, even when calorie intake is not reduced.

But I haven't told you the whole story. The eleven obese women who completed this study actually represented less than one-third of the total number of persons who entered it initially. Thirty-four subjects started, but only eleven were able to maintain the required thirty minutes or more of daily walking.

Q. What happened to the rest of them?

A. Only five of the original thirty-four were men, and they all stopped exercising. The usual excuse was that they worked full time and could not regularly devote the necessary time to exercise, even though three achieved marked weight loss prior to dropping out. Many of the rest chose jogging as their exercise, but were so plagued by injuries that they could not continue. The others had a variety of excuses.

THE CALORIE COST OF EXERCISE

Q. Wouldn't it make sense then to combine regular exercise with calorie reduction? Could we then reduce the daily exercise time and make it more acceptable to many people?

A. This would seem to be the method most likely to achieve reasonable weight loss safely. To help put this into perspective, let's talk a bit about the calorie cost of exercise. Many people already know how to count calories. Indeed, many overweight patients know far more about calories than their doctors do. But most people know relatively little about the number of calories consumed by common physical activities. Many are horrified to find out that they would have to jog a mile or two to burn the calories contained in a couple of cookies or a before-dinner martini.

55

Remember this: *There are about 3500 calories in every pound of body fat,* and loss of fat tissue is the only real method of losing weight in the long run. Many of the diets which promise, and frequently deliver, considerable initial weight loss take advantage of the fact that with carbohydrate restriction, you will quickly lose a lot of fluid. But this is only temporary—eventually you will regain the fluid.

So forgetting the transient ups and downs of the body's fluid or water balance, we are left with the fact that *we must burn about 3500 calories more than we consume if we are to lose a pound of fat.*

Remember another figure: If we jog for an hour at about 6 miles per hour, a speed of 1 mile in 10 minutes, we use between 600 and 800 calories in that hour depending on our weight. Discouraging, isn't it? We would have to jog 5 or 6 hours to lose a pound. We talked earlier about how evolution provided us with such an efficient musculo-skeletal system that we can perform prodigious amounts of aerobic activity without burning many calories. We are now paying the price for this. Remember the Bushmen!

But let's look at these figures another way. If each of us could jog for an hour each day, six days a week, with a two-week vacation and Sundays off, we could still lose 50 pounds a year even if we did not reduce our food consumption by a single calorie. Or we could eat a lot of tempting food without gaining weight.

Few people will have the time, energy, or inclination to spend an hour each day jogging. But these figures help put the issue in perspective. They show how hard it is to lose weight by exercise alone. It's easier by far to combine moderate calorie restriction with a modest exercise program.

For example, the expenditure through exercise of just 200 calories a day, about 20 minutes of slow jogging, puts you 1400 calories ahead at the end of a week. After a month you are nearly 6000 calories ahead. Combine this with a reduction of just 200 calories in your daily food intake and now you are 12,000 calories ahead each month. This is nearly 4 pounds, and you are achieving the reasonable goal of a 1-pound weight loss each week. Even a mile jog each day will consume about 100 calories and can serve as the exercise base for a weight loss program.

Q. This seems too simple. Why aren't more people doing it?

A. Often the biggest obstacle to getting started is the feeling that you're in such poor condition, or so overweight, that you can't possibly make any significant progress. How could your flabby bones and muscles, and rusty cardiovascular system, possibly allow you to perform enough calorie-consuming exercise to make a real difference? People who feel this way should take heart from a recent study which shows that fat people have an almost unfair advantage. Lugging all that extra weight around, even at a slow pace, makes them burn considerably more calories than their thinner colleagues performing exactly the same exercise.

A group of Air Force physicians measured the calories consumed by subjects of different weights and ages as they ran a distance of 1.5 miles at different speeds. Dr. Bruce F. Harger and his associates, writing in the *Journal of the American Medical Association* (April, 1974), showed that the pace at which their subjects ran—that is, how fast they completed the 1.5 miles—had surprisingly little effect on the calories they burned. Much more important was the weight of each subject. The heaviest among them burned considerably more calories when performing exactly the same exercise. Table 4 shows some of the data presented by Dr. Harger and his colleagues. Note the difference in the calories burned between the fast and slow speeds for your own weight.

TABLE 4. *The Calorie Cost of Running 1.5 Miles*

WEIGHT		CALORIES	
POUNDS	KILOGRAMS*	FAST SPEED	SLOW SPEED
120	54.5	125	112
130	59	135	121
140	63.9	145	130
150	68.1	155	139
160	72.6	165	148
170	77.2	175	157
180	81.7	185	166
190	86.3	195	175
200	90.8	205	184
210	95.3	215	193
220	99.9	225	202

*1 kilogram = 2.2 pounds.

There really is not that much difference. But look at the difference between the 120-pound and the 220-pound man. The heavier subject used almost twice as many calories in running his mile and a half.

Similar experiments have not yet been performed for other types of aerobic exercise, but' it's reasonable to assume that an activity of similar intensity performed for a similar period of time will require about the same amount of energy. (Calorie costs of other types of exercise have been given in Table 2, page 20.) An exception may be swimming. The buoyancy effect of water may make weight differences less important.

COUNTING CALORIES

Q. What is the best way to estimate the number of calories we consume each day?

A. By far the best way, in my experience, is to make a careful list of everything you eat for a period of time, perhaps a couple of weeks. Then look up the caloric content of each food in one of the widely available charts containing this information, and add up the total for each 24 hours. Make sure you account for the size of the portions of each type of food. Often counting calories for even this short period gives people a realistic estimate of how much they are eating. Many people are horrified to find out how much they really eat. Table 5 contains the calorie content of many common foods. Far more complete tables are available at any good bookstore.

The average adult American male consumes between 2000 and 3000 calories each day. If your usual daily intake is more than 2500 calories you are probably overeating, unless you perform a great deal of physical activity each day. At very low levels of activity, during a very lazy Sunday, or when you are recovering from an illness, you might consume only 1200 to 1500 calories. This is about the basic minimum. During the average work day behind a desk, or doing light housework, you might expend an additional 500 to 700 calories.

You might also keep a log of your daily physical activity. Are you really doing enough to balance the calories you eat? Your

TABLE 5. *The Calorie Content of Common Foods*[1]

ITEM	PORTION	CALORIES
Meat and Poultry[2]		
Bacon	1 strip (1 oz.)	156
Beef		
Corned beef (canned)	3 slices	184
Hamburger	¼ pound	224
Pot roast (rump)	½ pound	188
Sirloin steak	½ pound	260
Chicken (broiler)	3½ oz.	151
Duck	3½ oz.	326
Frankfurter (all beef)	⅛ lb.	129
Ham		
Fresh	¼ lb.	126
Cured, butt	¼ lb.	123
Cured, shank	¼ lb.	91
Lamb		
Shoulder chop (1)	½ lb.	260
Rib chop (2)	½ lb.	238
Leg roast	¼ lb.	96
Liver		
Beef	3½ oz.	136
Calf	3½ oz.	141
Pork		
Loin chop	6 oz.	314
Spareribs (3 or 4)	3½ oz.	209
Sausage (link or bulk)	3½ oz.	450
Turkey	3½ oz.	268
Veal		
Cutlet	6 oz.	235
Loin chop (1)	½ lb.	514
Rump roast	¼ lb.	84
Fish		
Clams (4 lg, 9 sm.)	3½ oz.	82
Cod	3½ oz.	78
Flounder or sole	3½ oz.	68

[1]From *Food Values of Portions Commonly Used, ed. 11* by C.F. and N.H. Church (Philadelphia: J.B. Lippincott Co., 1970). Reprinted by permission.
[2]Weight is before cooking.

TABLE 5, cont.

ITEM	PORTION	CALORIES
Lobster (1, boiled with 2 T. butter)	¾ lb.	308
Oysters (5 to 8, fresh or frozen)	3½ oz.	66
Salmon (pink, canned)	3½ oz.	141
Sardines (canned in oil)	3½ oz.	311
Shrimp	3½ oz.	91
Tuna		
Canned in oil	3½ oz.	288
Canned in water	3½ oz.	127
Snacks		
Candy		
Chocolate creams	1 candy	51
Milk chocolate	1 oz.	152
Ice cream		
Chocolate	½ pint	300
Vanilla	½ pint	290
Nuts		
Cashews (roasted)	6–8	84
Peanuts (roasted)		
Salted	1 T.	85
Unsalted	1 T.	86
Olives		
Green	2 medium	15
Ripe	2 large	37
Potato chips	5 chips	54
Pretzels (3 ring)	1 average	12
Dairy Products		
Butter (salted or unsalted)	1 pat	72
Cheese		
American, cheddar	1 oz.	112
American, processed	1 oz.	107
Cottage, creamed	3½ oz.	106
Cream (heavy)	1 T.	52
Egg	1 large	88
Milk (whole)	8 oz.	159
Oleomargarine (salted)	1 pat	72

TABLE 5, cont.

ITEM	PORTION	CALORIES
Breads, cereals, etc.		
Bread		
Rye	1 slice	56
White (enriched)	1 slice	62
Whole wheat	1 slice	56
Corn flakes	1 cup	95
Macaroni (enriched, cooked tender)	1 cup	151
Noodles (enriched, cooked)	1 cup	200
Oatmeal (cooked)	1 cup	148
Rice (white, dry)	¼ cup	178
Spaghetti (enriched, cooked tender)	1 cup	166
Waffles (enriched)	1 waffle	209
Wheat germ	3 T.	102
Beverages		
Apple juice	6 oz.	87
Beer	8 oz.	114
Coca-cola	6 oz.	78
Coffee (brewed)	1 cup	5
Cranberry cocktail	7 oz.	130
Ginger ale	8 oz.	80
Orange juice		
Canned	8 oz.	120
Fresh	8 oz.	111
Prune juice	6 oz.	138
Tea	8 oz.	2
Fruits[3]		
Apple	1 medium	87
Apricot		
Fresh	2–3	51
Canned (in syrup)	3 halves	86
Dried	17 halves	260
Banana	1 6-inch	85
Blueberries	1 cup	62
Cantaloupe	¼ melon	30
Cherries		
Fresh	½ cup	58

[3]All portions weigh 3½ oz., unless otherwise noted.

TABLE 5, cont.

Item	Portion	Calories
Canned (in syrup)	½ cup	89
Dates		
Fresh	10 medium	274
Dried (pitted)	1 cup (6 oz.)	448
Fruit cocktail	½ cup	76
Grapefruit	½ medium	41
Grapes	22 grapes	69
Orange	1 small	49
Peaches		
Fresh	1 medium	38
Canned	2 halves, 2 T syrup	78
Pears		
Fresh	½ pear	61
Canned	2 halves, 2 T. syrup	76
Pineapple		
Fresh	¾ cup	52
Canned	1 slice and syrup	74
Plums		
Fresh	2 medium	66
Canned	3 medium, 2 T. syrup	83
Prunes, dried	10 large	255
Strawberries	10 large	37
Watermelon	½ cup	26
Vegetables[4]		
Artichoke (base and soft end of leaves)	1 large bud	44
Asparagus		
Fresh	⅔ cup	20
Canned	6 spears	21
Beans, baked	⅝ cup	159
Beans, green		
Fresh	1 cup	31
Canned	1 cup	30

[4]Note: Because vegetable counts vary greatly from raw to cooked state, values are for cooked vegetables with no added salt unless otherwise noted. Frozen vegetables have virtually the same count as fresh vegetables when cooked, unless otherwise noted.

TABLE 5, cont.

ITEM	PORTION	CALORIES
Beans, lima		
Fresh	⅝ cup	111
Canned	½ cup	110
Frozen	⅝ cup	118
Beets		
Fresh	½ cup	27
Canned	½ cup	31
Broccoli, fresh	⅔ cup	26
Brussels sprouts	6–7 medium	36
Cabbage		
Raw, shredded	1 cup	24
Cooked	⅗ cup	20
Carrots		
Raw	1 large	42
Cooked	⅔ cup	31
Canned	⅔ cup	30
Cauliflower	⅞ cup	22
Celery	1 outer, 3 inner stalks	8
Corn		
Fresh	1 medium ear	100
Canned	½ cup	70
Cucumber, pared	½ medium	7
Lettuce, iceberg	3½ oz.	14
Mushrooms, uncooked	10 sm., 4 lg.	28
Onions, uncooked	1 medium	38
Peas		
Fresh	⅔ cup	71
Canned	¾ cup	88
Frozen	3½ oz.	68
Potatoes		
Boiled (in skin)	1 medium	76
French fried	10 pieces	137
Radishes	10 small	17
Sauerkraut	⅔ cup	18
Spinach	½ cup	21
Tomatoes		
Raw	1 medium	33
Canned	½ cup	21
Paste	3½ oz.	82

scales of course will tell you this in the long run, but it helps to estimate activity also.

However, many of you may find such a program too tedious. You are not going to keep food and exercise diaries. You will judge your results solely by the scales. Be careful! Don't weigh yourself too often, lest your slow progress discourage you. Most bathroom scales are so inaccurate that your weight may seem to vary by several pounds from day to day, even though your real weight remains essentially the same. Altered fluid balance, for example fluid retention just before the menstrual cycle, may temporarily elevate your weight. Don't let this discourage you. If you are exercising regularly, and are being careful about your eating, your weight will slowly fall. If it does not, get help from a nutritionist or physician.

THE BEST WEIGHT FOR YOU

Q. How can we find out how much we should weigh?

A. When patients ask this question, they often are surprised by the answer. I may give them a figure that seems distressingly low and impossible to attain. Perhaps they are asking the wrong question. Perhaps what they want to know is "How much *can* I weigh?"

Look back for a moment. How much did you weigh when you graduated from high school, when you were discharged from the service, or when you were married? Most of you certainly are no more muscular now. The difference between what you weighed then and what you weigh now is all fat. Even then you may have been heavier than you should have been; thus, your excessive fat may be even more than you calculate. This fat is doing you no good. It is producing an extra burden on your cardiovascular and musculo-skeletal systems which becomes increasingly dangerous as you grow older.

Height–weight tables have long been available to serve as guides to your proper weight. But don't be misled. The weights recommended in these tables are invariably too high, since they are based on average weights, not ideal weights. A better height–weight table is reproduced in Table 6. The weights recommended in this table are based on insurance company data for optimal weights for longevity, a much more realistic assessment of what constitutes "ideal weight." Even these weights may be 5 to 10 percent higher than ideal. So far as your health and future well-being are concerned, the thinner you are the better.

Height–weight tables also do not take into consideration the effect of body composition. For example, the usual fat content of men and women differs considerably. Young men have approximately 12 percent body fat when their weights are close to ideal. Young women have about 25 percent. "Obesity" is really defined as an increased percentage of body fat, regardless of total weight. A top athlete, during an intense training program, may actually gain weight if he increases his muscle mass. His percentage of body fat is low and he is clearly not obese, despite what the tables may say.

Still, you should not scuttle your weight losing program by setting impossible goals for yourself. It is far better to lose 10 pounds and keep them off than it is to lose 30 pounds only to gain most of them back when the stress of a stringent diet and intense exercise program can no longer be tolerated.

How far you continue on your weight loss program will then depend largely on your own motivation and needs. I suspect that

TABLE 6. *Height–Weight Table*

			MEN		
HEIGHT	AGE 20–29	AGE 30–39	AGE 40–49	AGE 50–59	AGE 60–69
5'3"	125 lbs	129 lbs	130 lbs	131 lbs	130 lbs
5'6"	135 lbs	140 lbs	142 lbs	143 lbs	142 lbs
5'9"	149 lbs	153 lbs	155 lbs	156 lbs	155 lbs
6'0"	161 lbs	166 lbs	167 lbs	168 lbs	167 lbs
6'3"	176 lbs	181 lbs	183 lbs	184 lbs	180 lbs
			WOMEN		
HEIGHT	AGE 20–29	AGE 30–39	AGE 40–49	AGE 50–59	AGE 60–69
4'10"	97 lbs	102 lbs	106 lbs	109 lbs	111 lbs
5'1"	106 lbs	109 lbs	114 lbs	118 lbs	120 lbs
5'4"	114 lbs	118 lbs	122 lbs	127 lbs	129 lbs
5'7"	123 lbs	127 lbs	132 lbs	137 lbs	140 lbs
5'10"	134 lbs	138 lbs	142 lbs	146 lbs	147 lbs

The Boston Globe, June 17, 1979. Reprinted by permission.

many of you may be so delighted with how you feel and look that you may want to approach your "ideal" weight. When I changed from a moderate but hardly strenuous program to a more vigorous one, I lost 15 more pounds, even though I thought I was not overweight to begin with. My family thought I looked too thin, but I felt great.

ESTIMATING YOUR BODY FAT CONTENT

Q. How can we find out how much body fat we have?

A. Body fat is most accurately estimated by submerging the subject in a tank of water and measuring the amount of water displaced. This method takes advantage of the fact that fat tissue is not as dense as other body tissues, such as bone and muscle. The more water displaced at any given weight, the higher percentage of fat in the body. For example, if a fat person and a muscular person, each weighing 200 pounds, are measured by the water displacement method, the fat person will displace much more water.

But this technique is cumbersome and requires relatively expensive equipment. A simpler, reasonably reliable method is based on the fact that about half the body fat is under the skin. By using instruments called calipers to measure the thickness of skin folds in various body locations, an estimate of total body fat can be made.

But you really don't even need calipers to obtain a fairly accurate estimation of your own fat content. At the back of your upper arm, over the triceps muscle, pinch a fold of skin and underlying fat (Figure 5), making sure not to include the muscle itself. The distance between your fingers is an excellent approximation of the amount of fat in your body. Remove your fingers from the skin without changing the distance between them. Measure the distance with a ruler (Figure 6). If it is more than an inch, you probably have excessive body fat. For obvious reasons we call this technique "the pinch test."

Yet, for most of us, even this simple measurement is really unnecessary. We know when we are overweight. Our stomachs hanging over our belts, the slacks that won't quite zip, or the role of fat around our middles when we bend slightly to the side, are all the proof we need. Men tend to add their extra weight in the

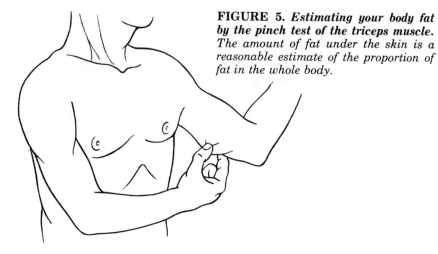

FIGURE 5. *Estimating your body fat by the pinch test of the triceps muscle. The amount of fat under the skin is a reasonable estimate of the proportion of fat in the whole body.*

stomach or abdomen. Women are more likely to spread it out more, although they tend to put a lot of it below the waist in the buttock area.

I would like to add one word here about alcohol. We forget that alcohol contains a lot of calories. There are perhaps 100 calories in a glass of beer, and at least that much in every drink of whiskey. These must be included in our calorie counts. Moderate reduction in daily alcohol intake may be the simplest way for some of you to reduce daily calorie consumption.

Q. You have discussed risk factors in considerable detail. It might be helpful at this point to summarize your recommendations.

A. What you're really asking is what I would recommend to anyone who wants to do everything possible to lead a long and healthy life. My advice is really very simple.

Smoking is out, unless you can restrict yourself to only an occasional cigar or pipe which you don't inhale.

You should eat sparingly, emphasizing a low fat diet which is relatively high in complex carbohydrates. We'll talk more about this in Chapter 9.

You should become as thin as possible. Don't worry about the comments of friends or family that you are "too thin" or actually appear ill.

67

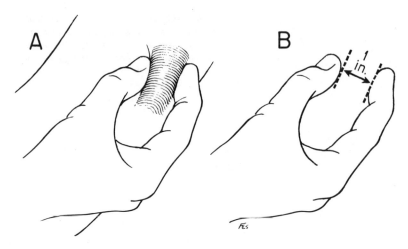

FIGURE 6. *Estimating your body fat by the pinch test. If the distance between your thumb and index finger is more than 1 inch, you probably have excess body fat.*

Exercise vigorously several days each week.

Try to arrange your life so that excessive stress is avoided.

I suspect that if all of us followed this prescription from an early age, the incidence of heart attacks, strokes, and other vascular diseases would be strikingly reduced, particularly in young and middle-aged people. Interestingly, heart disease and stroke are less common than they used to be. The reasons for this are not entirely clear. Perhaps reduced smoking in the adult population and better blood pressure control contribute. The fact that more people are exercising might be important. Most likely all these factors play a role.

The earlier this type of life style is begun the better. But atherosclerosis takes years to develop. Even if you are beginning late, you can do something to arrest its progression.

CHAPTER 4

Running and the Heart

Q. WE HAVE HEARD a great deal about the good effects of running on the heart. What actually happens to the heart during an aerobic exercise program?

A. Let's divide this question into two areas of discussion. The first is the effects of training on the normal heart. The second is the possible prevention and treatment of some types of heart problems by the development of cardiovascular fitness.

In Chapter 2, we covered some aspects of both these questions, but I would like to go into somewhat greater detail now. It is important for all of us, the healthy as well as the heart patients, to understand what happens when we exercise.

First let's discuss the changes produced in the normal heart during an effective, aerobic exercise program.

"Athlete's Heart": The Normal Response to Intensive Aerobic Training

Q. Are these changes what is meant by "athlete's heart"?

A. Yes. Fortunately, we now recognize that these changes can be a normal response to training. But even just a few years ago, many doctors felt that something might be wrong when they saw these changes, that intensive exercise was dangerous and might permanently harm the heart.

Q. What are the changes in the heart caused by training?

A. Both the heart's structure and its function are altered. After all, the heart's sole function is to pump blood. When it is required to work very hard for long periods of time—during long distance running for example—it is hardly surprising that it must change to meet these demands.

A major goal of training is to improve performance by increasing the maximum amount of blood the heart can pump to the exercising muscles. The distance runner's heart can increase its pumping capacity or output at peak exercise to five or six times its output at rest.

This dramatic increase in cardiac output is achieved in two ways, by raising the heart rate and by increasing the amount of blood the heart pumps with each beat.

In Chapter 2 we emphasized that the maximum rate the heart can achieve is largely independent of the level of fitness, depending rather on age. If the maximum heart rate of the well-trained distance runner can go no higher than that of poorly conditioned individuals his own age, how can we account for the significantly higher peak output the distance runner's heart can produce? The answer, of course, is that his heart must have developed the ability to pump more blood with each beat.

To do this, the distance runner's heart enlarges to increase its capacity to store blood between heartbeats. Then it contracts more vigorously and empties more completely to increase the amount of blood pumped with each beat. The heart enlargement, a key feature of the heart's normal response to training, was for years a source of concern to physicians. They worried that it signified a serious heart problem, since enlargement of the heart is a warning sign of heart trouble in other situations. Their concern was further increased when they noted that murmurs of the heart seemed to occur more frequently in well-trained athletes. Murmurs too may be a sign of a serious heart problem, but in an athlete they are usually the result of good training.

The athlete's heart also beats more slowly at rest, sometimes so slowly that doctors feared something might be wrong with the heart's pacemaker system. This too is now recognized as an expected result of training, caused by a change in the nervous system's control of the heart rate. Pulse rates as low as 30 per minute no longer cause concern; they too are a sign of good conditioning.

When doctors first began to take cardiograms to see what the hearts of healthy athletes might show, they were alarmed to find so many major changes from what was then considered to be normal. Gradually we have learned that an abnormal resting cardiogram may be the rule rather than the exception in athletes. They also often develop rather unusual changes during a stress test. If the resting ECG shows changes, these will often disappear during the exercise. If the resting ECG is normal, exercise may produce suspicious changes. These too are a normal training response.

So it is important that physicians take a careful history of patients who have suspicious cardiograms. They may be athletes. This was vividly illustrated to me recently when a surgeon at another hospital asked me to see his patient in consultation because of possible heart trouble.

The patient was a 40-year-old man who had badly damaged his knee during a ski race. In preparation for surgery, a routine cardiogram was performed. It was markedly abnormal. The attending cardiologists strongly advised against the operation because it might be dangerous to someone with such a potentially severe heart problem. They also recommended further heart testing to find out the cause of the trouble.

By the time I saw the patient, he was understandably very concerned. To the worry about whether he could ever ski again because of his badly damaged knee was now added the even greater problem of a bad heart. But I could find nothing wrong with his heart except for the abnormal ECG. In fact, he was in superb physical condition, well muscled without an ounce of fat. He looked like a college middle-weight wrestler, rather than a 40-year-old business executive. He had no symptoms remotely suggesting a heart problem.

Why the ECG changes? The answer was easy once I did a little detective work. His well-muscled body had not developed spontaneously, but was the result of extremely intense and lengthy daily workouts which combined both aerobic and muscle-strengthening exercises. Once I knew this, I became quite certain that his heart was normal and that the ECG changes were the result of his fitness program. I urged the surgeon to proceed with the knee operation.

A few months later, after a successful rehabilitation program for his knee, he demonstrated his superb physical condition in our exercise laboratory. Not only did he complete the stress test without difficulty, but the abnormalities of his resting cardiogram totally disappeared during exercise.

Q. What causes these ECG changes in athletes?

A. We are not sure, but they may be related in some way to both the enlargement of the heart and the altered nervous system control over the heart.

Q. How does the nervous control of the heart change?

A. As mentioned earlier, at any given moment there is an interplay between the two main parts of the autonomic nervous system, *the sympathetic,* which speeds up the heart and strengthens its contractions, and *the parasympathetic,* which slows and relaxes the heart. When we are frightened or tense, the sympathetic influence dominates. The heart speeds up and beats more forcefully. When we sleep, the parasympathetic system is dominant. Our heart rate slows and the heart beats less vigorously unless we have a disturbing dream which activates the sympathetic system.

As we become fit, the influence of the sympathetic system is lessened at rest. The parasympathetic system dominates and the heart slows and relaxes. Once exercise begins, of course, the sympathetic nervous system is activated, and its influence becomes even stronger than in the unfit person.

Q. Does the heart respond the same way to all types of exercise?

A. It clearly does not. This question has recently aroused much interest, and recent studies using the echocardiogram, which can accurately measure the size of the heart chambers and also the thickness and function of the heart muscle itself, suggest that the idea that there is a single type of "athlete's heart" is much too simple.

Just as the weight lifter's muscles respond completely differently to his training program than the runner's muscles do to his, so the responses of their heart muscles differ. The heart of the weight lifter is altered chiefly by increased thickness and strength of the heart muscle. As you might expect, it is a compact, strong heart, only slightly increased in overall size, designed to perform short bursts of intense work when the blood pressure is very high. The major change in the runner's heart is enlargement of the heart chambers. The muscle itself is thickened only a little. His heart changes reflect the need to pump large volumes of blood for long periods of time. Even the cardiograms of runners and weight lifters tend to be different. The weight lifter's ECG commonly shows a "strain" pattern, typical of thickened heart muscle. The runner's cardiogram suggests enlargement without strain.

Q.   What happens to an athlete's heart when he stops training?

A.   It tends to decondition rapidly, just like his other muscles. But that is about where heart muscle's similarity to skeletal muscle ends. Let us clear up some misconceptions about the effects of aerobic training on the heart.

THE HEART IS NOT JUST ANOTHER MUSCLE

We are frequently told that exercise must be good for the heart, because the more we stress the heart, like any other muscle, the stronger it becomes. This of course implies that the stronger the heart gets, the less likely it will be damaged by disease. If this were true, our weight lifting colleagues might have the best hearts of all. We know this is not the case. The actual strength of the heart muscle has little to do with prevention of heart disease.

Heart muscle is not like other muscle, and if aerobic exercise helps to prevent heart attacks, and most of us believe that it can, it does so by slowing the development of coronary artery disease or atherosclerosis, not by strengthening the heart muscle. Indeed, exercise is far more likely to weaken rather than improve the function of the already damaged heart muscle. We rarely recommend exercise to anyone whose heart muscle is already functioning poorly.

Even when the heart muscle is normal to begin with, and

73

changes occur to produce the picture of the "athlete's heart," these changes are of much lesser magnitude than those in the exercised skeletal muscles. The runner's leg muscles, for example, develop a more extensive blood supply, dramatically increase the concentration of enzymes so that they can use oxygen more efficiently, and also enlarge.

Normal heart muscle already has a full complement of enzymes to facilitate the use of oxygen, and training does not change this very much. No new arteries develop in the heart muscle, nor is its enlargement very great compared to skeletal muscle.

When coronary arteries are already narrowed by atherosclerosis, an exercise program helps not because it increases the amount of blood that the coronary arteries can bring to the heart muscle, but chiefly because training allows more efficient use by the exercising muscle of the blood the heart pumps to it at all levels of activity, thereby reducing the heart's work.

THE CORONARY ARTERIES OF CLARENCE DEMAR

Q. But we have heard that running can enlarge the coronary arteries. Isn't this true?

A. You are probably referring to the widely published case of Clarence DeMar. He won the Boston Marathon a record seven times and was probably the United States' most famous marathon runner. When he died, his autopsy examination showed very large, broad coronary arteries. Certainly one might conclude that running produced these changes in his coronary arteries. It is just as reasonable, however, to conclude that he was such a good runner because his coronary arteries were so big to begin with.

There is surprisingly little information available concerning humans to resolve this question. Animal experiments do not show much increase in the size of coronary arteries of animals who are exercised regularly. However, experimental animals have hardly been exposed to the intensity and duration of exercise that Clarence DeMar performed.

There is an interesting sidelight to DeMar's case. It is not generally known that he stopped running for several years at the peak of his career on the advice of doctors who heard a heart murmur and feared that running might be dangerous for him. Fortunately, he finally disregarded this colossal error and started to run again on his own. We are not told whether his murmur disappeared during his period of inactivity, but we do know that it must have been an innocent or functional murmur, because the autopsy showed a perfectly normal heart.

Exercise for People with Coronary Artery Disease

I suspect that many readers of this book may have coronary problems, either a previous heart attack or angina. They have heard that running might help them, and want to know more about it. They are particularly interested, of course, in whether it is safe for them to run, and if running can help them feel better and live longer. I firmly believe that a running program can be helpful to such people in a number of ways, provided that the pumping function of the heart is still reasonably normal, and the exercise program is properly supervised.

Q. Will you describe a good program for patients with coronary disease?

A. No single program is best. The patient's age, occupation, and motivation, as well as his heart function and general health, all strongly influence what might be recommended. It is very important to individualize each program. This requires the help of a knowledgeable physician.

Some coronary patients develop severe pain at low levels of exercise, and are never able to exercise enough to develop much cardiovascular fitness. They may require coronary bypass surgery to improve blood flow to the heart muscle. Then they may be able to participate in an effective exercise program. For others progress may be distressingly slow, and months may pass before they can go beyond the walking stage.

While I cannot outline a program suitable for everyone, it may help to describe one for a fairly typical patient. Let me outline an exercise rehabilitation program for a 50-year-old man, otherwise in good health, who has just had a myocardial infarction or heart attack.

Q. What actually happens to the heart during a heart attack?

A. A continuous supply of oxygen-containing blood is crucial for maintaining the life and normal function of the heart muscle cells. A heart attack occurs when the blood supply to part of the heart muscle, almost always the muscle of the left ventricle, the heart's main pumping chamber, falls too low to maintain the life of the muscle cells. They are permanently and irreversibly damaged. The attack is produced when one of the already narrowed coronary arteries becomes completely blocked either by further atherosclerosis, blood clot, or spasm of the artery. The damaged heart muscle cells must be replaced by fibrous or scar tissue, a process which usually requires several months to complete. During this healing period, the heart should not be subjected to heavy work loads.

Q. Can the heart ever function normally again after it has been damaged by a heart attack?

A. Fortunately the heart, like most of the organs of our body, has considerable reserve. If the area of damage is not too large, and a strong scar is formed, the remainder of the undamaged heart muscle takes over very well. Although heart function may never return to absolutely peak performance, it is usually good enough to allow most heart attack patients to lead reasonably normal lives.

As I note elsewhere, some heart attack patients have run marathons, finishing with quite respectable times. Their hearts function much better now than they ever did before the attack, largely because they are in much better general physical condition.

This is the key to rehabilitation of coronary patients by exercise. Because the whole oxygen transport system (Chapter 2, page 12) functions more efficiently, the fit person's heart, whether it is normal or has previously been damaged by a heart attack, works better at all levels of physical activity. The body makes more efficient use of the blood the heart pumps to it, so the heart need not work as hard. Whether you are cleaning the house, walking the beach, shouting at your children, or having sexual relations, your heart will be less strained if you are fit. This training effect can produce crucial improvement in the patient with severe angina pectoris who develops chest pain every time his heart must do extra work.

ANGINA PECTORIS

Q. How does angina differ from a heart attack?

A. The major difference is that angina pectoris is reversible. An attack of angina does not cause permanent heart damage. Angina patients also have significantly narrowed coronary arteries, but the arteries are still able to transport enough blood to the heart muscle to meet its resting needs. During exercise or stress, when the heart must work harder and requires more oxygen, the narrowed arteries cannot bring enough blood to meet its needs. This oxygen deficiency causes symptoms of pain or pressure in the chest or arms. This is a warning to the patient to stop the activity that is causing the angina. Once he does this, the angina symptoms abate, signifying the end of the temporary oxygen lack before any permanent damage to the heart has occurred.

Q. What if the patient doesn't stop the activity, despite the warning signs?

A. That could be dangerous. Continued activity could cause permanent heart damage or a heart attack.

EXERCISE AFTER A HEART ATTACK

We used to keep patients in bed for weeks after a heart attack. They were not allowed even to shave or wash themselves, much less walk around. This treatment was designed to lessen the load on the damaged heart while it was healing. Unfortunately, we probably did more harm than good with this treatment. *Now our exercise program begins soon after the patient enters the hospital*, when the initial pain and other acute problems have subsided. Physiotherapists start passive muscle exercises to prevent the rapid deconditioning which occurs with bed rest. If the heart attack is uncomplicated, we let the patient sit in a chair and walk a little a day or two after the attack. Of course during these early stages we carefully watch the patient and monitor his cardiogram to be sure the activity does not strain the heart. We do not want him to do too much until heart damage is reasonably well repaired, but moderate physical activity seems to speed rather than hinder the patient's recovery.

Q. How soon can he begin a more vigorous program?

A. Some cardiologists begin a fairly vigorous program just a few weeks after a heart attack. They have demonstrated that this can be done safely. I am a little more conservative at this point. I see no need to rush as long as the patient can do some walking. Several months must pass before the heart's healing is completed, and it makes no sense to me to strain the heart before then.

In the 6 or 8 weeks following the heart attack we encourage the patient to increase his activity slowly so that at the end of this period he can walk fairly briskly for short periods, and perhaps can perform light arm work. If his job is not too taxing physically or mentally, he may be able to return to work at this time.

Then we begin a more vigorous walking program. During the next 3 or 4 months the patient is instructed to increase the duration and speed of his walking gradually, until he can walk 3 or 4 miles comfortably at a brisk pace. Many patients find that adding a quarter of a mile each week to their daily walking distance is a convenient way to reach this goal.

During this time I examine the patient regularly and perform an exercise stress test to about 50 or 60 percent of his maximum expected heart rate, a level of exercise somewhat above that required for walking. If no worrisome changes are seen during the stress test, I am fairly confident that the brisk walking program is safe for him. Of course if he does develop chest discomfort or breathlessness at some point during his walking program, or if his stress test is severely abnormal, we adjust the activity level to just below that which causes the changes or symptoms. We may also slow any subsequent advance in his exercise program.

About six months after the heart attack, the patient should be ready to begin a more vigorous fitness program. From now on the program we recommend should not differ appreciably from those given to patients whose heart attacks occurred years before or whose only sign of coronary disease is mild angina pectoris.

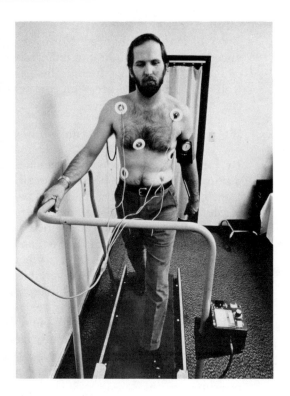

THE SUPERVISED EXERCISE PROGRAM

Before this program is begun, certain requirements must be met. The patient should find an exercise rehabilitation program supervised by trained personnel. He should not start this program on his own. In a supervised program, his physician's recommendations can be translated into an effective, safe exercise routine. The patient will also be prevented from overdoing, and even pushed a bit if he is too cautious or tentative. Many programs have physicians in constant attendance. All have the capacity to provide prompt treatment for any emergencies.

Q. Are you implying that an exercise program can be dangerous for coronary patients?

A. It certainly can be, but it is extremely safe if proper precautions are taken.

Most cardiologists agree that in the long run it is best for

79

coronary patients to exercise. They feel better and their long-term survival may be enhanced. However, these benefits must be balanced against the slight, but definitely increased, risk of a cardiac emergency occurring during the exercise itself. Fortunately a well-run, supervised program can handle any of these emergencies quite successfully.

Q.   What kind of emergencies do you mean?

A.   By far the most important is sudden cessation of the effective pumping action of the heart, generally due to ventricular fibrillation. This dread complication is the most common cause of death in coronary patients. Left untreated for more than a couple of minutes, ventricular fibrillation is invariably fatal. A major problem in its prevention is that it is frequently unpredictable, occurring suddenly in a patient who felt perfectly well the moment before. Yet it is usually completely reversible if it is treated soon enough. The only way to do this is to have proper equipment and personnel trained in cardiopulmonary resuscitation immediately available. These facilities are available only in supervised programs. Since no coronary patient is totally free of this risk, and since it is particularly high in the first year or two after the heart attack, it seems sensible to me that coronary patients run in a supervised program.

Q.   Are there other emergency situations?

A.   Yes there are, although none so urgent as ventricular fibrillation. They include severe dizziness or fainting, marked breathlessness, and chest pain that does not disappear when the exercise is stopped.

Q.   Are supervised exercise programs generally available for coronary patients who want them?

A.   Unfortunately there are not nearly enough. If no program is available in your area, I would urge you to lobby to get one started. If there is enough demand, a local hospital, YMCA, or community center can usually be persuaded to start one.

Q.   Aren't they very expensive to start?

A. Of course they can be if new facilities must be built, but the physical requirements for an exercise rehabilitation program are not complex. Existing facilities can often be utilized. Even the smallest towns generally have a gym and other athletic facilities which can be used at off hours such as early in the morning. The only costs will be the salaries for the few personnel required to staff the program part time and the emergency equipment. Usually you can find a physician willing to donate a few hours of his time each week to supervise, and it has been my experience that once one physician gets involved, others are quick to join.

Q. If you have a patient who wants to start exercising, but no supervised facility is readily available, do you still recommend that he exercise?

A. If his examination is good, and the stress test shows no worrisome changes, then I may encourage some type of exercise. However, the patient must begin very cautiously, exercising at a much lower intensity, and increasing his program very slowly.

THE EXERCISE PRESCRIPTION

Q. Let's go back to your heart attack patient. It is now 6 months after attack, he feels well, and he can walk 3 miles briskly without discomfort. A supervised program is easily accessible. What happens next?

A. First, I examine him, and then repeat his stress test. Only this time I make him exercise until he achieves his maximum expected heart rate, or until symptoms or electrocardiographic changes make us stop the test. If he has an essentially normal response, or if the changes are only minor, we design a program in stages quite similar to those recommended for a normal person (described in Chapter 5, pages 108–14).

If the response is not normal, we carefully measure at what stage of the exercise stress test the abnormalities first appeared. Then we design a program which allows the patient to exercise at an intensity just below that which caused the abnormal signs or symptoms. Some have called this the _"exercise prescription."_ A prescription for a patient who developed significant changes in the ECG during the third stage of his stress test, when his pulse rate was 140, is shown in Table 7. His pulse rate, an accurate guide to the intensity of his exercise, should not go beyond 135, and to assure a margin of safety, we have recommended that he exercise, after an adequate warm-up, at an intensity which will produce a heart rate of 120 to 130.

How quickly we increase the duration and intensity of the exercise may vary tremendously, but each time we consider a significant change, another stress test is done to see if the amount of exercise we are recommending will overburden the heart. The exercise prescription may then be changed accordingly.

The majority of heart attack patients managed this way do very well. Many are able to run enough to develop significant improvement in their cardiovascular fitness. Others advance much more slowly, or never are able to run very far. Yet almost all patients who stick to the program feel better and want to continue no matter what their activity level.

This is an important point. Even if heart attack and angina patients who exercise did not live a moment longer, I would still

TABLE 7. *The Exercise Prescription*

Date: May 15, 1980   *Name:* John Smith
Height: 5' 10"   *Weight:* 150 pounds
Age: 50

---

1. Maximum expected heart rate for your age is 170 (220–50).
2. Maximum heart rate during your exercise test was 140.
3. Your target (training) heart rate must not exceed 130.
4. You will achieve significant training effect if you exercise for:
   a. 20 to 30 minutes
   b. three or four times a week
   c. at a pulse rate between 120 and 130.
5. You must warm up by running slowly for at least 5 to 10 minutes before you reach your target heart rate.
6. At the end, slow your pace gradually over at least 5 minutes before you stop.
7. If you become short of breath or develop chest pain during your run, *stop.* Try again tomorrow at a slightly slower pace.
8. If symptoms continue at this slower pace, see your doctor.
9. The date of your next stress test is *June 12, 1980.*

---

recommend a group exercise program for most of them. The group can be extremely supportive. Its members share their fears and talk about their problems with others similarly afflicted in a way which rarely can be achieved with doctors and nurses. And of course exercise helps relieve tension and may strikingly reduce the depression which is so common in heart attack patients. Many of the fears about becoming an invalid or a burden to the family are reduced when the patient finds that he can perform moderately intensive exercise and that his performance is steadily improving.

Q. At what point can the patient leave the supervised program and run on his own?

A. Ideally I would like him to stay in a supervised program for as long as he runs. Even though his risks are low, they are still present, and I see no reason to increase the risks of running by doing it alone. However, I might make one concession. If he is in top condition, and able to run long distances comfortably, I might allow him to do some road running. However, even here he should always run with a group, or at least with one person skilled in CPR. The heart attack patients who have run in marathons are in superb physical condition, but they always run in groups.

Q. Earlier you mentioned that running did not change the coronary circulation very much if the heart is normal to begin with. Is this also true if atherosclerosis is present?

A. New arteries, called collaterals, have been described in the hearts of experimental animals who have been exercised after blockage of the coronary arteries has been produced, but there is little evidence that this happens in humans. Current thinking is that this is not an important effect of exercise.

Other animal studies are of some interest. If an experimental heart attack is produced in rats previously conditioned by an exercise program, smaller areas of the heart are damaged compared to rats who have not exercised. Also fewer serious heart rhythm disorders have been reported in previously exercised animals after experimental heart attacks. Whether humans might be similarly protected is at present unclear.

Other Kinds of Heart Disease

Q. Until now you have talked only about exercise in patients with coronary artery disease. Can patients with other kinds of heart problems also benefit from exercise?

A. Not nearly as much. In fact, an exercise program may be harmful. In many patients with coronary disease, only a relatively small part of the heart muscle is damaged, and the heart's pumping function is nearly normal. In most other types of heart disease for example when the valves of the heart are damaged or the heart muscle itself is inflamed, the pumping function is impaired, and it would not be reasonable to expect that exercise, which further stresses the pumping function, could help very much. This does not imply that such patients should remain inactive. They should be active within the limits of comfort. Rather it means that a graded aerobic exercise program will probably not help their hearts. Treatment should be aimed at correcting the underlying mechanical or structural problem if one exists, or using drugs to aid the poorly functioning heart muscle.

Rehabilitation of coronary patients with exercise is an exciting area of medical research and treatment. It will take years to prove without doubt that it produces long-term benefits. Until that proof is forthcoming, we must rely on a strong hunch that it may be a very useful way to treat coronary patients who are suitable for it. Nevertheless, no matter how effective it may prove to be, it will never be nearly as effective as the prevention of coronary atherosclerosis by following a healthy life style from an early age.

CHAPTER 5

How to Begin Your Running Program

Q. WE SUSPECT that by now most readers are anxious to learn how to begin a running program. How should we start?

A. This is not complicated, provided one uses good judgment and common sense. But remember that I am a physician, not a coach or trainer. My remarks are not directed toward extracting maximal performance from a training program. Rather, I want to outline a running program that will be as safe as possible, while at the same time gradually improving your aerobic capacity to the desired level. Remember also that there is considerable room for individual variation depending on age, health, psychological needs, and the unique problems posed by each person's bones, joints, and muscles. Take my comments only as general guidelines. There may be tremendous variation depending on your individual talents.

Many running books outline very precise recommendations for the beginner. They tell him exactly how much to do and how fast to do it. I'm a little uneasy about such blanket prescriptions. Some might find them too easy and become discouraged by their slow progress. Others may find them too difficult and become equally discouraged.

Should You See a Doctor?

Q. Perhaps the first question many would-be runners want to know is should they see a doctor before beginning, and what examinations and tests should he perform?

A. First let's look at the extremes. An 18-year-old, active person who has had normal exams in the past does not need a complex medical examination. Usually he can just begin his running program and do it safely. But a 60-year-old, sedentary male who has high blood pressure and smokes too much should be closely examined and followed by his physician. But examinations and tests are time consuming and expensive. There is an understandable tendency to avoid them if possible. When is that safe? Where should one draw the line?

Ideally I would like everyone who is beginning to run to have a thorough examination. The need to do so is less urgent if your health has been perfect over the years, if you do not have any of the known risk factors for heart disease, or any abnormality of your bones, joints, or muscles, and if you have been fairly active physically much of your life.

It would certainly seem prudent for men above the age of 35 to be examined. Potentially serious heart disease which does not cause symptoms, so-called "silent" heart disease, is not uncommon in men over 35. It should be looked for carefully. Because women are far less likely to develop atherosclerosis at this age, perhaps the age limit for examination can be raised safely to 40 or 45 for women who feel well.

The Stress Test

Q. What type of examination is best, and what tests do you recommend?

A. Before I answer this specifically, I would like to comment about the undue, grossly distorted importance placed on the stress or exercise electrocardiogram (ECG). Most running books enthusiastically endorse this test, stating in glowing terms that it's the key to a safe exercise program. I would be the first to agree that the exercise ECG, properly done, is a very useful medical test. However, it has major limitations. It is far less important than a careful medical history and a physical examination by a physician who understands runners and running.

Most potentially serious heart problems can at least be suspected from a history and physical exam with a far higher degree of accuracy than an isolated stress test can achieve. The examination should also include a blood count and simple tests of liver and kidney function, plus accurate measurement of the blood levels of sugar, cholesterol, and triglycerides. These values would then serve as a baseline to define changes produced by the exercise program. If a chest x-ray has not been done in the previous few years, it should be performed. I would advise such an x-ray for anyone, whether he runs or not.

Q. Why aren't you more enthusiastic about stress tests?

A. In theory the stress ECG is an excellent test. We know that a normal resting electrocardiogram certainly does not preclude serious heart disease. You have all heard about patients who had normal cardiograms, were told they were in good health by the doctor, and then dropped dead soon thereafter. The exercise ECG, by stressing the heart to its limits, should uncover potentially serious heart disease. Figure 7 shows an example of just that. The patient is a 47-year-old man who had chest pain. His resting ECG was normal. The stress ECG is strongly positive. During the test the patient developed his typical pain. On the basis of this result, treatment for his heart problem was begun.

Unfortunately the exercise test is not always that accurate. In fact, if it's used as a screening test to identify people with silent but potentially serious heart disease, it may be so grossly inaccurate that more harm is done than good.

Let me give you an example. If you did stress tests in one hundred healthy young people, a few, perhaps five or six, will have changes in the ECG during exercise that are consistent with or suspicious for heart disease. But most of these will actually have perfectly normal hearts. The test will be _falsely positive_.

Figure 8 is an example of a false positive stress test in a young man with a normal heart. Compare it to the abnormal test

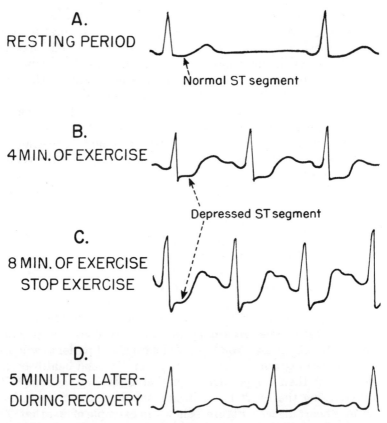

A.
RESTING PERIOD

Normal ST segment

B.
4 MIN. OF EXERCISE

Depressed ST segment

C.
8 MIN. OF EXERCISE
STOP EXERCISE

D.
5 MINUTES LATER-
DURING RECOVERY

FIGURE 7. *Exercise (stress) cardiogram of a 47-year-old man with chest pain and heart disease.* (**A**) *The resting ECG is normal.* (**B**) *After 4 minutes of exercise, note the changes: The heart rate is much faster, and the ST segments, the chief indicators of abnormal coronary arteries, are already depressed.* (**C**) *Here the test was stopped because of chest pain. Note the marked depression of the ST segment, the sign of a strongly positive test.* (**D**) *Five minutes later the ECG had returned to normal and the chest pain had stopped.*

in Figure 7; it's not much different. On the basis of the stress test alone we would have to make a diagnosis of heart disease, and this young man might be prevented from exercising normally. Worse still would be the worry and concern about a serious heart problem which really was not present. Unfortunately there is no easy way to distinguish those people with false positive tests from

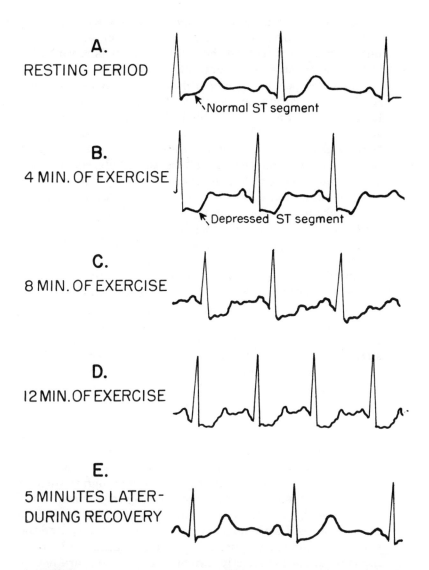

A.
RESTING PERIOD

Normal ST segment

B.
4 MIN. OF EXERCISE

Depressed ST segment

C.
8 MIN. OF EXERCISE

D.
12 MIN. OF EXERCISE

E.
5 MINUTES LATER–
DURING RECOVERY

FIGURE 8. *False positive exercise ECG in a 20-year-old male with a normal heart.* *The ST segment changes suggesting coronary disease appear in **B**, but get no worse later as exercise intensity increases (**C** and **D**), and disappear after exercise is stopped (**E**). The changes are similar to those in Figure 7, but not as marked. This young, athletic man had no heart disease.*

those who have truly positive results. To do so with certainty, we would have to perform a heart catheterization and coronary arteriography. This requires hospitalization. It is reasonably safe, but it is expensive and somewhat painful.

In older people, an abnormal exercise test is much more likely to be accurate; the person with a positive test will probably have a significant heart problem. But many older people with severe narrowing and even complete blocks of their coronary arteries will still have a normal stress test; that is, a *falsely negative response*. Strict reliance on the stress test results would produce an unwarranted sense of security about the safety of a vigorous exercise program. I am still extra cautious about prescribing an exercise program for a fat, smoking 60-year-old man with high blood pressure, even if his stress test is normal.

False positive stress tests occur so frequently in healthy young women that exercise testing should not be performed routinely for this group. Athletes also frequently have abnormal stress tests. Other causes of false positive tests include high blood pressure, anxiety and over-breathing, changes in posture, unusual body build, and many drugs. Perhaps now you can understand why I am so concerned about blanket endorsements of stress testing for runners. It isn't all it's cracked up to be by a long shot. Undoubtedly some exercise tests are performed to help the physician, not the patient. In our litiginous society, when malpractice cases are so common, the physician often feels compelled to protect himself as much as possible. A negative exercise test allows him to endorse an exercise program more confidently and perhaps, should disaster occur, it will aid him in court.

It is crucially important that the stress test not be performed as an isolated procedure, but as part of a thorough medical examination by a competent physician. Equally important, it must be interpreted by someone who truly understands its subtleties. Stress test results are not easy to interpret correctly, and there is a common tendency among less sophisticated cardiologists to interpret them too strictly. Minor changes often are not important.

Despite their shortcomings, I recommend exercise tests for most men above age 40, particularly if I suspect the presence of coronary disease, and for women above 55 or 60. I rarely perform a stress test on younger women, for the reason mentioned.

Q. What do you recommend to the person who feels well but whose stress test is positive?

A. It's a difficult decision. The findings cannot be ignored, particularly if the test is strongly positive. But even if there is some chance of coronary disease, I believe it is better in the long run for such patients to exercise. However, as stated in Chapter 4, it is safest for them to exercise in a supervised program so that potential emergencies can be treated promptly and potential disaster avoided.

Q. Are there other reasons for performing a stress test?

A. A doctor administering a stress test must look for a lot more than just changes in the electrocardiogram. The blood pressure response during exercise furnishes much useful information. Listening to the heart during or immediately after peak exercise will often provide clues to abnormal heart performance which are not present at rest. Exercise tests can also be used to judge the effectiveness of a treatment, such as drugs or heart surgery, particularly the coronary by-pass operations which are so frequently performed to treat coronary disease. Because the exercise test is divided into stages of increasing intensity of exercise, it becomes a good method for estimating cardiovascular fitness, or aerobic capacity. Any improvement from a training program can be documented by the patient's ability to proceed further in the exercise protocol before exhaustion occurs. This graded or staged type of test allows the physiologist to compare the effects of different training procedures.

Despite its considerable limitations, a negative exercise test in an older person does make me feel a bit more comfortable about recommending an exercise program. A well-performed treadmill test reproduces the type of heart stress that occurs during running. If the stress test remains negative at the levels of activity likely to be achieved during a running program, it seems reasonably safe to recommend one. Whenever I have doubts, I remind myself that the appropriate question perhaps is not "Is it safe to exercise?" but rather "Is it safe _not_ to exercise?"

Finally, as mentioned in Chapter 4, doctors use the exercise test to write a "prescription" for their heart patients. For example, a person may feel fine and have no changes in the cardiogram during the third stage of his treadmill test, but may develop chest pain and ECG changes when the intensity of the exercise is increased during the fourth stage. The patient should then limit the exercise intensity to that achieved during Stage 3. This can be estimated by measuring the pulse rate during Stage 3 of the test and making certain that the exercise performed never raises the pulse rate higher.

Buying the Right Equipment

Q. What's next for those of us who have passed the medical exam?

A. Before you go off to the road or track, you should know something about equipment, particularly running shoes.

SHOES

You might as well purchase shoes right at the beginning, although some people like to delay a while until they are sure they will continue to run. Don't delay too long. Bad shoes may cause discomfort or an annoying injury and discourage you from going further.

Shoes are by far the most important part of your equipment. If your funds are limited, spend your money here. No matter how comfortable you feel in sneakers or other types of athletic shoes, if you run very far, you should have running shoes. They have features which will protect your feet from injury. Shop carefully, preferably in a store that specializes in running equipment. Talk to salesmen and other runners. Take your time before you buy. Everyone's foot is different. There is no single shoe that is best for everyone.

The perfect running shoe is inexpensive, maintenance free, very light, yet excellently cushioned. It provides excellent support in the heel and has plenty of room for the toes. The sole is flexible over the ball of the foot, sturdy, and long lasting. The shoe should be comfortable when you first try it on in the store.

Unfortunately, the perfect shoe does not yet exist. But the

increasing variety and quality of shoes available should allow you to choose a suitable pair. Shoes are divided into two types, training and racing. For the present, at least, forget about racing shoes. They weigh much less than training shoes but offer too little cushioning and support for the beginner. Training shoes are no longer heavy and cumbersome. In fact, many good runners race in them. Make your choice from among this group.

Until recently most manufacturers made only D width shoes. If your foot was too wide or narrow, you had to improvise. But now some manufacturers offer a variety of widths. Women, whose feet tend to be narrower, no longer must wear shoes designed for men. The boom in women's running has the manufacturers falling all over each other to produce shoes specially made for women.

If you plan to wear socks while running, bring a pair with you and wear them when you try on your shoes. Make sure the shoes are flexible; the sole should bend easily under the ball of your foot. A stiff sole can turn running into torture. Just like any other shoes you buy, _running shoes should immediately feel comfortable. If they are snug, don't try to break them in. Try another pair._

There should be at least ½ inch between the end of the shoe and the tip of your longest toe. Look particularly for enough room in the toe box. Every time your foot strikes the ground it flattens and the toes spread out. They need plenty of room. At the same time be sure that your heel is well supported. As you gently run in the store, your heel should not lift out of the shoe. If it does, you'll soon have blisters, and you won't get the support needed to prevent injury.

Recognizing the importance of a firm, stable heel for injury-free running, several manufacturers now offer training shoes with exaggerated, flared heels, far wider than those found in walking shoes. Some beginners like them. Others find them a bit awkward. I suggest avoiding them for your first pair. You can experiment later.

Another absolute must for a good pair of shoes is a high heel. The lifted heel reduces stress and stretch on the Achilles tendon during running. Fortunately today it's virtually impossible to purchase a running shoe which does not provide such a heel. However, other types of athletic shoes do not have it. Don't wear them!

It's best to buy shoes that are too loose rather than too tight. You can always add inserts if your shoes are loose somewhere, but if they are too tight, nothing short of ripping them open will make them comfortable.

Also make sure your shoes are well cushioned. Your feet weren't constructed to pound hard pavement mile after mile, and they need all the help they can get. Some runners will need more cushioning than others, depending on their foot type. Since it is impossible to tell at the beginning just how susceptible you may be to foot aches and pains later when your running program advances, make sure your shoes are adequately cushioned. Later you may want to try a lighter, less well cushioned pair.

High price does not always ensure quality, and low-priced shoes may fit more comfortably and be better for you. However, it's unlikely that you will find a good pair of shoes for under $25. Some will cost much more. Try to buy one of the standard, well-known brands whose models have passed the test of the marketplace. As competition increases and manufacturers feel required to change the cosmetics of their shoes every year, it's becoming easier to pick up bargains by buying "last year's model."

You should examine your shoes regularly; they wear out all too quickly. Often the first sign of wear occurs at the outer heel. Proper maintenance will prevent injury and lengthen shoe life. Maintenance consists chiefly of applying shoe cement, widely available in running and hardware stores, to the worn areas of the sole. Once the upper shoe itself begins to break down, important support, chiefly in the heel, is lost. This can't be fixed and it's time to buy a new pair.

Once you've committed yourself to a running program, and if you possibly can afford it, purchase a second pair of shoes. If you are extremely happy with your first pair, by all means buy the same kind. But many runners like to experiment a bit to find another shoe they may like even better.

SOCKS

Q. What kind of socks should be worn? Is it really necessary to wear them at all?

A. You would think this question might have a simple answer, but the experts seem to have different opinions. Some runners don't wear any socks and are perfectly comfortable running without them. I've tried it and much prefer to run with socks. But they must fit properly. If they are too loose, they'll wrinkle, which may cause pressure points and blisters. If they are too tight, normal toe and foot mobility may be compromised. If they are too short, you will soon wear through them. Sometimes mending the sock is possible, but often the mended area causes a slight pressure point. While this may cause no trouble when walking, a blister may develop if you run in mended socks.

Many prefer thin, cotton socks, others wool, wool mixtures, or bulk orlon. Some runners wear two pairs of thin socks. I am in the minority, preferring a single, fairly thick pair of socks. Experiment to find what suits you best. A lot of runners tend to wear high socks, even in warm weather. There is really no need to lug around this extra weight, which can be considerable when the socks become heavy with absorbed sweat.

SHORTS AND TOPS

Q.   Do you have any recommendations about other clothing for runners?

A.   Don't spend much money, at least at the beginning, on shorts and tops. Wear a comfortable top that is not too tight. A cotton shirt will do. As the weather gets warmer, you should wear a light-colored top to reflect rather than absorb the sun's heat.

If you can afford them, a very light pair of nylon shorts is best. They will dry quickly. But any pair of loose-fitting shorts will do, even cut-offs. Make sure there is no constriction or thick inner seam which might cause irritation or chafing. Some of the more expensive men's shorts come with a built-in supporter. Some men prefer to wear a separate jock. Many, myself included, find jockey-type underwear most comfortable. Again, find out what seems best for you. If you do develop areas of chronic irritation or chafing, use petroleum jelly or other lubricants generously.

BRAS

A few years ago women runners complained there were no bras available that provided enough support yet were still comfortable. Now there are dozens to choose from. Most of the good ones have no metal clips to cause irritation. Running bras should be comfortable and above all not constricting. Some women don't wear a bra when they run. In most cases this is not harmful, provided the runner can withstand the leers and comments of male chauvinist bystanders. There is no good evidence that the unsupported breast will be damaged by running, although large-breasted women usually feel more comfortable if they wear a bra. Running ordinarily does not affect breast size, unless the runner loses a lot of weight. But because the chest wall muscles around the breast may be strengthened by running, breast contour may be improved.

OTHER EQUIPMENT

I almost always wear a sweat band around the forehead because sweat runs into my eyes no matter what the temperature, and also fogs my glasses. Many runners prefer a lightweight mesh cap which serves the dual purpose of absorbing sweat and protecting the head from the sun in hot weather. We'll talk more about other running gear in Chapter 16 when we discuss running in temperature extremes, rain, and snow.

As you progress, you may want to "look" like a runner. Be careful! You may end up looking foolish or fake. Don't buy a fancy warm-up suit if you really want to be taken seriously by other runners, or unless you are very good. If you must splurge, or if your family or friends want to give you a present, get a very lightweight pair of runner's shorts. Although I doubt they will let you run faster, they are so light that they may make you think you are running faster, and really that's almost as good. I treat myself to a new pair before each marathon.

Tops are another problem. The T-shirt explosion may tempt you. Stay away from the cruder ones. Recently I have seen seemingly respectable, middle-aged runners wearing such slogans as "Runners do it longer" and "It's easier downhill." I like to wear shirts that advertise the races I have run in. In fact I confess that one of the attractions of a race is the T-shirt it offers. Once at the Falmouth Road Race, I received two shirts as a reward for giving a brief talk at a runners' conference the night before. I was in heaven and would have gladly talked all night for another.

A variety of other gadgets are also available to the affluent runner. Fancy watches, pulse-rate counters, headphone radios, special water bottles, and dozens of other baubles are widely advertised to tempt the unwary. The pages of running magazines are beginning, sadly, I believe, to look like ski magazines.

Starting

Q. Are we finally ready to hit the road?

A. I think it's time.

Remember that what I am going to recommend should serve only as a very broad general outline. Each of you, if you approach your program intelligently, should be able to judge your own best pace and intensity. How you start and how quickly you advance depend on many factors, including your age, previous level of fitness, and most importantly the condition of your bones, joints, and muscles. The conditioning of these structures, which we collectively call the musculo-skeletal system, takes priority during the early part of your training program. The surest way to injure them and scuttle the whole program is to advance too quickly.

I understand that once you have made the commitment to run, you really want to get on with it. This is precisely the time to curb your enthusiasm and start slowly. If you are 18 years old you can probably start right in by jogging at a comfortable pace. But for most of you, the first few weeks (for want of a better name let's call it Stage I) should be devoted to strengthening and conditioning your musculo-skeletal system. The best way to do this is to begin a gentle stretching and strengthening program combined with brisk walking.

97

Stretching and Strengthening Exercises

Q. Why do you and so many other writers stress exercises?

A. Running does not provide balanced exercise for all muscle groups. Some muscles, particularly those in the back of the leg and lower back, are strengthened by repeated contraction during running. (See Figure 9.) With conditioning these muscles also become thicker and shorter. The muscles in the front of the leg and the lower abdomen, less involved in the muscular effort of running, become relatively weaker. This gradual process alters the normal muscle balance at each joint of the leg, and may cause abnormal

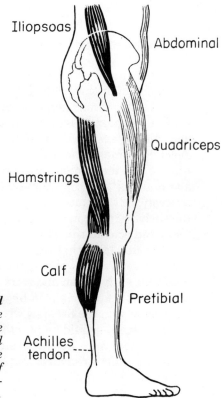

Iliopsoas

Abdominal

Quadriceps

Hamstrings

Calf

Pretibial

Achilles tendon

FIGURE 9. *Strengthening and stretching the leg muscles. The muscles in the back of the leg and the low back become much stronger and shorter when you run. They must be stretched. The muscles in the front of the leg and the abdomen become relatively weaker and need strengthening.*

leg motion and injury. Such injuries become much more frequent as mileage is increased.

To prevent these injuries, exercises must be performed which stretch the shortened, stronger muscles and strengthen the weaker ones. The value of any particular exercise to an individual runner will of course depend on particular musculo-skeletal characteristics. For example, some of us have unfortunately inherited "tight joints" and may need to do extensive stretching to prevent injury. A few lucky runners say they never have to stretch.

Q. Do you always stretch before a run?

A. I used to skip my stretching whenever I was rushed. A couple of annoying, relatively minor, but still disabling injuries, plus a stern lecture from a podiatrist friend who assured me the injuries would disappear if I behaved myself, cured me. As long as I stretch before and after running, the injuries rarely bother me.

Once you have changed into your running gear, there is an understandable desire to get out and run. Time is short, and you would rather spend it on the road than stretching in your bedroom. But curb your enthusiasm. Stretch before and after each

run, and if you have special problems, you may well need to stretch at other times during the day. As your program increases in intensity and duration, the importance of these exercises increases tremendously. Don't neglect them!

Several of the popular running books describe excellent stretching–strengthening programs, some of them so complex that all but the most enthusiastic might be discouraged. These programs seem designed more for the serious runner intent upon maximizing his performance. I will describe a simpler program, one I have found useful personally, as have many of my friends and patients. It is based on the "Magic 6" first described by Dr. George Sheehan, with some additions of my own.

STRETCHING EXERCISES

Stretching the Calf Muscles and the Achilles Tendon
This can effectively be done by performing a *wall pushup* (Figure 10). Stand flat-footed, 3 or 4 feet from the wall, bracing yourself against the wall with your outstretched arms (Figure 10A). With your knees locked and legs straight, lean into the wall until your calf muscles begin to hurt (Figure 10B). Hold this position for 20 seconds, and then repeat for a minute or two. Sometimes toeing in just a little, so that your toes are slightly closer together than your heels, increases the stretch.

Some runners prefer a variation of this exercise. Instead of keeping both feet together, put one leg back and the other forward. Then bend the knee of the forward leg, keeping the back leg straight and the back foot planted flat on the floor (Figure 11A). Hold this position for 20 seconds, then repeat for a minute or two. Then change legs and repeat. Even more Achilles tendon stretch can be achieved if you then bend the back knee as well, keeping the back foot firmly planted (Figure 11B).

These exercises are very important. Achilles tendon injuries are common, often serious, and difficult to cure. They are particularly common in women who have worn high heels for years, because their Achilles tendons are likely to be short.

Stretching the Hamstrings Place your straight leg, with knee locked, on a low chair, while the other leg, also straight with

FIGURE 10. *Wall pushup.* An exercise to stretch the Achilles tendon. Be sure to keep your heels flat and your knees straight. You should feel a pulling sensation or tension in your lower calf.

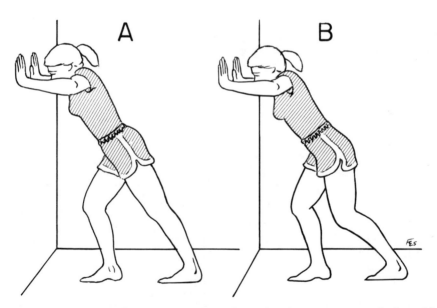

FIGURE 11. *Variation of the wall pushup.* Another way to stretch the calf muscles and Achilles tendon.

101

knee locked, supports you (Figure 12A). Then bring your head toward the knee of the elevated leg until you feel the pulling (Figure 12B). Hold this for 15 or 20 seconds and repeat for a minute or two. Don't bounce! Repeat for the other leg.

It may help to grasp the extended foot with your hands to steady yourself. As you become more limber, raise the extended leg higher by changing to a bureau or table. Ideally you should eventually be able to touch your chin to your knee, but I must confess I have never been able to manage it. This is an excellent exercise and is highly recommended.

Stretching the Low Back and the Hamstrings   To do this perform a simple toe touching exercise with knees locked and legs absolutely straight (Figure 13). Although this exercise is not part of Dr. Sheehan's basic program, I have found it very helpful. During long runs, while waiting for traffic or stopping for water, I perform it regularly, because it so effectively loosens my rather tight low back muscles. If you have chronic low back strain, how-

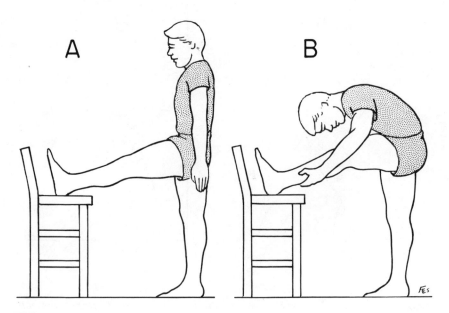

FIGURE 12. *Stretching the hamstrings.*

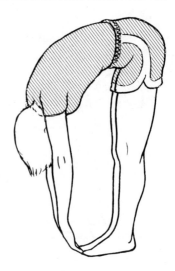

FIGURE 13. *Toe touching to stretch the lower back and hamstrings.*

ever, you may find this exercise painful, and it may aggravate your pain. So go easy.

A common error when performing all stretching exercises, but this one in particular, is to bounce instead of stretch. Bouncing is self-defeating, because it provokes neuromuscular reflexes which tend to contract the muscles instead of lengthening them. Stay in place when you bend, and don't bob up and down. You will feel the gradual lengthening of the low back and hamstring muscles, and your fingers will gradually come closer to the floor. Some recommend staying down for 15 or 20 seconds, and then repeating. I prefer to hold it much longer. Either way, do the exercise for 2 minutes.

When I stretch in the morning, my muscles are still stiff from lying in bed. At first I can't come close to touching my toes. After a couple of minutes, I can generally plant my palms on the floor. This exercise has seemed particularly helpful in preventing the mild, recurrent hip pain that regularly bothers me whenever I up my mileage.

Q. Are there alternative exercises for people who have low back pain?

A. If your back bothers you, and you still must stretch the lower hamstrings, a useful exercise is shown in Figure 14. Squat with

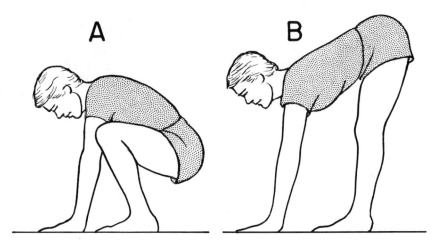

FIGURE 14. *An alternative way to stretch the hamstrings. This exercise can be used if you have low back problems.*

your knees bent and your hands on the floor (Figure 14A). Then slowly rise by straightening your knees without moving your hands or feet (Figure 14B).

Still another exercise to stretch the low back and hamstrings is the *backover*. Perform this by lying on the floor and bringing your straight legs over your head. Try to touch the floor with your toes (Figure 15). Hold your position steady for 20 seconds and then relax by bending your knees. Repeat, again attempting to touch the floor with your legs straight. Do this for two minutes.

A final method for stretching the low back is to lie flat on your back with legs straight (Figure 16A). Then unroll your back

FIGURE 15. *The backover to stretch the lower back and hamstrings.*

104

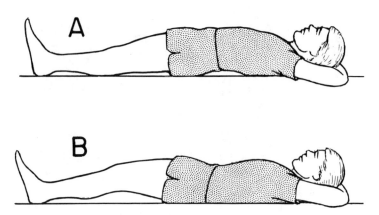

FIGURE 16. *Stretching the lower back.*

muscles by trying to make your whole lower back touch the floor (Figure 16B). Hold for 20 seconds, relax, and then repeat for 2 minutes.

MUSCLE STRENGTHENING EXERCISES

Although muscle strengthening exercises may be crucially important to prevent muscular imbalance, somehow the stimulus to perform them seems to be much less than for the stretching program. By trial and error, I have found that I don't need to perform the first two exercises described below; my quadriceps and shin muscles are relatively strong. But my abdominal muscles are weak; I get into trouble every time I skip the bent-leg situps which strengthen them. Each of you will have to define for yourself which parts of the strengthening program are necessary.

Strengthening the Shin Muscles Sit on a table high enough so that your feet don't touch the floor. Place a 3- to 5-pound weight over your toes. Then bend your foot at the ankle (Figure 17). Don't move the rest of your leg. Hold this for 15 or 20 seconds, then relax. Repeat for 2 minutes, then switch to the other leg.

A simple way to make a satisfactory weight is to fill an old

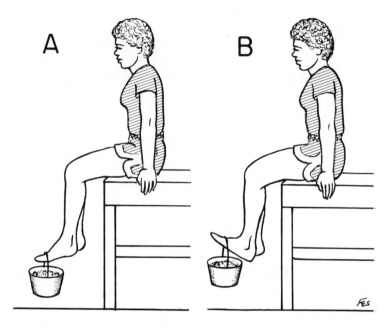

FIGURE 17. *Strengthening the shin muscles.*

paint can with sand. You can also purchase weights at some running stores.

Strengthening the Quadriceps (Front Thigh) Muscles Use the same position and the same weight as just described, but this time straighten the knee without bending the ankle (Figure 18). Hold this for 15 or 20 seconds and then relax. Repeat for 2 minutes. Then do the same thing for the other leg.

As strength is acquired by performing both these exercises, you might want to increase the weight lifted (add more sand to the paint can) and the total time the exercises are performed.

Strengthening the Abdominal Muscles This is achieved by performing a bent-leg situp (Figure 19). For me regular performance of 20 of these situps each day is the key to preventing low back pain. The knees must be kept bent so that the necessary

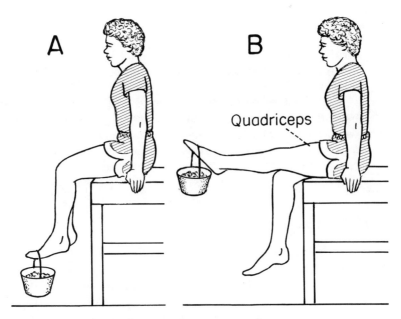

FIGURE 18. *Strengthening the quadriceps.*

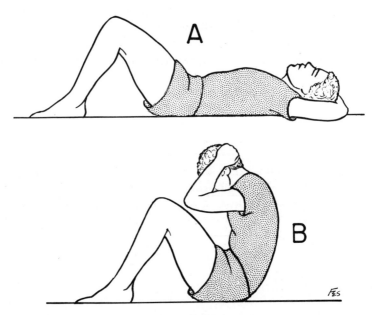

FIGURE 19. *The bent-leg situp for strengthening the abdominal muscles.*

strain is applied to your abdominal muscles. If you keep your legs straight, you stress the low back muscles, exactly what you don't want to do.

It's best to perform this exercise with your hands clasped behind your head, but at first, if your abdominal muscles are weak, you may have to keep your arms at your sides. Start with a few situps each day, and gradually increase the number until you can do 15 or 20 without stopping. If you have a severe low back problem, you may be helped by performing even more.

OTHER EXERCISES

Watch runners before a race. You will see a varied, at times punishing, frequently grotesque or even comical set of strengthening and stretching exercises. No two runners do them the same way. Each seems to have worked out a routine which best suits him. So should you.

Many of you will want to stretch your neck and shoulder muscles. You can do this by gently rotating them. Slowly touching your chin to your chest also stretches the neck. Some find it relaxing to bend from the waist and swing in a gentle circle.

Q. Do you recommend doing exercises such as pushups or chinups to strengthen the upper body and arms?

A. Some of the better runners are convinced that doing mild strengthening exercises for the upper body helps them run better. Some even do light work with weights.

I have no objection to this kind of exercise provided you like it. But remember that it will not make you more fit or reduce your risk factors. There is no compelling reason for a runner to perform such exercises unless vanity requires him to have bulging muscles. Personally, I prefer not to have to lug around this extra muscle mass when I run.

Stage I—Walking

Q. Now that we know the proper exercises, can we begin the running part of the program?

A. For the first few weeks, you should concentrate on brisk walking. We might call this Stage I.

Some of you may be in such dreadful physical condition that even a few minutes of walking will make you breathless. Don't become discouraged. If you are basically healthy, your performance will slowly improve. The older you are the longer you will probably remain in Stage I. Don't leave it until you are comfortable walking at a brisk pace, perhaps 15 to 20 minutes per mile, for a distance of at least 2 or 3 miles.

Stage II—Walk–Jog

Once you've accomplished this, you can begin Stage II. Here walking and *very slow* jogging are combined. Some of you may remember doing this as youngsters. Then you called it Scout's Pace. Again take plenty of time in Stage II. There is no rush. Start by jogging just a few steps, then *slowly* increase the proportion of jogging to walking. It may be weeks or even months before you can jog the majority of the distance, which should remain about 2 to 3 miles. Try to do this every day, but don't hesitate to take a day or two off if you begin to hurt or have other things to do. However, try not to take off more than two days in a row unless injuries stop you.

Q. At what pace should we jog?

A. Probably between 10 to 12 minutes per mile. Go a little faster if you can, but be careful not to hurt yourself. At this point speed is less important than time. You should continue for 20 to 30 minutes. It's tempting to do more. Don't! *If you exercise for much more than 30 minutes, your chances of hurting yourself rise considerably.*

Once you can complete 2 or 3 miles, you are ready to advance to the next stage. If, after many weeks, you still can't make it, you are in all likelihood jogging too fast. Slow down, even if your pace seems agonizingly slow. You will eventually get there if you are patient and don't hurt yourself.

109

Stage III—Jogging

Stage III is the stage of consistent jogging, when you do not have to slow to a walk. Early in Stage III many regress because they are tired, bored, or have musculo-skeletal aches and pains. Don't be disappointed if this happens to you also. Steady improvement will continue, provided you are patient. Also remember that jogging is different from walking. You are using your muscles differently. For a brief period, with each step, you are airborne. Both feet are off the ground. Even at a slow jog, the impact your feet, ankles, knees, and hips must tolerate increases enormously. The faster you go, the greater the impact. Almost certainly you will at least ache a lot. Respect these early warnings and slow down when they occur.

Some runners have trouble at this point because they are going too fast. A chance encounter with an old friend vividly demonstrated this to me recently. Barbara had simultaneously embarked on a fairly strict diet and a jogging program to lose weight and become fit. Weight loss was easy, but she had become impatient, annoyed, and frustrated by her inability to run farther than a mile without becoming extremely fatigued. She had always enjoyed good health and had never smoked, but she wondered if something serious might be wrong with her. She felt fine when she was not running, and had added iron and multivitamins to protect herself from any deficiencies her diet might have caused.

She certainly looked healthy enough, and I asked her if she might be going too fast. She assured me that she always ran slowly, but she did admit that she was frequently breathless, particularly early in the run.

The breathlessness of course was the clue that no matter how slowly she thought she was running, she was still going too fast for her present level of fitness. I urged her to slow down considerably, despite her protests that if she jogged any slower she would be walking. She promised to try.

When I next met her a few weeks later, she greeted me enthusiastically. She had indeed slowed her pace, never developed breathlessness, and had recently completed her first 3-mile run without difficulty at 11 minutes per mile.

Our aim in Stage III is to maintain high enough intensity and duration of exercise to increase cardiovascular fitness. Earlier we defined this level: exercise performed at least three or four times a week, for 20 to 30 minutes, at an intensity high enough to increase the pulse rate to about 70 percent of the maximum expected heart rate for your age. Early in Stage III this may not be possible because of fatigue or pain. But if you avoid injury, you will gradually achieve it.

This is done of course by *gradually increasing your speed.* Don't jog beyond 30 minutes at this point. Measure your pulse rate regularly to make sure you are gradually reaching the necessary intensity. If you are very slightly breathless, and still comfortable, this is almost certainly an adequate pace for you, and you can dispense with taking your pulse if you don't have a heart problem.

INJURIES OF OVERUSE

It's at this stage that defects in your running form or any intrinsic abnormalities of your musculo-skeletal system may show up. Your injury pattern will change. You have now graduated from the aches and pains of the unfit beginner to the many possible injuries and annoyances of runners, which we collectively call "injuries of overuse." These injuries are discussed in Chapter 7. Sometimes consultation with a sports podiatrist or orthopedic surgeon is needed to cure these nagging problems.

At this point in your development it is often best to take days off. Run four or five days each week rather than every day. But do your stretching exercises at least once every day, and preferably twice on the days you run.

You'll soon find that as your fitness increases, you must exercise a little more vigorously to maintain your pulse rate. This, of course, is a sign of increasing fitness, the desired effect of a training program. At this level of training you can expect to derive most of the benefits of running discussed earlier. Many joggers are content to stay at this level. However, we will soon see that just a bit higher level of intensity may provide the maximum health benefit.

111

Stage IV—Distance Running

Q. Suppose we do want to run longer distances. What should we do next?

A. First you have to ask yourself several important questions.

> What are my goals?
> Do I want to train for longer distances, a marathon perhaps?
> How much time do I have to devote to running?
> How fit do I really want to become?

I am hopeful many of you will want to go further, into what I call *Stage IV. At this stage the goal is to increase both the duration and the speed of running.* Let me emphasize that the duration is far more important, so long as the intensity is enough to keep your pulse rate at the desired level. I mentioned earlier that maximal protection from a heart attack may be provided by running 20 miles a week at a pace of 9 to 10 minutes per mile. This translates to about five runs of 4 miles each week, and this is a minimum goal to aim for in Stage IV. Again let me emphasize that the increase in daily mileage should be very gradual, perhaps no more than adding a mile each week to your total until you reach your goal.

Later (in Chapter 10) I will discuss more intensive training for those of you who want to run longer races. The principles remain the same, however—*change slowly and emphasize increased duration rather than increased running speed.*

Many experts feel that the best way to progress at this stage is to vary your daily program. An every other day run may be preferable, since it allows your muscles to rest in between. If you want to run 20 miles each week, dividing the mileage into three or four equal parts may be preferable to shorter daily runs. In general I agree with this approach. If nothing else it's more convenient for those who have trouble finding enough time to run every day. I also agree with the increasingly accepted notion that training is improved if one of your runs each week is somewhat longer. The weekly long run gives you a goal to shoot for, and that's increasingly necessary as you increase your running program. It's also an integral part of training for a longer run.

We might divide our 20-mile week in the following way:

Sunday	stretching only
Monday	4 miles
Tuesday	stretching only
Wednesday	5 miles
Thursday	4 miles
Friday	stretching only
Saturday	7 miles

Of course each of you should alter this rough guideline to fit your own physical and psychological needs. Work out the plan that best suits you.

At this point you also should consider doing some speed or interval work. I know this sounds a bit strange after all my exhortations to take it slowly. But by now your musculo-skeletal system is in the kind of shape that can take the added stresses of a faster pace. Not only will interval work probably improve your overall capacity, but, equally important perhaps, it will make your running more interesting. Of your total mileage, 5 or 10 percent, that is about 2 miles, might be performed at a decidedly faster pace. It's easiest for me to accomplish this by running a couple of hundred yards of each mile at a faster speed. I usually don't include speed work in my weekly long run, but do try to include some in each of my shorter ones. Speed work particularly lends itself to running on a track, where the distances are easily calculated. Initially your attempts to quicken your pace may leave you breathless, but you will improve with practice. As you improve, you may want to increase gradually the length and speed of your intervals.

The four stages discussed in this chapter are summarized in Table 8. Many of you will proceed no further. Your health benefits will be considerable. You will feel better, and probably you will be reasonably thin. You will be able to hold your head up and even join in when runners begin to discuss their times, courses run, equipment, and psychological highs. But I hope that many of you will be tempted to go still further, to the point at which the run itself becomes the important factor, not the possible health benefits you might derive from it. This phase of running is discussed in Chapter 10.

TABLE 8. *The Stages of a Running Program*

	ACTIVITY	PACE	TIME OR DISTANCE
Stage I	brisk walking	15 minutes/mile	2–3 miles daily
Stage II	walk–jog–walk	10–15 minutes/mile	20–30 minutes daily
Stage III	slow jogging	8–12 minutes/mile	20–30 minutes four times a week
Stage IV	jogging–running	6–10 minutes/mile*	20 miles per week

*Interval or speed work for 5–10 percent of the total mileage may be added.

Running Style and Form

Q. Is there a preferred running style or form that we should try to use?

A. Everyone's form will differ somewhat and these differences are usually not too important. But watch good runners. All share certain characteristics which even the beginner should strive for. Particularly, they seem loose and relaxed, unlike us plodders who so often tend to tighten our muscles, particularly at the neck and shoulders. Such tightening wastes energy, and, if it lasts long enough, may cause real pain. I have to remind myself constantly of this during my longer runs.

Most experts agree on the following recommendations:

1. *Use a heel–toe gait.* Running on the toes is for sprinters, and running this way for long distances will cause muscle strain and tears. Some writers have recommended a flat foot plant, with the heel and toe striking the ground nearly simultaneously. Very fast distance runners may prefer to run this way. For the rest of us the best way to run is to plant the heel first, then the toe.
2. *Run straight up.* Don't lean forward. Straight up is the best balanced position by far, as well as the least tiring and most comfortable.
3. *Keep your arms loose and relaxed.* Many runners carry their

arms much too high. Some flail them wildly. Try to keep your hands at waist level. Sometimes it helps to think of your arms as propelling you forward. They can't do that if they are swinging from side to side. Try instead to move them parallel to your legs, not letting your arms move across the midline of your body. Don't clench your fists. Keep your arms and hands relaxed by touching your thumb lightly to the tip of your index finger and running that way for a while.

4. *Don't bounce!* It's wasted energy and usually happens when you are trying to run too fast or take too long a stride.

5. *Take short, compact strides.* It's more efficient, more comfortable, and less likely to cause injury. Your stride will naturally lengthen as your speed increases. You should not make a conscious effort to lengthen it.

Breathing Correctly

Q. Is there a proper way to breathe during running?

A. Good runners use their diaphragms. They expand their lungs not only by pushing out their rib cage but also by contracting the diaphragm, the muscle that separates the chest from the abdomen. As the diaphragm contracts it pushes down on the abdominal contents, making the abdominal cavity smaller and the chest larger. This pulls air into the lungs and tends to push out the abdominal contents. You can tell if you are breathing with your diaphragm if you see your stomach expand with each breath.

Check this when you run. Many of you may already be breathing correctly. If not, slow your pace a little, and consciously try to push out your stomach each time you breathe in. If you still can't do it—and many runners have trouble with this—try diaphragmatic breathing at rest. It's often easiest to develop the proper rhythm and coordination if you lie flat on your back and place a book or magazine on your stomach. Try to lift the book each time you breathe in, while at the same time not moving your rib cage. You should soon develop the knack of proper breathing with your diaphragm. The next step is to breathe this way while you are standing. Place your hand lightly on your abdomen. Each time you inhale it should move outward or forward. Once you can do this, you should be able, with a little practice, to breathe with your diaphragm when you run.

Not only is this type of breathing more efficient, but it will also help prevent the side "stitches" that are so common among novice runners. Most stitches appear to be caused by spasm or cramp-like contraction of the diaphragm in runners who are not breathing properly.

Q. We know many runners who reached this level and then stopped. Some were bored. Others began to hate the drudgery. How do you manage to continue and still enjoy it?

A. Even after twenty years of running, there are still times when I have to drag myself into my running gear, when the idea of going out into the cold, heat, snow, or rain is positively loathsome. Everyone has periods like this. But there are ways to keep going through these low periods, and in the next chapter we will discuss them.

CHAPTER 6

How to Continue to Enjoy Running

Running Alone

Q. What do you think about when you are running alone? Don't you get bored?

A. It's surprising how often this question is raised. Many beginning runners, and even some veterans, find it difficult to concentrate on anything except their aching bones and joints. Often this stops them from running as long as they would like. Many runners use mental tricks to dissociate themselves from their bodies during their routine daily runs. Conversation, of course, does this very nicely, but when you're running alone you are left to your own devices.

Sometimes you can develop a reflective, meditative mood, isolating yourself completely from the environment. At times I have achieved a near trance-like state with little recollection of the events that occurred. But this happens rarely and lasts only a short time. Of course such a state can be dangerous if you are running on a road and must watch for cars. You might want to try it if you do much running on a track.

Or you may consciously try to solve problems or even come up with new ideas. Some very creative thinking can be done while running. It's the one time of the day when you can be by yourself, away from the telephone and other intrusions. In fact the isolation is one of the most attractive aspects of running. Many of the ideas in this book, and indeed the idea to write it in the first place, were generated during my daily runs.

Most commonly, perhaps, runners find themselves intensely investigating their environment. Running offers a chance to notice things often completely overlooked at other times. I often study the old Boston homes in detail as I plod by them. Somehow my sensitivity and appreciation for detail seem heightened during a run. Much of this heightened awareness undoubtedly occurs because running provides isolation from other intrusions. There are courses I have run hundreds of times, and yet each time I see something new.

Runner's High

Q. Just what is meant by "runner's high"?

A. There is no uniform definition of this phenomenon, because it has been so differently described by so many different people.

Running often produces a feeling of elation or high spirits. I suppose this could be called a mild runner's high. During slow running, some have described a sense of floating, of feeling as if their legs were moving automatically. Such runners seem to become passive witnesses to their bodies' movements rather than active participants. This too must be a kind of runner's high. At faster pace, some runners describe a heightened awareness of their bodies and the environment, another kind of runner's high. Beginners and novices often describe vivid, new sensations when they run, but I suspect that they have literally let their enthusiasm for their new-found activity "run away" with them. Finally, some have described a much more powerful experience, an almost transcendental feeling, as if they had taken a mind-altering drug. This feeling must be rare. I have never experienced it, and I have never met a veteran runner who has.

It's important to differentiate these various sensations I have called "runner's high" from the general feeling of well being and good health that most runners have. This latter is a long-lasting, fairly constant feeling; "runner's high" is short-lived, usually ending during the run itself or shortly after.

Q. Are there any other tricks to keep us going on a running program?

A. It is extremely helpful to set goals. One of the major reasons to enter races is to have something to train for. If I want to run a marathon, I plan several months ahead. As soon as it is over, I take it easy and let my body recover. My mileage drops to 15 or 20 miles a week. Sometimes I may even stop running completely for a while. I then return to running refreshed and anxious to begin once more.

Don't let your running become a strict routine. Nothing can be more boring than running the same course, at the same speed and distance each day. Choose an interesting course even if you must drive to it. Vary your mileage. Never run hard two days in a row.

Q. Do you think it is better to run alone or with company?

A. You should learn to enjoy both. Most runners prefer a group, particularly if they plan to run more than just a few miles. However, group running can become competitive. Choose companions who run at about your level. Otherwise, you may push too hard, making your running less enjoyable and increasing your chance of injury.

It is also worthwhile to get used to running alone. One of running's major advantages is that it can be squeezed into even the busiest schedule. You lose this flexibility if you always require company.

Keeping a Log

Q. Does it help to keep a diary or running log?

A. Every running book I have read enthusiastically recommends keeping a log, so there must be something to it. Not only will the diary furnish you with an accurate record of your recent mileage, but it may help your training by comparing your performances after different training programs. A log may spur the beginning runner on, giving concrete evidence of improvement and thus helping to prevent discouragement.

119

I have never had much trouble remembering as much as I want to about my mileage and previous training programs, so I have never kept a log. But you may find that a log is helpful, and if so, you should by all means keep one. If you are particularly affluent, rather handsome logs are now available at some running and bookstores.

When Should We Run?

Q. Is there a preferred time of day to run?

A. I used to love to run early in the morning. Now I find it virtually impossible to muster the determination to do it. I would rather have a cup of coffee and start the day more slowly. Some runners so welcome the quiet, pollution-free environment of early morning running that they poke away the morning cobwebs with no trouble. They prepare for their day by exercising. Others prefer to rid themselves of the day's tensions by running after work.

Varying the time of day you run helps to prevent running from becoming boring. Weekends I like to run in the late afternoon, so that I can spend the last couple of miles dreaming of how good a beer will taste at the end of the run. Weekdays I prefer to run in the late morning or at noon. Often this means I must start my day very early to make enough time. In winter it is best to run around mid-day when there is enough light and the temperature is warmer. Many find that running after work, just before supper, helps to curb their appetite. Lunchtime running is popular. Runners can socialize while they run and also avoid the temptations of a high calorie lunch. I try to run at lunch with friends at least once each week.

Q. Is it safe to skip lunch and exercise instead?

A. It certainly is, although most runners have a light snack after their run, rather than skipping the meal entirely. Many runners have found that the three-meal day is a custom, but hardly a necessity. A piece of fruit after a lunchtime run is often enough.

WHEN TO EAT

Q.   How soon after eating is it safe to run?

A.   There is tremendous individual variation. I never run well once I have eaten a large meal, no matter how many hours I wait. I prefer to wait at least a couple of hours after even a light meal. Others have much more tolerance. Each of you will have to experiment to find what suits you best.

How soon you can run after eating will also depend on what you eat. Carbohydrate is much more quickly absorbed than protein and fat. Water doesn't count. Moderate amounts should be consumed before running, particularly in warm weather. Other liquids will have to be tested individually. Some, like coffee, may upset the stomach.

Don't bound out of bed first thing in the morning and go off running. First drink some water. You are relatively dehydrated in the morning and need fluid. You also must stretch even longer than you might at other times of the day. There is some evidence that early morning runners, particularly older runners, are more prone to injuries, presumably because their musculo-skeletal systems are not sufficiently warmed up.

MAKING THE TIME

Q.   How do you find time to run?

A.   One doesn't find time, one *makes* time. One of the most frequent excuses patients give for not continuing their exercise programs is the lack of time. I don't accept that excuse. They can find time if they try hard enough. I do it by beginning my work day very early so that I can squeeze out the time somewhere in the middle. Obviously there are some days when this is impossible, but not often. I carry a pair of jogging shorts and running shoes in the car. If I haven't been able to run earlier, I may try to run on the way home, using the car to change. After the run, it's back to the car and home, sweaty but hopefully on time for supper.

Some people run to work. Others run home. This is a perfect

121

way to make time, provided you have shower facilities, or at least a place to change at work. Few work harder than medical and surgical residents, who are on duty many nights and weekends, and regularly work at least a 12-hour day. Yet many of them find time to run regularly and even manage to train for marathons. They do it by running to and from work, carrying a change of clothing in a light backpack.

Others have tried to solve the time problem by running at night. This may appeal to some of you, but I suspect that most will have difficulty doing it regularly. Running in the dark is dangerous unless you run on a well-lit course and wear reflective clothing. Most people make supper their biggest meal and may be uncomfortable running even several hours later. Running is often a stimulant. Many runners have difficulty sleeping for several hours after a good run. I would not recommend evening running unless you like to retire fairly late.

Where to Run

Q. How about track running? Do you recommend running indoors in bad weather?

A. Actually, there aren't many days, even in winter, when you can't run outdoors on the road. I avoid running indoors whenever possible. Indoor tracks are short, often steeply banked, and the surfaces are hard. They are very tough on the feet and legs.

Outdoor tracks are a little better, and sometimes even fun if you are trying to do a little speed work or have decided to meditate. The boredom of running around and around them may be welcome. When I am increasing my mileage, during marathon training, for example, I prefer to run part of the time on a softer surface to prevent injury. Most outdoor tracks are soft enough for such training.

Q. Can you run in the rain?

A. Strange as it may seem, running in the rain can be enjoyable if the rain isn't too heavy and it's not too cold. The major difficulty is keeping your shoes dry. Heavy, water-logged shoes can take all the fun out of running. Wet feet also can cause blisters.

Q. Which kind of course is preferable?

A. Feet were not constructed to run on hard pavement. Even the best-cushioned shoes will not completely protect your feet if you run long distances on paved roads. Yet roads do have some advantages. The surface is relatively smooth, and, if you are careful, you can avoid ruts and holes, since they are seen easily. In theory grassy surfaces are fine, but I am always a little uncomfortable running on grass, since the holes and bumps are often hidden. Best of all would be a course with a consistent, moderately resilient running surface. Outdoor tracks are good, but boring. I heartily endorse the construction of outdoor running trails and paths through scenic areas, and urge you to lobby to encourage building such trails in your own areas.

ROAD RUNNING

Q. I like to run on the road. Do you have any suggestions for running in traffic?

A. Whenever possible run facing traffic. Despite stories to the contrary, most drivers are not really out to get you. But it is a lot easier to avoid the careless driver, who may see you too late, if you can see him approaching. Whenever I run in traffic, I keep a sharp eye to my left to make certain there is room enough to jump off the road if necessary.

The exception is running around sharp curves. It may be smart to run with the traffic, because the oncoming cars, often taking these turns tightly, can't see you until they are almost through the turn. It's better still to avoid narrow, tightly curved roads. You are asking for trouble if you run them often.

There is another disadvantage to road running. Most roads are not flat. They slope gently downward from the center to help drainage. Therefore, if you run facing traffic, your right leg will consistently strike the pavement a little higher than your left. Your pelvis and hips will be tilted downward to the left. If you

regularly run long distances this way, you are likely to injure yourself. However, my right leg is about ½ inch shorter than my left, so I am most comfortable running against traffic. The slope of the road corrects my skeletal deficiency.

If you're not so "fortunate" as to have one leg shorter than the other, you should try to find roads that are sparsely traveled so that it will be safe to run in the middle, at the crown, where the road is relatively flat. Or you may have to do some running _with_ the traffic for some distance to restore muscular balance. But do so only when the traffic is sparse and the road is wide.

Any time you run when visibility is not good, you should wear brightly colored, reflective clothing so that you can be seen easily.

CARS

Q. How should a runner deal with cars?

A. Cars are joggers' natural enemy and you should never relax your guard. I have never seen a jogger win an argument with a car, so I recommend running "scared" whenever there is traffic. Most drivers are reasonably polite and I doubt any, save for a few psychotic ones, deliberately try to injure runners. Still, you may encounter one who enjoys scaring you a bit.

Runners can also be obnoxious and antagonistic. They often act as if the roads belonged to them, as if they expected drivers to alter their usual practices to accommodate their whims. Some run two or three abreast in the road, forcing the cars toward the center or provoking the drivers to lean on their horns. I have seen runners curse drivers who would not slow down or stop to let them cross, even though the light was green. Runners also seem to have a penchant for darting out from between parked cars and looking surprised and angry when they are almost hit by an unsuspecting driver.

In addition to arousing hostility, cars also pollute. In some parts of the country, running becomes impossible during the morning and late afternoon rush hours. The air smells terrible and carbon monoxide levels become appallingly high. At such times running should be avoided. Instead, run early in the morning when the air has had a chance to clear overnight.

CARBON MONOXIDE

Q.   What effect does carbon monoxide have on the body?

A.   The long-term effects of carbon monoxide are not known, but this pollutant can hardly do the body much good. The short-term effects are better understood and more easily measured. Carbon monoxide competes with oxygen and displaces it in the red blood cells. Because its affinity for the blood cells is much greater than oxygen's, even small amounts of carbon monoxide may significantly decrease the oxygen-carrying capacity of the blood and hence its ability to bring oxygen to the exercising muscle. If carbon monoxide levels are high enough, death will occur, since oxygen can no longer be transported from the lungs to the tissues. The runner who runs outside will not be exposed to lethal carbon monoxide levels, but the levels may be high enough to cause dizziness, decreased mental acuity, and poor performance.

DOGS

A dog may be man's best friend, but there is something about running that often brings out the worst in them. Next to cars, they seem to be runners' most dangerous enemies. I have been attacked, scratched, treed, and frightened half to death by dogs. I respect them enormously and avoid them whenever I can.

Q.   Do you have any hints for handling them?

A.   Run in familiar areas which have leash laws. I have never been bothered in my own town because the leash laws are strictly enforced. Dogs know their own territory and often guard it jealously. When I see one growling in his yard, I cross to the other side of the street. This is often enough to prevent the encounter.

When running in a strange area, it may be wise to carry a long stick. Most aggressive dogs will keep their distance if you keep swinging the stick, and will eventually stop chasing you after you have passed their territory. Sometimes it helps to turn and face the dog, pick something up and throw it at him. Shouting and screaming also may help.

RUNNING HILLS

Q. Do you have any hints about hill running? Is it necessary to change running style and pace?

A. Some runners have real problems with hills, and they try to avoid them like the plague. I really don't mind them at all. In fact, hills seem to be the only place I ever pass people during a race.

Shortening your stride and leaning into the hill a bit may help considerably. Try to keep your head down and not lift your legs as high as you would on level ground. This almost shuffling gait seems less taxing running uphill. You might also pump your arms more vigorously and slow your pace a bit.

Running uphill is likely to aggravate any underlying knee problem. If your knees hurt, avoid hills for a while, and do more quadriceps strengthening exercises. (See pages 106–7.)

Running down a gently rolling hill is one of the sport's greatest pleasures. But when the hill is steep, you may tend to tighten your leg muscles to check your speed and avoid losing control. Many runners check themselves too much. You should relax a bit and run more freely when you run down hills.

HIGH ALTITUDE RUNNING

Different problems are presented by high altitude running. Above 5000 feet, the oxygen content of the air begins to fall, decreasing progressively as the altitude increases. Less oxygen is thus available for the exercising muscles.

If you travel to a higher altitude and attempt to run at your usual pace and distance, you may be very unpleasantly surprised. Your running capacity will be considerably reduced. If you run at a high altitude, you must decrease both speed and duration until you acclimate. The body does this in part by increasing the number of red blood cells which carry oxygen from the lungs to the exercising muscles. Some runners take advantage of this adaptive mechanism and regularly train at high altitude for competition at sea level. They believe that the extra oxygen-carrying capacity of the red blood cells improves performance. Not everyone agrees with this theory, however, and it has yet to be proved conclusively.

127

Q.   How long does it take to acclimate to high altitude completely?

A.   Some say it takes a few weeks; others say much longer. Peak long distance performance is never as good at high altitude as at sea level, as the 1968 Olympics in Mexico City clearly demonstrated. From this point of view complete adaptation never occurs. You probably will acclimate as much as you can within a few weeks, as long as you continue to exercise near peak capacity.

Running in Cold Weather

Most runners want to run throughout the year and should know how to protect themselves against the very real dangers of temperature extremes. If you understand what happens to your body during prolonged running, and the often profound effects of climate, you are likely to run more intelligently.

Exercising muscles generate heat which the body must eliminate. Otherwise the central body temperature, called the core temperature, will gradually increase, eventually to dangerous levels.

In cool weather there is little problem losing the heat produced by muscular activity, unless you are severely overdressed. Heat generated by the muscles is carried away by the blood, whose temperature is in turn increased. The warmed blood circulates to the skin where the extra heat is lost by several different mechanisms which include conduction, convection, radiation, and evaporation.

In very cold weather we are confronted with an opposite problem, excessive heat loss. The body needs the heat to maintain adequate core temperature. One mechanism for reducing excessive heat loss is to reduce blood flow to the skin and nonexercising areas. When we run in cold weather our feet and legs stay warm because of the considerable heat generated locally by the exercising muscles. But blood flow to other parts of the body, the hands for example, is reduced. That's why it is often necessary to wear gloves when the weather is only moderately cold. In extremely cold weather mittens more effectively warm the hands than gloves. Blood flow to the head and scalp remains fairly brisk even when the temperature is low, and considerable heat can be lost this way. To prevent this, a hat should be worn in cold weather. The ears are quite susceptible to cold injury and should also be well covered.

It's important to cover all exposed areas in very cold weather. I recommend the liberal use of petroleum jelly over exposed areas of the face and neck. An alternative would be to wear a ski mask. These are available at most ski shops, but I find them uncomfortable and messy. They tend to get wet around the mouth and nose and then freeze up.

There is tremendous variability in susceptibility to the cold. Once the temperature goes much below 55 degrees F., I must wear gloves, yet I rarely need a hat until it is well below freezing. For others the opposite occurs: their heads and ears get cold early and their hands only at much lower temperatures.

HOW TO DRESS

Q. What kind of clothing do you recommend for cold-weather running?

A. We must distinguish between the upper and lower body. There is usually no problem from the waist down because the legs are generating so much heat. There is little risk of cold injury unless the toes get wet. Long underwear and warm-up pants are enough for almost any temperature. Some runners prefer running shorts over sweat pants or long underwear. Many women wear leotards. You won't need to add extra socks. Your feet will stay warm unless they get wet.

The upper body is different. The key here is to dress in layers. The air trapped between the layers serves as good insulation to reduce heat loss. I start with a cotton undershirt and long thermal underwear. Cotton is comfortable, it doesn't itch, and it absorbs sweat well. I then add a long-sleeved cotton turtleneck, and, if it is really cold, a wool turtleneck. A light nylon warm-up jacket is finally added to serve as a windbreaker.

Turtlenecks are particularly useful because they cover the neck and even part of the face if necessary. Make sure the sleeves are long enough so that no gap exists between your gloves and the end of your sleeve. As you become warmer during the run, you may want to shed some clothing. The wool turtleneck goes first. It can be carried or conveniently tied around your waist.

Inexperienced runners often overdress in the cold. When you start your run, expect to feel a bit chilly. Within a few minutes you'll generally feel warm and comfortable.

Wind is another problem. It magnifies the effects of the cold, since the air rushing past the body carries away heat from the skin. Be sure to dress warmly on a windy day. A wind-proof nylon shell is a necessity. Running into a strong wind when your body is wet with sweat can become very uncomfortable. If possible, plan so that the first half of your run, when you are not so sweaty and warm, is into the wind. The second half, or return trip, when you are sweating more heavily, is more comfortably run with the wind at your back.

Rarely is it too cold to run in winter. But it can be a problem to find time to run during the day when it's light enough. If I cannot manage a midday run, I am forced to turn elsewhere, either to an indoor track, an exercise bicycle at home, or even to running in place.

Running on ice and other slippery surfaces is dangerous. If you must run on them, make sure you have the right kind of shoe. Some ripple soles, fine for hard, dry surfaces, are disastrous on snow or ice. The studded type of sole or cleats are preferable.

Q. We've heard that running in cold weather may be harmful to the lungs. Is this true?

A. Not for most people. Even in extremely cold weather, the air we breathe is warmed up so quickly in the upper airways that it is at normal body temperature by the time it reaches the lung tissue itself. It is unnecessary, in fact burdensome, to wear a scarf or mask.

A few unfortunate individuals develop asthma when they are exposed to cold air, but this is an allergic type of reaction, and fortunately need not concern most of us.

However, cold air may be dangerous for runners with heart problems, particularly coronary artery disease. The heart pumps much more vigorously in the cold in all of us because of constriction of the arteries. But in coronary patients, the coronary arteries, already narrowed by atherosclerosis, seem particularly susceptible to further spasm and constriction by the cold. That is why people with angina or other heart symptoms usually feel worse in cold weather. I strongly urge my coronary patients to reduce the intensity of their outdoor physical activity in winter, or to exercise indoors.

To summarize: When you are properly dressed, and assuming that you are healthy, there is really little danger in running in cold weather. Dress in layers, wear gloves or mittens, protect your head and ears with a proper hat, cover all exposed parts with petroleum jelly, and you will probably be safe and even comfortable. Some of my best runs have taken place in temperatures well below freezing. Even sub-zero temperatures are less dangerous than extremely hot and humid weather.

FROSTBITE

Q. People talk about frostbite as a real danger. What is it and how do we treat it?

A. *Prevention* is the key to the problem of frostbite. You can do this by observing the dressing instructions for cold weather we have just discussed. When frostbite first occurs it is often painless; the victim is often totally unaware it has happened. Those who look at him, however, can quickly detect it. The skin is blanched, often nearly white, or mottled with white areas mixed with red patches. The area may be numb to the touch, but later it will become quite painful.

The skin changes color because the response of the body to extreme cold is to maintain the central body temperature at all costs. A major way of doing this is to shut down blood flow to the skin where heat is lost to the cold air. If not enough blood goes to the skin, the skin temperature itself falls significantly. Damage to the skin and even to the underlying tissues may begin. When the skin temperature falls below 60 degrees F., the body makes a last-ditch effort to save it by reopening some of the constricted blood vessels to bring in warm blood to raise the temperature. This causes the patchy redness or mottling of the skin seen during the second stage of cold exposure. Sometimes this response is successful and no serious injury occurs, but often it is inadequate and permanent tissue damage results.

If frostbite is suspected, treatment is simple and straightforward. The subject must be moved to a warmer environment and moderate heat must be applied to the involved areas. Two precautions must be taken: First, make sure that the frostbitten area, once rewarmed, is not exposed again to the cold lest even more severe damage to the skin and underlying tissues occur. Second, do not expose the frostbitten area to excessively high temperatures, certainly no higher than 110 degrees F., and preferably no higher than 100–105 degrees. Also remember that the warming process may be very painful and pain-killing medication may be helpful if it is available.

The warmed skin will become red as blood rushes into it. Fluid will leak from the damaged tissues and blisters will form. If the subject is lucky, the skin will eventually heal. If he is not so fortunate, permanent skin damage will occur and scar tissue may form. If the underlying tissues and bones are frozen, gangrene may occur.

Years ago I contracted a mild case of frostbite of the forehead when I was foolish enough to try skiing when the wind-chill factor was nearly minus 100 at the top of the mountain. I receive a reminder of this every time the temperature falls below freezing. The skin of my forehead aches, feels numb, and blanches white. The blood vessels are permanently damaged and probably will never respond normally to the cold.

Guard against frostbite on windy days particularly. The combination of moderate cold plus a brisk wind is deceptive but dangerous, often more dangerous than severe cold alone.

Running in Hot Weather

Q. Why is it so dangerous to run in hot weather?

A. It's dangerous because runners are often foolish. In their eagerness to get in their daily runs, come hell or high water, they take unnecessary risks. I have seen world class runners, even in relatively short races, nearly die because they have not handled the heat problem sensibly.

Q. We don't want to stop running in the summer. Is there a way to do it safely?

A.   The most important advice I can give you is to avoid strenuous running during the peak heat and humidity of the day. If it's hot, run in the early morning or in the evening when it is cooler. If you must run in hot weather, acclimate yourself gradually. Start slowly, initially decreasing your speed and distance. Then training in hot weather can be relatively safe.

Even if you are acclimated to warm-weather running, I would strongly advise against racing in hot weather. When you can't maintain a comfortable pace, and instead push yourself during a race, dehydration and soaring body temperatures may cause serious problems. In most parts of this country, races should not be scheduled in summer between 10 A.M. and 4 P.M. Unfortunately some race directors have yet to learn this lesson.

The real danger from hot-weather running is that the body is unable to dissipate the heat generated by the exercising muscles. Earlier I mentioned that heat loss can occur through several different mechanisms. But as the environmental temperature approaches that of the body, 98.6 degrees F., heat loss by radiation, convection, and conduction is nullified. Significant heat loss occurs only through cooling of the skin by the evaporation of sweat. If you add high humidity to high temperature, the evaporation of sweat is also seriously impaired. Running on very hot, humid days poses a real danger. If the body temperature soars too high, heat stroke can occur.

To acclimate to running in hot weather you must slowly increase the duration and intensity of your running. Such a slow increase allows your circulation to function more efficiently. Blood flow to the skin will increase and the capacity of the sweat glands to make sweat will be greatly enhanced.

Q.   Why is sweating so important?

A.   It is the only way the body can dissipate the heat generated during running in hot weather.

Sweat is basically water with small amounts of salt or sodium chloride and tiny amounts of other minerals. It is formed by the specialized sweat glands in the skin which extract this water from the blood. As sweat is formed, the water lost in the sweat must be replaced to maintain an adequate volume of blood and to prevent the tissues from becoming dry or dehydrated. During a long workout in hot weather, even a well-conditioned runner may lose 10 percent or more of his body weight as sweat if he doesn't replace it with fluids.

When fluid replacement is inadequate, the blood volume falls and the sweating mechanism is seriously impaired because blood flow to the skin is reduced. Some of this deficit is repaired by a transfer of fluid from the tissues to the blood, but this too may have dire consequences, since water-depleted tissues do not function normally. Muscles won't work as well and, equally important, the brain may not function normally. Mental acuity is clouded and the victim may not realize what is happening to him. At this stage he may become quite combative if someone comes to help him. *Crucial to preventing this condition is an adequate supply of fluid before, during, and after the exercise.* The only fluid necessary is water.

Q. How do you make sure you have enough fluid?

A. I have never had too much trouble with hot weather because I observe a few simple principles.

First, do not wait until you are thirsty before you start drinking. Just before I begin my hot-weather run I drink at least two cups of *cold* water (about 8 ounces). I emphasize that the water should be *cold.* Contrary to popular belief, the body handles cold water more easily than warm. Cold water is absorbed faster from the intestine and is thus available sooner to the blood and tissues. It is also less likely to cause a stomach ache, provided you don't drink too much. Cold water also will obviously have a greater cooling effect.

Runners have been reluctant to drink much water before they run because they are afraid they will have to stop to urinate. But once running begins, blood flow to the kidneys is markedly reduced and urine formation practically ceases. The water you drink just before starting goes directly from the intestinal tract to the bloodstream to maintain adequate blood and tissue volume. It is not lost in the urine.

Second, drink a cup or two of water every 2 or 3 miles at least, and keep drinking right through to the end of your run. Of course you should cut back this intake if your stomach feels full.

Third, if you don't feel quite right, *stop!* Don't be a hero in hot, humid weather. Walk home, making certain you drink plenty of water en route.

Fourth, don't expect your best performance in this type of weather. Be satisfied with a lower intensity of exercise.

Fifth, use water liberally to cool your head and skin. Pour it over your head and body whenever you have the chance. But don't get your shoes wet.

Q. You have emphasized water as the only necessary fluid. Why don't you use the prepared athletic drinks which also contain minerals and sugar? Don't you need to replenish the sugar you burn during your run as well as the minerals you lose in your sweat?

A. Very low concentrations of sugar, less than 2 or 3 percent, are thought to be helpful, but even this is uncertain. In most of the commercially available preparations, the sugar concentration is much higher. A high sugar concentration can cause abdominal cramps and may actually slow down the absorption of the fluid from the intestine into the blood. These preparations may be fine for the football player at halftime or the baseball player who rests between innings, but they are not helpful, indeed may be harmful, for the athlete who exercises continually. If you use these preparations at all, dilute them with at least equal parts of water.

Even these dilute solutions don't sit well in my stomach, and since there is no convincing evidence that they really help, I never drink them during a run. The small amount of glucose that is absorbed is not going to make much of a dent in my energy needs, although it may help a world class athlete to reduce his time by a few seconds. Also, these preparations are expensive. If you are certain they help you, you can make your own by diluting your favorite sugar-containing soft drink, or adding small amounts of sugar or honey to tea and then chilling it.

Q. Would it not be helpful at least to replace the minerals lost in the sweat?

A. Of course it's important, but the time to do this is after you exercise so that your body's mineral content is normal before you run the next time. The well-conditioned, acclimated runner develops enormously effective methods for retaining salt. He has plenty in his body to meet any of his needs during exercise. I would strongly advise you never to take any salt pills _during_ your exercise period

135

or shortly before. The salt is too concentrated and may have the same adverse effects as the concentrated sugar solutions. There will be plenty of time to replenish your salt by normal eating after you run. In extremely warm weather, you might want to salt your food a little more liberally, but even this is rarely needed.

Other minerals are also lost from the body during a run, particularly potassium. Fortunately this important mineral is contained in most foods, particularly fruits and vegetables. Orange juice and bananas are particularly rich sources. A reasonable diet will furnish all the potassium you need, and leave plenty in reserve. There is no need to take added potassium during a run.

WHAT TO WEAR IN HOT WEATHER

Q. What kind of clothing is best during hot-weather running?

A. As little as possible. Some men prefer no top at all, but the direct exposure of the skin to the hot sun does interfere with the heat loss mechanisms. It is probably preferable to wear a mesh or cotton top that is light in both weight and color. It will absorb sweat and help transmit heat from the skin to the air, reflect rather than absorb the sun's rays as a dark top would do, and also hold on better to the cooling water you pour over yourself from time to time. Your shorts also should be as lightweight as possible.

A lightweight hat with a visor, preferably made of a mesh or porous material will also help. It will absorb sweat from your forehead and keep it out of your eyes, protect your skull, and shield your eyes from the sun. When you pour water over your head, the hat will also help to retain it a bit more efficiently.

A small hand towel and plastic drinking straw complete my hot-weather outfit. I use the towel to wipe the sweat away and keep my glasses dry and clean. The straw helps me sip water from cups without having to stop. This is most helpful during races.

HEAT STROKE

Q. You mentioned heat stroke earlier. Could you describe what happens and how to treat it?

A.   Heat stroke can occur if the central or core body temperature goes above 105 or 106 degrees. Dehydration (that is, fluid loss) is almost always a major cause. The fluid content of all the body's tissues, as well as the blood, is reduced. Muscle and other tissues, now starved for water, stop functioning normally. There is also excessive dilation or widening of all the blood vessels, which may cause a major drop in blood pressure. The flow of blood to the brain is often reduced; dizziness or even fainting may follow.

The dehydration, responsible for the high core temperature in the first place, prevents adequate loss of heat via the sweating mechanism. The temperature soars even higher, and this vicious cycle tends to perpetuate itself. If the cycle is not quickly broken, heat stroke and death may follow. Prevention is the key, but once heat stroke happens, the important remedies are a rapid reduction in body temperature and replacement of the water deficit.

Victims of heat stroke are easy to recognize. They may complain of severe weakness and fatigue. They may feel nauseated. The skin is invariably very warm and dry, and the pulse is quite rapid and faint. The victim's mental status is almost always altered. Some may be disoriented and talk incoherently. Some become angry and combative when you try to help them. If heat stroke is severe, the victim may become unconscious and unrousable.

This is a major medical emergency. Don't wait. First place the patient lying down in the shade. Sometimes raising the legs will help to increase the return of blood to the heart, which can then pump more blood to the brain. Cold water should be splashed liberally all over the patient. Rubbing him down with ice is also very effective. If a tub is available, the patient should be placed in it in a bath of ice water.

Most heat stroke victims will respond to this program and will soon be able to drink enough water to improve their dehydration. Some, however, will require replacement of fluid by vein. This can be accomplished only by trained personnel. Most well-managed races run in hot weather will have this capacity in at least some of their aide stations. If not, the victim must be rushed to a hospital.

It's also important not to lower the body temperature too much. Rectal temperatures should be regularly checked. Mouth temperatures are grossly inaccurate in this situation. Once the temperature has fallen several degrees, and the subject is alert and able to drink, remove him from the ice-water tub and stop the other methods of cooling. But continue to watch carefully. Some patients may relapse and require more cooling. At first water alone is the preferred fluid. Later fruit juices, beer, or other mineral-containing fluids are added.

Heat-stroke victims should go easy for the next few weeks, since they seem particularly prone to develop the condition again. It is almost as if the body's regulatory mechanisms have been upset by the event and take a while to regain their equilibrium.

Finally, don't confuse early heat stroke with the much more common phenomenon of "heat exhaustion." This is much less serious. The early symptoms are the same—weakness and often severe fatigue—but the heat regulatory mechanisms are still intact. Heat exhaustion is probably caused by moderate dehydration and salt depletion. it is the result of inadequate heat acclimation, excessive intensity or duration of activity, or more likely a combination of the two. The immediate cure is to stop running and take fluids. Heat exhaustion can be prevented by lowering the intensity and duration of your workouts for a while.

CHAPTER 7

How to Take Care of Yourself

Q. EVERYONE WE KNOW who runs seems to suffer from one injury after another. Why can't injuries be prevented?

A. I suspect the injury frequency is greatly exaggerated. The runner who is hurt makes a lot of noise, and often delights in telling about an injury to anyone who is willing to listen. The healthy runner keeps quiet and runs.

But the injury frequency is still fairly high, perhaps because many runners are constantly pushing themselves to run longer distances or faster times. It has been repeatedly stated that anyone who runs long enough will eventually get hurt. However, if you keep the demands on your musculo-skeletal system reasonable, and are not overly competitive, you should be able to avoid serious injury. The key here is prevention. I cannot emphasize too strongly the importance of the four major ways you can prevent serious injury:

1. Make sure your running shoes fit properly and are well-cushioned.
2. Perform your stretching and strengthening exercises regularly.
3. Increase your distance and pace slowly.
4. Treat minor injuries early, before they become major ones.

Nonetheless, even if you follow these recommendations carefully, some of you will still be troubled by one or more injuries. To deal with them intelligently, you should be aware of the injuries common to runners, their early symptoms and signs, and what should be done about them.

Ideally each one of us would have very supple joints, no curvature of the spine, equal leg lengths, and feet whose arches were neither too high and stiff, nor too low and flat. Our shoes would fit perfectly, with good support in the heel and arch, proper cushioning, and enough room for the toes, although not too much lest we develop blisters.

The older runner particularly may be injury prone because he already possesses one or more of a variety of degenerative musculo-skeletal problems, better termed perhaps "diseases of aging." Particularly common are degenerative or osteoarthritis of the hip, knee, and ankle joints, chondromalaccia of the knee (see p. 158), and a variety of spinal abnormalities. These may cause little trouble when activity is limited, but the likelihood of injury dramatically rises as the intensity and duration of running are increased.

A regular stretching–strengthening program and good care of your shoes help, but if basic musculo-skeletal problems are left uncorrected, injuries will occur. In this section I would like to discuss the cause and treatment of some of the more important ones.

Treating Acute Injuries

Every runner probably will either sustain acute injuries or witness them in other runners or friends. Therefore, you should understand a few basic principles about their treatment. *Prompt and proper treatment can significantly reduce the initial swelling, pain, and tissue damage, which in turn will decrease the period of disability.*

Whether the injury is just a mild muscle pull or sprain, or a serious fracture, the steps are the same.

1. *The injured part should be rested and elevated. Weight bearing should be avoided. Obvious fractures should be immobilized.*

2. Ice should be applied immediately to the injured part.
3. A compression bandage should be applied.

The value of rest, elevation, and compression have long been known. Only recently has the often remarkable benefit of aggressive *icing* of the acute injury been fully appreciated. Ice is also useful for the regular care of many chronic injuries.

Muscle Injuries

Muscle soreness and stiffness will occur in virtually every beginning runner. This condition is really not an injury, but the expected result of early training. The stress of running does cause microscopic tears of muscle fibers, which the runner senses as pain and stiffness. These symptoms are usually worse in the morning on arising, and subside with moving around. They generally disappear completely during the daily run, only to reappear the next morning.

Q. Are sore muscles a danger signal?

A. With one important exception, pain and stiffness which behave this way are not serious. If you are really bothered by them, skip a day or cut back on your running speed and duration.
   The one exception is the pain caused by injury and inflammation of tendons. Characteristically, symptoms of potentially serious tendon injuries subside with activity, reappearing when you rest. Injuries to the Achilles tendon must be particularly looked for (pp. 153–55).
   Respect pain which gets worse as you run. It may signify an injury which requires treatment.
   A *pulled muscle* presents a much more serious problem. It is caused by a major tearing or rupture of muscle fibers. Pulls usually occur abruptly during sudden, intense activity. They are far more common in sprinters than in distance runners, and are likely to occur when there has been insufficient warm-up. A good stretching–strengthening program helps prevent them. Ice and rest for the acute injury will shorten the recovery time.
   Trauma can also damage muscle fibers, producing pain, swell-

141

ing, and sometimes a large collection of blood, the so-called "black and blue" area or hematoma. The treatment is the same as for acute muscle pulls.

Q.   Is a "Charley horse" a type of muscle pull?

A.   The term "Charley horse" means a number of different things to different people. Most of the time the term does refer to a muscle injury of the type described, but it is also loosely used to include injuries to the tendons, the ends of the muscles that attach to bones. Some people also refer to muscle cramps as "Charley horses," even though cramps are really quite different.

Q.   How does a sprain differ from a muscle tear or pull?

A.   We generally use the term "sprain" to refer to partial or even complete tearing of the ligaments. Ligaments are special structures, not part of the muscles, which hold the ends of the bones together at each joint.

Pain directly in the joint itself may be due to a ligamentous sprain. If it occurs suddenly, treat it as you would any acute injury. If it persists, see your doctor. Joint injuries can be serious.

Ankle sprains are particularly common in runners. They are usually the result of running on uneven surfaces, or of poor arch support or flat feet. We will discuss ankle sprains in greater detail on page 155.

Q.   How about muscle cramps? Are they dangerous?

A.   Muscle cramps may disable some runners, while others seem virtually immune to them. Cramps result from strong contractions of muscles which are then unable to relax. In runners, cramps usually involve the leg or abdominal muscles, and often appear after the run is finished, or during brief rest periods in the middle of vigorous workouts. Sometimes they appear toward the end of long, intense runs. Occasionally they appear suddenly at night, waking you from sleep. Rarely are they serious, but the pain can be excruciating. Most marathoners have experienced them at some point in their running careers.

The immediate treatment, of course, is to slowly stretch the cramped muscle. Recently a report in _The New England Journal of Medicine_ described the prevention of calf cramps, probably the most common type of cramps in runners, by regular performance of wall pushups (see page 101).

Muscle cramps are more common in hot weather, perhaps because the proper balance of certain minerals—particularly sodium, potassium, and magnesium—is disturbed by losses in the sweat. The best way to prevent them is to eat a lot of fruits, vegetables, and grains, foods with high content of potassium and magnesium. Reduction of salt may also help.

Q.   We have always been taught that salt is good for cramps. Won't the low salt diet you recommend make cramps worse?

A.   Surprisingly not. Why cramps are prevented by a low salt diet, when lack of salt may sometimes cause them, is still uncertain. Perhaps a low salt diet actually improves our ability to conserve or hold onto salt. The urine of a well-trained distance runner on a low salt diet contains only a tiny amount of salt. His sweat also has a much reduced salt content. His body seems more sensitive to changes in salt and other mineral levels, and is better able to compensate for those changes. This, of course, is precisely what happens when you acclimate to running in warm weather (Chapter 6).

Leg cramps that occur during exercise, and then promptly subside when the exercise is stopped, are an entirely different problem. They are not due to the inability of the contracted muscle to relax, but rather may be a warning that the flow of blood to the cramped muscles is inadequate. In older people, atherosclerotic narrowing of the leg arteries is often the cause. The calf muscles are most frequently involved. In younger runners, cramps and even severe pain may occur in the front of the lower leg, the shin, where a combination of extremely well developed, enlarged muscles, tightly encased by tough fibrous tissue called _fascia_, plus increased tissue pressure interfere with blood flow to the muscle. This is usually a chronic problem, appearing every time vigorous running is performed, and subsiding with rest. I understand that this was the problem that recently plagued John Walker, the 1976 Olympic 1500 meter champion. Surgery to relieve the excessive tissue pressure was required to remedy the condition. Occasionally the pain occurs acutely and does not subside with rest. Then emergency surgery may be required to reduce tissue pressure and prevent permanent muscle damage.

Q.   What causes side stitches?

A.   A special kind of muscle cramp usually causes the common "stitch in the side" which may appear in the lower part of the rib cage during a vigorous workout. Most stitches result from improper breathing techniques (see Chapter 5), and are caused by powerful contractions of the diaphragm, the muscle which separates the chest from the abdomen. If a stitch occurs while you are running, it is best treated by slowing your pace and concentrating on proper diaphragmatic breathing.

A less common cause of a stitch is the distension of one of the various abdominal structures which press on the diaphragm, particularly the large intestine or colon as it bends acutely in the upper, right part of the abdomen. Food allergies, especially to milk or wheat products, may also cause side stitches, but more commonly these symptoms appear lower down in the abdomen.

Overuse Injuries—The Crucial Role of the Foot

Only relatively recently have we come to realize that abnormalities of the foot can cause many of the common, often serious overuse injuries. Even though your pain may be in your ankles, knees, or hips, your foot is often to blame.

The foot is a complicated structure with twenty-six bones and scores of ligaments and muscles. It was not designed to pound hard pavement for long periods of time. Even seemingly trivial abnormalities of foot structure and function may become important as your training program becomes more intense.

NORMAL FOOT PLANT

Q. Why is the foot so important?

A. To comprehend properly the role of the foot in the production of injuries, we must understand the *normal foot plant.*

When we run, the first part of the foot to strike the ground, the one which absorbs the full impact, is the outside of the heel (Figure 20A). If you doubt this, look at the soles of your running shoes. Invariably the area of greatest wear is the outside of the heel where the impact of foot strike is greatest.

As we move forward, weight is transferred to the outside of the ball of the foot, an area which is composed chiefly of the tips or "heads" of the metatarsal bones (Figure 20B). Weight then is rapidly transferred to the inner part of the ball of the foot, and the foot *pronates* or flattens. The forces of impact are then more evenly distributed to the longest and strongest parts of the ball of the foot, the heads of the first two or three metatarsal bones. At this point, with the weight shifted forward and properly distributed on the ball of the foot, normal forward thrust or takeoff can begin (Figure 20C).

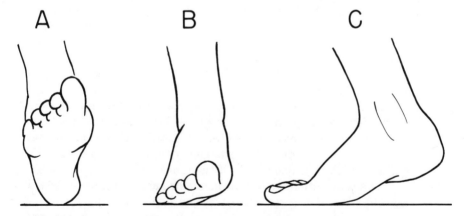

FIGURE 20. *The normal foot plant.* (A) *The outer heel touches the ground first and absorbs the full impact of initial heel strike.* **(B)** *As we move forward, the weight is transferred to the outside part of the ball of the foot.* **(C)** *Weight is then quickly transferred more equitably to the inner part of the foot as the arch flattens (pronation). The foot is now ready for normal thrust or takeoff.*

INADEQUATE FLATTENING OR PRONATION —THE HIGH-ARCHED FOOT

If the arch of the foot is too high or inflexible, normal flattening or pronation of the foot is interfered with, and the force of impact is unevenly distributed. Increased stress is put on the arch, the outer part of the foot, the knee, and the hip. A variety of injuries may result, among them local foot pain, stress fractures of the metatarsal bones, and pain in the outer knee and hip.

Treatment for this problem is designed to reduce the impact of foot strike. A well-cushioned shoe is absolutely essential. An arch support or a soft, but not rigid, orthotic (p. 149) may remedy the problem. Running on softer surfaces at reduced speed may be necessary until the injury heals.

STRESS FRACTURES

Q. Are stress fractures real fractures?

A. They are cracks in the surface of a bone, not complete fractures. In runners they most commonly occur in the third and fourth metatarsal bones, less commonly in the second, when a high, stiff arch is present. Such an arch prevents adequate pronation, which in turn causes uneven distribution of the forces of foot impact. The third and fourth metatarsals bear an excessive load and are more likely to sustain stress fractures during periods of intense training (Figure 21).

Stress fractures are usually very painful, with marked local tenderness at the point of the fracture. They may not be seen on the initial x-rays because the crack is so thin. X-rays taken a few weeks later may show only a shadow at the fracture site, called a callus, which signifies repair of the crack in the bone surface.

The only satisfactory treatment for such fractures is rest. It may be several weeks before you can begin running again. An extra cushion in your walking shoes may help. Sometimes crutches or a cane may be necessary to reduce weight bearing. Casts or other methods of immobilization are not necessary, since only the surface of the bone is injured, and there is no bone displacement.

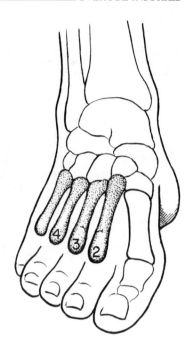

FIGURE 21. *The most common places for stress fractures—the third and fourth metatarsals.* *Such fractures are more likely to occur when the arch is high and stiff.*

EXCESSIVE FLATTENING AND INWARD ROTATION (PRONATION) OF THE FOOT

This problem, caused by a number of different biomechanical abnormalities of the foot, seems to be the most important cause of many running overuse injuries.

Q. What causes this excessive flattening?

A. If the arch is too flat or poorly supported, if the support structure of the inner ball of the foot is abnormal, or if the ankle is too weak, the foot flattens excessively, the ankle rolls inward, and a torque or force is exerted upon the whole leg which turns it inward (Figure 22). Abnormal motion of the ankle, knee, and hip joints results, and injury is likely to follow soon thereafter.

The key to treatment is to find the particular cause of the excessive pronation. But first some general treatment guidelines can be offered.

147

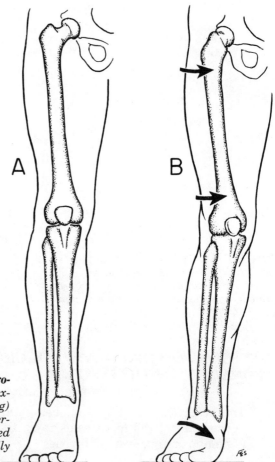

FIGURE 22. *Excessive pronation of the foot. If excessive pronation (flattening) occurs, excessive counterclockwise rotation is placed on the knee and occasionally the hip.*

Arch Supports and Orthotics Most good athletic shoes have built-in arch supports whose major function is to reduce excessive pronation. Often these supports are not enough. Extra support can be supplied by shoe inserts. If you suffer from one of the injuries caused by excessive pronation, you might first try one of supports that are widely available in running, specialized shoe, or even drug stores. These often work and have the real advantage of being relatively inexpensive. If the injury persists, you should next get help from a sports podiatrist.

Q.   How can a podiatrist help?

A.   If your symptoms are in fact caused by excessive pronation, the podiatrist may custom-make a support from a cast of your foot. These arch supports, called _orthotics_, offer heel lift and support as well (Figure 23). My nagging right hip pain, which 5 years ago made running more than 5 miles nearly impossible, disappeared the first time I wore my orthotic. Not only did it prevent my excessive pronation, but it corrected the ½-inch discrepancy in my leg lengths. Frequently I wear my orthotic all day if I plan to do a lot of walking. It has helped my chronic low back pain as well.

Orthotics can be "soft" (flexible) or "hard" (rigid). The hard ones, made of stiff plastic material, will last longer, but most runners find them relatively uncomfortable, and prefer the softer ones. My soft orthotics are five years old and still going strong. I expect at least a couple of more years from them.

Orthotics obviously take up space in your shoes. If you use them, you may have to change to a wider, longer shoe.

The price charged for custom-made orthotics varies widely. But it can be very high, sometimes more than $100. Some podiatrists justify these prices because so much professional skill and time are required to fit and make them. You might want to ask

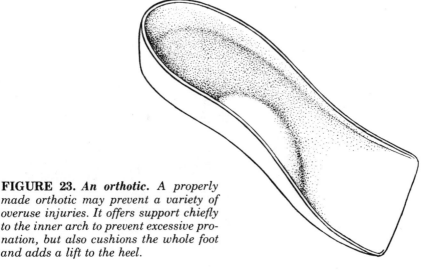

FIGURE 23. _An orthotic. A properly made orthotic may prevent a variety of overuse injuries. It offers support chiefly to the inner arch to prevent excessive pronation, but also cushions the whole foot and adds a lift to the heel._

149

about the cost before consulting a particular podiatrist. If the price seems steep, you may find as good an orthotic elsewhere for less money.

Shoe Care   If you have excessive pronation, the outer heels of your shoes may show excessive wear. It's vitally important that you examine your shoes regularly and prevent excessive heel wear. Use the special glues or shoe cement at the first sign of wear. Don't wait until your heels are visibly worn. I learned early that the best way to prolong shoe life, as well as prevent injury, was to build up the outer heel with cement after having run in them just a few times, before any real wear can be detected.

Morton's Syndrome   Flat arches and weak ankles that roll inward are obvious causes of excessive pronation. Less obvious, but perhaps the most common cause is referred to, somewhat erroneously, as "Morton's toe," or more accurately as "Morton's syndrome."

Look down at your feet. If your second toe is longer than your first (Figure 24) you have Morton's toe. Initially it was thought

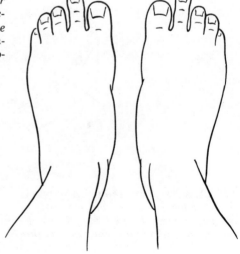

FIGURE 24. *Morton's toe.* *If your first toe is shorter than the second, you may be prone to excessive pronation of the foot and the injuries associated with it. An orthotic may help.*

that in Morton's toe excessive pronation was caused by the short first metatarsal bone, which was not long enough to provide adequate support for the foot as weight was transferred inward during normal foot plant. Now podiatrists point out that the shortened first metatarsal is only the most obvious of several abnormalities of the important support structures on the inner side of the foot which are ordinarily responsible for normal pronation. Of course, not everyone with Morton's syndrome has excessive pronation, but whenever I hear a friend or patient describe one of the injuries commonly associated with excessive pronation, I look at their toes.

Q. What are the injuries associated with excessive pronation?

A. I'll describe them in greater detail soon, but I can list them here. Perhaps the most common injury is to the knee, called by some "runner's knee." Other injuries include inflammation of the Achilles tendon at the back of the heel and inflammation of the supporting structure of the bottom of the foot, the plantar fascia. The excessive pronation associated with Morton's toe also causes a variety of less common ankle and hip injuries.

  Plantar Fasciitis The *plantar fascia* is the sheet of strong fibrous tissue which supports the bottom of the foot (Figure 25). It can be torn or injured by a number of causes, including excessive foot pronation. If the foot flattens too much with impact, the plantar fascia will be stretched too far and will eventually become inflamed. Pain can occur anywhere along the bottom of the foot, most commonly along the inner part of the heel.

  Other causes of plantar fasciitis are a sudden wrenching or turning of the foot and excessively stiff soles in the running shoes. Treatment is aimed primarily at providing better support of the foot and arch. Sometimes just a heel lift cures the symptoms. More often either an arch support, a soft orthotic, or taping the arch is required. Icing the painful part of the foot after running may reduce inflammation. Some authorities also believe that plantar fasciitis may be one of the few conditions in which an injection of cortisone or similar anti-inflammatory agent may produce long-term benefits.

151

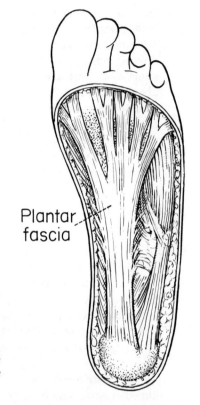

Plantar
fascia

FIGURE 25. *The plantar fascia.*
This is a view of the bottom of the foot.
The plantar fascia is a strong, fibrous
sheet which supports the bottom of the
foot.

Heel Spurs and Bruises   Plantar fasciitis must be distin-
guished from *heel spurs*, which also may cause local heel pain.
The spur is really a small outgrowth from the heel bone itself,
usually in the area where the plantar fascia attaches. Heel spurs
are common. Often they cause no symptoms and are noted as an
incidental finding in foot x-rays. Indeed, some orthopedic surgeons feel that heel spurs alone rarely if ever cause pain, and that
plantar fasciitis in the area of the heel spur is the real cause.
Nonetheless, the severe local heel pain is often dramatically relieved by inserting a doughnut-type heel cushion (Figure 26),
which reduces pressure on the painful area. Here, too, cortisone
injections may occasionally be indicated. I am surprised that heel
bruises are not more common, considering the punishment the
heel takes. Well-cushioned running shoes have almost certainly

FIGURE 26. *A   doughnut   can   be used to cushion the pain from a heel spur.*

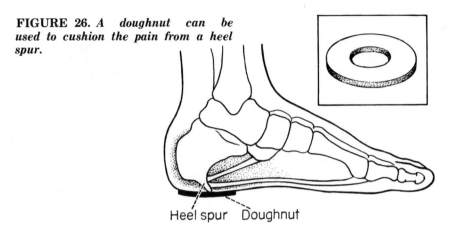

Heel spur   Doughnut

helped. If you do sustain a bruised heel, cut back your mileage for a while and wear an extra cushion in your heel.

    Achilles Tendonitis   Tendons are the extensions or ends of muscles which attach muscles to bone. Unlike muscle, tendons are composed chiefly of tough, fibrous tissue which cannot change its length very much. Thus, when muscles are regularly exercised and undergo strengthening and shortening, the tendons may be stretched and injured. Tendons throughout the body are subject to great stress. In distance runners, perhaps the most frequently injured is the *Achilles tendon* at the back of the calf, which attaches the calf muscles to the heel (Figure 27).

    Running shortens the calf muscles, and the Achilles tendon is secondarily stretched. If the muscle shortening is great enough, the Achilles tendon is overstretched, and becomes inflamed and painful. Rarely, when the calf muscles are very short, and a sudden great stress is applied to the tendon, actual Achilles tendon rupture can occur.

    Tendon injuries are unique in at least one respect: symptoms often improve with activity, returning afterwards. The runner with an Achilles tendon injury may be encouraged to keep running in hopes of "working out" the injury. This may eventually prove disastrous because Achilles tendonitis is often very slow to heal once it becomes severe.

    The diagnosis of Achilles tendonitis is easy. There is in-

153

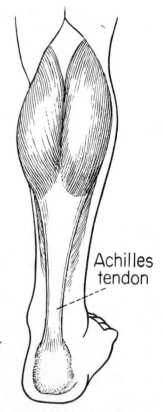

FIGURE 27. *A normal Achilles tendon.*
During a regular exercise program, the calf
muscles are shortened, in turn stretching the
Achilles tendon. This tendon is the largest
in the body and is very vulnerable to
inflammation and even rupture.

variably local tenderness in the tendon itself or at its bony at-
tachment. Look for this if you have suggestive signs and
symptoms. Begin treatment immediately. The following measures are strongly advised:

1. Decrease the intensity and duration of your running until
   symptoms subside. If the pain is severe, stop running for a
   while.
2. Avoid hills. Running uphill markedly increases the stress and
   strain on the Achilles tendon.
3. Ice the painful area immediately after running. This will reduce inflammation.
4. Use a heel lift and stretch the calf muscles. Some people are
   born with short tendons or tight muscles. Women who regu-

larly wear high heels will develop short calf muscles. They must stretch extra vigorously and advance their running program very slowly.

5. Try an orthotic. Excessive pronation may cause Achilles tendonitis. An orthotic will help remedy this as well as provide a welcome heel lift.

6. Take good care of your shoes. All good running shoes are built with an elevated heel. Have you let yours run down? In my experience this is often a problem for susceptible runners. Cure it by fixing your heels or buying new shoes.

If none of the above measures work, you should see a doctor. Anti-inflammatory drugs or even surgery may be necessary if you still want to run. Cortisone or other steroid injections directly into the inflamed area should be avoided. There is increasing evidence that this may weaken the tendon, making it more likely to rupture during strenuous running.

Ankle Injuries   Most ankle problems in runners are acute and not due to chronic overuse. Sprains are by far the most common injury. Usually they result from running on uneven surfaces. In the North, stepping into the potholes which appear in the roads every winter is a particularly common cause. Like many injuries, sprains seem more likely to occur toward the end of the run when you are tired and perhaps a bit careless. Treatment for acute sprains has already been discussed (page 140–41).

Q.   Do sore ankles indicate a serious problem?

A.   Chronic ankle soreness is common in beginning runners. Their ligaments and muscles are weak, but they will strengthen as the running program progresses. Runners are also likely to have chronic ankle pain if they pronate excessively. A good example of this is the frequent occurrence of _right ankle_ soreness in runners who regularly run facing traffic. An easy solution is to run on flatter surfaces or to vary your program and run carefully with the traffic.

Ankle pain may also be caused by shoes that do not offer good heel stability and support. Sometimes a heel cup solves the problem. The major weakness of the brand of shoes I wear is relatively poor heel support. Virtually the only problem I ever have with my left leg is slight aching of the ankle when I run long distances, particularly if I have let the heels of my running shoes wear down a little.

Stress fractures of the outer bone of the ankle (the fibula) have been reported, but are fortunately rare. These fractures are far more common in activities in which foot impact is greater, for example landing hard coming off a mogul when you are downhill skiing.

Shin Splints   This term is used to describe virtually every ache or pain that occurs in the front part of the calf (Figure 28A).

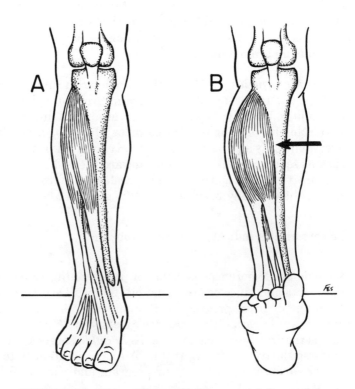

FIGURE 28. *Shin splints.* **(A)** *The normal front of the lower leg where shin splints occur.* **(B)** *Production of pain from shin splints when the ankle is flexed.*

Orthopedic surgeons not surprisingly wince when they hear it, because they know the term is being used to describe a variety of symptoms resulting from an even wider variety of vastly different causes, including muscle injury, cracks in the shin bone itself, nerve entrapment, or interference with the blood flow to the shin muscles because of increased tissue pressure.

Q. What causes these symptoms?

A. The muscles of the front of the calf are contained in a fairly tight compartment. As they enlarge during a training program, the compartment may become too tight and pressure may be exerted on the nerves and blood vessels which supply these muscles, causing a number of distressing symptoms. These should not be referred to as "shin splints." Rather, we should limit the term to the fairly common, and usually not too serious, soreness and tenderness in the front of the shin bone where the muscles attach to the bone. The symptoms and signs are due to small tears and inflammation of the muscle fibers, although the bone itself seems tender. There is local soreness, and pain is often produced when the ankle is flexed by moving the foot upward (Figure 28B).

Shin splints may occur because a vigorous running program has strengthened and shortened the calf muscles more than those of the shin, pulling the foot into a relatively extended position. In such a case, the calf muscles must work harder to pull the foot upward. Treatment is easy and effective: stretch the calf muscles (page 100) and strengthen the shin muscles (page 105).

Shin splints may also be caused by running too long or fast on hard surfaces, running uphill, running on your toes, or wearing poorly fitting shoes. The cure for these is obvious. Icing will help reduce the pain. But if you have tried all the remedies above, and are still having symptoms, see an orthopedic surgeon.

Runner's Knee "Runner's knee" is a general term for a variety of different knee injuries related to overuse. Many, although certainly not all, are caused by excessive pronation.

The knee has a relatively simple task. Unlike the ankle, which moves in many directions, the knee is designed to move only back and forth. Any structural or functional abnormality which interferes with this motion may cause knee injuries.

It's not difficult to see how excessive pronation, which causes inward rotation of the leg with every foot plant, changes this normal motion (Figure 29). The kneecap or patella, is pulled to one side, and its normal smooth gliding movement over the bones of the lower leg is hampered. The inner surface of the patella is roughened, and pain behind the kneecap is produced. Some writers call this condition *chondromalaccia*.

Q. Is there a cure for this condition?

A. The treatment is straightforward: prevent the excessive pronation with an orthotic. Sometimes hill running, particularly downhill increases the pain, or the knees will hurt if you walk up-

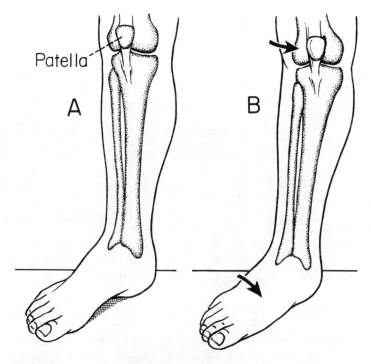

FIGURE 29. *Runner's knee, caused by excessive pronation.* *With excessive pronation, each time the foot strikes the knee is rotated inward (counter-clockwise), interfering with normal knee joint motion. Normal movement of the patella (kneecap) may also be hindered.*

stairs or try to rise from a squatting position. Obviously these pain-producing activities should be stopped.

I develop a slight right knee pain if I run long distances on roads facing traffic. The experts say this is common, because the inside leg, the right in this case, strikes the gently banked road higher than the outer one, and then is required to pronate excessively. If this happens to you, run on flat surfaces, or with your back to the traffic if you dare.

Q. Are there other types of knee injuries?

A. Normal knee joint movement and stability are also partly controlled by the hamstring and quadriceps tendons which insert into the bones of the lower leg below the joint space itself. We have repeatedly mentioned the muscle imbalance that running produces. The knee, of course, is no exception. As the hamstrings in the back of the leg become relatively stronger and shorter than the quadriceps muscle in the front of the leg, abnormal movement is produced. This results in added stress and strain on the tendons which in turn become inflamed (tendonitis). The best treatment for this condition is to strengthen the quadriceps muscle (p. 106). Some orthopedic surgeons also recommend isometric contraction exercises for the quadriceps. Occasionally a knee brace of the unrestricted type is helpful.

Knee function and stability are also provided by the ligaments which hold the bones of the knee together, and the other structures which cushion the joint. Injuries to these are usually caused by acute trauma, common in football running backs but less frequent in runners. Distance runners can, however, aggravate preexisting abnormalities. If you are so troubled, consult a good orthopedic surgeon.

Every September, football team physicians see an epidemic of "runner's knee," almost certainly due to the widespread, and, I believe, harmful practice of making the players run up stadium steps as part of their conditioning program. One orthopedic surgeon I know has called this practice "idiotic." Unfortunately I now see many runners also doing it, presumably to strengthen their legs and help them run hills. World class runners may get away with such an exercise. The rest of us should forget about it, lest we ruin our knees.

Hip Injuries   These are relatively uncommon in runners. They are due to one of the following causes:

1. Excessive pronation which may produce abnormal rotation of the hip just as it does at the knee.
2. A stiff, high-arched foot which prevents normal pronation.
3. Abnormalities of the low back and spine which may cause one hip to be higher than the other.
4. Structural abnormalities within the hip joint itself.
5. Inequality of leg length.
6. Other injuries which interfere with normal stride and running style.

For years many of my nonrunning physician friends have been predicting, sometimes almost gleefully, that running long distances regularly would damage the hip joint, hastening the onset of degenerative arthritis, by far the most important adult hip problem. To my knowledge there is not a shred of evidence that running will do this if the hip joint is reasonably normal to begin with. In fact, some authorities are beginning to think that running in some way protects the hip from this type of arthritis.

If your chronic hip symptoms are not helped by the usual measures for remedying abnormal pronation, you should see a podiatrist or an orthopedic surgeon. The cure is likely to be easy, but to determine the cause often requires a fairly sophisticated examination.

Low Back Pain   This problem seems to afflict much of the adult population of the Western world. It is especially common in women, the obese, the unfit, and those with structural abnormalities of the spine. Often symptoms begin acutely, for example after heavy lifting, and never completely disappear. Often such pain plagues its victims for decades. Low back pain has become one of the major causes of chronic disability in the working population. Its cost to our society is measured in billions of dollars. Most physicians do not understand it or treat it very well.

Q. Do runners suffer from low back pain?

A. Low back pain is less common in runners, perhaps because they are fit and unlikely to be obese. When it does appear in a runner, it often is due either to a structural abnormality of the low back or legs, or to our old nemesis muscle imbalance.

Running strengthens the low back muscles more than the muscles of the abdomen. The ligaments of the spine are stretched, and abnormal motion of the low back is produced. The initial treatment is straightforward: abdominal muscles must be strengthened by performing bent-knee situps (page 107), and the low back muscles stretched by performing toe touching exercises (page 103) and backovers (page 104).

A visit to an orthopedic surgeon or podiatrist may be necessary to detect any structural abnormalities which might cause low back pain. Sometimes a discrepancy of even ½ inch in leg length, caused either by minimal curvature of the spine, or actual difference in the lengths of the legs themselves, can throw the back out of line enough to cause symptoms. A heel lift is all that is needed.

Sciatica   If the back pain does not stay localized to the back, but shoots down the back of the leg, pressure on the nerves to the leg is often present somewhere. This condition is called sciatica.

Q.   What causes this problem?

A.   The cause is often protrusion of a disc, the cushion between two of the lower spinal vertebrae. Sometimes removal of the disc by surgery is required to relieve the pain.

My orthopedic colleagues tell me that curvature of the spine (called *scoliosis*), or unequal leg lengths, rarely if ever cause sciatica or similar problems. But a personal experience during my first marathon makes me question this. At the twenty-fifth mile, while I was feeling fine, breezing along at a pace faster than I believed I could possibly have run, I was suddenly pulled up short. My right leg had become totally numb, almost as if it no longer belonged to me. I felt no significant pain, but I could hardly move it. Nothing remotely resembling this sensation had ever happened before. I tried some stretching exercises which helped a little, and then hobbled the last two miles at about half my previous pace. Whenever I tried to go faster, the near paralysis would return.

Something obviously had interfered with the nerves that controlled my right leg muscles. But I had experienced no sharp pain, the hallmark of a disc problem. A thorough examination revealed only that my right leg was about ½ inch shorter than my left. It was at that time I was fitted for my orthotic, which corrected this discrepancy. I have never had even a hint of a similar problem.

Black (Runner's) Toe   You can sometimes spot a runner at the beach or in a shower by his blackened toes. Usually it's the large toenail that's involved, but in runners with Morton's toe it may be the second. The injury usually happens during runs longer than you are used to and is caused by jamming the toes into the front of a shoe that may be a bit too short. The continued jarring of the toenail causes rupture of some of the tiny blood vessels in the nail bed underneath the nail. If enough blood accumulates, exquisite pain may occur because the nail cannot expand to accommodate the added fluid. At this point the toenail is dark red, not black. Only later as the blood breaks down does the nail turn black.

Q.   Is there any way to relieve this condition?

A.   The only way to stop the pain is to evacuate the blood trapped under the nail. A number of methods are recommended. I prefer heating the end of a paper clip until it is red hot, and then quickly plunging it through the nail where the blood is collected (Figure 30). This is painful for a moment but dramatically effective. Of course the nail should be cleaned with antiseptic solution before and after you puncture it.

This painful problem can usually be prevented by running in shoes that are long enough for you, and by clipping your toenails fairly short.

Blisters   Blisters are produced when there is too much friction between the skin of the foot and the sock or running shoe. They may be caused by either too tight or too loose a fit. Poorly fitting socks, or those with wrinkles or bumps from mending, are responsible in some cases. To avoid blisters, make sure your shoes and socks fit well. Try not to get your feet wet because this too will cause blisters.

When you treat a blister, resist the tendency to pull off the

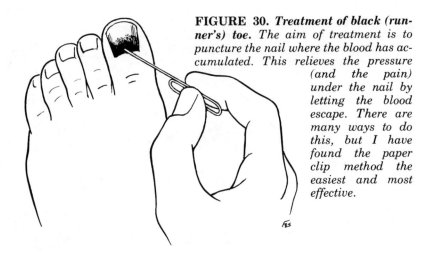

FIGURE 30. *Treatment of black (runner's) toe. The aim of treatment is to puncture the nail where the blood has accumulated. This relieves the pressure (and the pain) under the nail by letting the blood escape. There are many ways to do this, but I have found the paper clip method the easiest and most effective.*

loose outer skin. It should not be removed because the skin underneath is raw and undeveloped, and easily infected. It should not be exposed. If there is little fluid in the blister, you only need to cover it with adhesive tape or a bandaid. If there is considerable fluid, it should be removed. Prepare the skin with an antiseptic solution, then puncture the base of the blister with a sterile needle and withdraw the fluid (Figure 31). Cover the blister with adhesive tape or a bandaid.

Q. If I get a blister, should I reduce my running?

A. Usually a blister will not interfere with your regular running program. You can generally run the next day. If you are particularly blister-prone, you might try to cover the areas where blisters commonly appear with petroleum jelly.

Chafing Chafing is caused by the same general process as blisters: rubbing of harsh surfaces against the skin. It is most common during long runs. Ill-fitting clothing will cause chafing, particularly running shorts with thick seams that rub against your thighs, and bras and jock straps that are too tight. Get rid of the offending garments and use petroleum jelly if you need to.

163

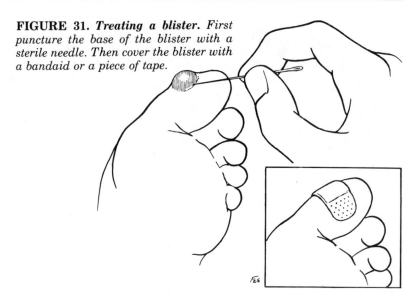

FIGURE 31. *Treating a blister. First puncture the base of the blister with a sterile needle. Then cover the blister with a bandaid or a piece of tape.*

Jogger's Nipples   The first time I developed this annoying problem I was less sophisticated about the medical difficulties runners might encounter. I was really frightened when my nipples became hard and painful, and actually bled. At the time I was training vigorously for my first marathon, running longer and faster than I ever had before. The problem kept recurring, but curiously never appeared when I ran without a shirt. This finally offered a clue to me about its possible cause: friction of a tight top rubbing against the nipples. I was now able to relax, certain that I did not have breast cancer or another serious medical problem. Only later did I find out how common a problem this was, and how easily it could be prevented. A generous coating of petroleum jelly over the nipples usually works. Placing corn plasters over the nipples or merely wearing a looser top may be all that is necessary.

Gastrointestinal Problems   Cramps, gas, heartburn, and diarrhea are only some of the gastrointestinal (GI) problems that plague runners. Some of these problems will be discussed in Chapters 9 and 10, but I would like to make some comments about specific ones.

164

The diets many runners prefer, particularly during their more intensive training periods, are likely to be gassy because they contain large amounts of fruits, vegetables, and other high roughage foods. Some runners foolishly make major changes in their diets just before a race. The GI tract is confronted with new demands. It often reacts belligerently with gas, cramps, and diarrhea.

Running does cause significant changes in stomach and intestinal function. Blood flow to the whole GI tract, normally so copious, falls precipitously during exercise as blood is shunted to the muscles. At the same time, peristalsis, the process by which the bowel churns the food and propels it down the GI tract, is increased. Sometimes its direction is even reversed. Abnormal bowel function and cramps may result. If an underlying problem is present, specific food intolerance for example, it may be fairly well tolerated at rest, yet cause very distressing symptoms during exercise.

Q. Are there any particularly common intolerances that tend to cause trouble?

A. Intolerance to milk and milk products is a fairly common cause of GI problems. It is caused by an inadequate level of an enzyme in the intestine called lactase, which helps digest milk sugar. The only known treatment is to avoid all milk products. The problem is said to be more common among Blacks.

Gluten sensitivity is also not rare. Gluten is a component of wheat and other grains. Ingestion of even tiny amounts can cause severe GI upset in susceptible people. Fortunately rice and corn are gluten-free, so the gluten-sensitive individual can obtain some nourishment from grains. But his choice of food is still restricted. A great many foods contain gluten, some of it "hidden," as in gravies, baked goods, and prepared foods.

Perhaps the most common cause of GI problems is, of course, *the nervous or overactive bowel*. This condition afflicts many non-runners as well, but intense training, and races particularly, seem to make the problem much worse. If you have an irritable bowel, you may need a doctor's help to choose the right diet. Occasionally drugs to "cool off" the GI tract are required to make running comfortable.

Q. How should we deal with such problems?

A. If you have a GI problem, you can start to solve it by experiment-
ing on yourself. Begin by eliminating foods likely to cause
difficulty. These include bran, certain fruits such as raisins and
bananas, nuts, salad ingredients, and corn. Blacks might try a
milk-free diet first.

If symptoms still persist, you can next try a gluten-free diet,
but it might be wiser to seek help from a doctor who specializes in
disorders of the GI tract.

We talked earlier about coffee. Runners have been drinking a
lot of it, as well as other caffeine-containing beverages such as soft
drinks, ever since the first reports that caffeine might improve
performance. I'm not certain what coffee does to performance, but
I know it is a very common cause of GI problems in runners.

CHAPTER 8

Other Risks of Running

Viruses and Other Annoyances

EVEN THOUGH I had run in other marathons, I never seemed able to train properly for the most important of them all, the Boston Marathon.

I live virtually at the top of Heartbreak Hill, perhaps the most famous point in the world's most famous long distance race. For years I had watched the world's best distance runners, along with friends and colleagues, run by me. Each year I returned home with very mixed emotions. My spirits were buoyed by the splendor of the event and by the enthusiasm and camaraderie of the huge crowds. But at the same time I was depressed because I wasn't running.

For the past several years I had planned to run, but each year I found that I could not sustain the high intensity of running required to get into proper shape. The long, hard Boston winters prevented me from running long enough. Each March, as the temperatures rose and the days lengthened, I would rapidly increase my daily mileage to speed up my training. Each year I suffered the consequences of this too rapid increase, sustaining overuse injuries which stopped my training program cold.

The 1979 Boston Marathon was going to be different. I was more determined than ever to run in it. Members of the American Medical Joggers Association, to which I belonged, had been given the privilege of running officially without having to achieve the necessary qualifying time, provided we started in the rear of the huge pack. There were rumors that this special treatment would soon end, and I might never have another chance to enter the Boston Marathon legally.

Fortunately, the winter was mild. Running outdoors was relatively easy. I lightened my usually heavy professional schedule and had time enough to train adequately. By April 1, two weeks before the race, I was certain not only that I would finish, but that I would perform respectably.

A week later, just one week before the race, I felt ill. A day later, for the first time in twenty years, I stopped work in the middle of the day to go home to bed. I had a whopping case of the flu. At any other time, I probably would have continued plodding along, muttering to myself that "I might as well be sick standing up as lying in bed," hoping that the awful symptoms would gradually disappear. This time I acted intelligently; I did not want to jeopardize my chances of running. I dutifully stayed in bed, drank plenty of fluids, even had some chicken soup, and took lots of aspirin. Forty-eight hours later, a bit weak but feeling reasonably well, I returned to my normal routine. I still had a few days to regain my strength, and the world seemed bright again.

The Boston Marathon is always run on a Monday, Patriots Day. The weekend before is filled with parties, meetings, and other gatherings which create a carnival-like atmosphere. I was really looking forward to the weekend. Many friends were coming from all over the country either to run or to join in the festivities. We would have a marvelous time.

But on the Friday night before the race, I was sick again. Either the original virus had become revitalized, or a new one was doing me in. This time I decided not to go to bed. There were meetings I wanted to attend and parties I certainly did not want to miss. Saturday night I barely made it through a "carbohydrate loading party" thronged with runners who cheerfully filled the air with newly discovered training techniques and ingeniously designed excuses as to why they would not be at their best on Monday. Runners are worse than fishermen this way.

Sunday I had a mild fever and felt miserable. When I went to sleep Sunday night, I was certain I would not run the next day. I awakened Monday morning feeling no better. I did not take my temperature, although I am sure I had a fever. But I could not stay in bed. I had to give it a try.

A group of us drove to the starting line in Hopkinton together. I vowed silently that if I was not feeling better by the time we arrived, I would return home with our driver.

But by then the adrenalin was starting to flow. Once I neared the starting line, there was absolutely no way I was going to return. I rationalized that I would start, and if I didn't feel well after a mile or two, I would drop out. I certainly would not want to do anything to jeopardize my health. Other people might do crazy things like that, but not me.

Patriots Day, 1979, was cold and drizzly; an excellent day to make good time in a marathon, but not so good for someone with the flu.

A few minutes before noon, the traditional starting time, standing with my friends far back in the huge throng, my teeth began to chatter and I developed a violent chill. The idea of running for the next 3 or 4 hours seemed absolutely ludicrous. "What the hell am I doing here?" I asked myself. But when the gun sounded and the mob moved forward, I moved with it. Seven minutes later, when we finally crossed the starting line, with Bill Rodgers and company already nearly a mile and a half ahead, I began to trot and shuffle forward with the others. A quarter of a mile later, when running room finally became available, my pace quickened. By then the adrenalin was really flowing, and all my symptoms miraculously disappeared. For the rest of the race I felt no different than I had during other marathons, better perhaps, because Boston was "home." The huge crowds, estimated at more than a million, provided enormous support. Cheering friends dotted the course from beginning to end. At about 18 miles, when I reached the top of Heartbreak Hill, traditionally the place where mediocre marathoners, and even some experts, hit "the wall," I felt better than ever because my family was there to cheer me on. I finished elated. I had run my first "Boston." I was already planning my strategy for next year's race.

Then it happened! My symptoms returned as quickly as they had disappeared, only much worse. I barely survived the next hour. A hot shower did nothing to relieve my shivering. Even a couple of very welcome beers didn't help much. I hardly remember driving home. For the next two weeks I was vaguely miserable. Never had I been so felled by an ordinary viral infection.

Was I incredibly stupid to run when I was sick? Absolutely. Would I do it again if I became ill just before next year's Marathon? I probably would.

If one of my patients had acted this way, I would have lectured him sternly about the dangers of running when he was sick. I would have reminded him that there are always other races to run, and emphasized that such stupid behavior might set back his regular training program weeks or even months. Yet secretly I would have been sympathetic. We tend to become so involved in our fitness programs, or, if training for a race, so determined to improve ourselves, that we often cease to act rationally. Yet clearly there are times when it is in your best interest to stop or cut back your running program. Running when you are sick can be dangerous, and it's important that we discuss the dangers and warning signs.

Although the facts are not clear, many feel that stress, either mental or physical, in some way may make us more susceptible to viral infections, and perhaps increases the consequences of an infection if we are already sick. For this reason, I believe there is some merit to resting more when we are sick. We certainly seem to recover more quickly when we do.

There is also some evidence that at least some of the viral illnesses—colds, the flu, and other respiratory infections we commonly consider as relatively minor annoyances—may actually involve important organs. Changes in the electrocardiogram, good evidence that the heart is involved, are surprisingly frequent during many viral infections. However, the patient is usually unaware that anything is wrong with his heart and, just like the cough and stuffed nose, the heart changes disappear gradually and recovery is complete. But during the time of heart involvement, I am concerned that high intensity exercise might have dire consequences. It seems reasonable not to stress the heart during this period.

Q. What then are your recommendations for running when you are sick?

A. It's very hard to be precise. If you are very sick, you obviously will have to stop running for a while. You should not begin to run

again until you feel entirely well. Surprisingly, the runner's response to severe illness is rarely a problem. Runners, while enthusiastic and often a bit foolish, are not totally crazy. They know that if they run when they really feel sick, they may break down completely, totally disrupting their training program. Most are willing to stop for a while. A much greater problem occurs when the illness is less severe, such as the flu or the typical head cold.

As a general rule, most physicians feel that the presence or absence of fever is an important criterion to help decide whether or not exercise should be stopped completely. In the absence of fever, they suggest that you can continue to run safely, but should reduce the speed and duration of your run. If you have a fever, you should stop running completely and wait a few days until it has subsided before starting again. It seems prudent to rest about twice the number of days the fever lasted.

While there is no evidence that these recommendations are any more than educated guesses, I generally go along with them. It makes no sense to jeopardize your health by over-enthusiastic exercise when your body is not functioning normally. But exceptions can be made if you have your heart set on participating in a particular event, although you must accept the fact that it might be risky to push yourself. Enjoy the participation and run well within your limits. You can worry about improving your performance some other time.

During the recovery period, make certain you get enough sleep, drink plenty of fluids, and take aspirin or similar medication to relieve your symptoms. Avoid getting chilled. It's also wise to avoid excessive use of many of the over-the-counter medications such as nasal decongestants which contain substances which may overly stimulate the heart. Antihistamines too can cause annoying side effects, which may be made worse by exercise. These drugs should be avoided in excess.

The "Overtraining Syndrome"

Q. Do you think that your heavy running program before the Boston Marathon contributed to your becoming ill?

A. There is an unproven feeling among physicians interested in exercise that high intensity training may do just that. The mechanism is not well understood. There is, however, a well-known series of events that seems to be the direct consequence of overtraining. I like to call it the "overtraining syndrome." It occurs when we push ourselves beyond reasonable limits. For the world class marathoner this may happen when he runs more than 120 miles per week. For us duffers, 5 miles a day may provoke it. It's almost as if the body is rebelling at being worked too hard. Some of the symptoms may be more prominent in some runners than others, but often they all occur together. They are not difficult to recognize.

The "overtraining syndrome" was most graphically demonstrated to me a couple of years ago. I had just finished a very popular local 7-mile road race at my usual slow pace, and I dropped into the medical tent at the finish to see some friends and help out if needed. One of the physicians in attendance, recognizing me, asked if I would take a look at a runner who was not feeling well.

From a distance he did not seem sick except for the worried look on his face. When I came closer, I recognized him. He was a world class runner, one of the best this country has produced.

He was concerned because his pulse rate had not yet returned to normal even though his race had ended 30 minutes before. Ordinarily it would take just a few minutes for him to recover, no matter how intense his effort. His blood pressure had also climbed a bit higher than usual, and he had an ill-defined, uneasy feeling. His wife confirmed that he had been short tempered and harder to get along with recently. His weight had dropped a bit, but he did not know why.

He had been training hard for years, but lately had been putting forth a little extra effort. He was soon to embark on an extensive European tour during which he would run in a number of important races. Over the past month, if he did not feel "right," he would run an extra 10 miles a day in hopes of curing his vague symptoms. Instead of making him stronger, the extra miles seemed to weaken him further. He became increasingly lethargic. Sometimes he had trouble sleeping, a problem he had never previously encountered. His enthusiasm for running, once boundless, had declined appreciably. He had great difficulty getting out of bed in the morning. Only his enormous discipline kept him going.

I approached him with considerable diffidence. Good athletes often know themselves better than any physician possibly can. Often they resent, usually with good reason, recommendations made by doctors used to treating ordinary people.

When he had finished his story, I told him that if one of my middle-aged running companions had complained of similar symptoms, I would have been certain of the diagnosis—he had pushed himself too hard and suffered from the "overtraining syndrome." I speculated that he too, on a much higher level to be sure, was suffering from the same problem.

An initial look of disbelief was followed by a somewhat puzzled look and then a more concerned one. His wife began to nod her head in vigorous assent. She was sure this was the answer. Reluctantly, he seemed to agree.

His next question was logical—"What should I do about it?"

The answer was easy, but I hesitated. He would not like what I was going to say. "The only cure is to stop running for a while and then begin at a much lower intensity. At the very least you must cut back your mileage considerably."

He shook his head vigorously. "Impossible. I have important races coming up soon."

"But if you don't cut back, your performance will suffer, and, more important, you run a great risk of injuring yourself." I was fairly confident of these two conclusions. Athletes and trainers have long known that performance declines, and injuries often follow, once a runner shows signs of overtraining. It is almost as if the ill-defined psychological upsets that characterize the syndrome's early stages are a warning that weakening of the whole body will soon follow.

We talked a while longer. Then he had to leave to catch a plane to Europe where he would soon compete. I wished him well and told him I would watch his progress with interest.

His European tour was a disaster. His times were well above his best, and toward the end he developed an apparently serious injury. I was sad but not surprised.

Foreign runners shake their heads at the intensity of American runners' training programs and the number of meets they enter, both indoors and out. They know that athletes can't maintain their competitive peaks for long, and must plan for peak efforts just a few times each year. If an athlete pushes too hard for too long, he breaks down.

Q. But isn't this condition peculiar to world class runners?

A. We plodders are equally prone to the problem. I've experienced the "overtraining syndrome" myself, as have many of my more enthusiastic running friends. You need to learn to recognize its early signs and symptoms, no matter what your present level of running duration and intensity. They include:

1. Fatigue and loss of enthusiasm for your daily exercise program. A slightly depressed and tired feeling all day.
2. An ill-defined edginess or frank nervousness.
3. Increased resting pulse rate when you first awaken. Some authorities feel that an increase of ten beats from normal is the earliest objective sign. However, my own pulse rate, even first thing in the morning, varies so much that I don't find this as much help as you may.
4. Difficulty falling asleep, or waking up several hours before you want to.
5. Slowed return of your pulse rate to normal after you have finished your run.
6. Pounding of the heart without obvious reason, or palpitations (skipped or extra heartbeats).
7. Change in appetite.
8. Weight loss without obvious cause.
9. Reduced performance.

A psychiatrist looking at this list of symptoms in a nonrunner would probably say that the patient was tense and depressed, and then begin his search for possible causes. In the runner the cause is easy to find if you are aware of the syndrome.

Q. To cure all this, all you have to do is stop?

A. This sounds simple, but of course it isn't. The last thing a runner wants to do is stop. His overenthusiasm placed him in this predicament in the first place, and it is hard to curb this enthusiasm, particularly if he is relying on self-diagnosis.

It is very important to listen to your body. If you have some of the symptoms listed, stop for a few days. If you can't do this, at least cut back. Sometimes this is enough to revive your feeling of well-being and improve your performance.

Q. What kind of injuries occur at this point? Are they any different from those that can happen to a runner at any time?

A. Earlier, you will remember, we used the term "injuries of over-use" and we discussed methods for preventing them. The same type of injuries occur with overtraining. Shin splints, runner's knee, Achilles tendonitis, ankle and foot pain can all occur, depending on your individual susceptibility. Cramps seem more common, and muscle aches after a long run are more persistent. The usual measures for treating these injuries may seem less effective. Their appearance is further reason to stop for a while.

Remember that the "overtraining syndrome" can occur at almost any level of fitness, although it is more likely to occur the fitter you become. It is unlikely to afflict the beginning jogger. But once you are up to 30 minutes or more, several times each week, beware! Listen to your body!

Serious Warning Signs and Symptoms

Q. What other health risks are there for runners?

A. Until now we have talked about important but not really danger-ous problems. Shin splints or insomnia never killed anyone. But there are some signs and symptoms which must be taken seri-ously, since they may herald important medical problems.

CHEST PAIN

One of the most important symptoms is chest pain. Most of you already know it may be a warning of a heart or coronary problem. Fortunately, it is usually not. Most chest pains in runners are due to other much less serious problems, such as minor injuries to the muscles of the chest wall or shoulder, or actual mild inflamma-tion of the joints of the chest (for example where the ribs join the sternum or breast bone). An injury to a rib or to the chest itself often causes pain when you move the chest cage or breathe. Minor digestive problems may also cause chest pain. Occasionally, infec-tion in the lung itself causes pain when you take a deep breath. We call this pleurisy.

Q. When should you see a doctor about chest pain?

A. If you are not sure of the cause of your chest pain, and particularly if you are older, if the pain is dull or aching—more a discomfort or pressure than a pain—and if it tends to begin when you start running and subsides promptly when you stop, you should see a physician soon. Heart pain may also show up as a discomfort in the throat, left arm, or shoulder. _Don't ignore it_!

HEART SKIPS AND POUNDING

Usually irregularities of the pulse rate, skipped or extra beats, or severe pounding of the heart, are not caused by serious heart problems and should not interfere with your running program. But they must be checked out. In some instances they may be serious and require treatment. I sometimes have skipped beats when I run, often when I have not had enough sleep or have drunk too much coffee. Even though I am quite sure they aren't serious, they make me uncomfortable. I can understand why they would frighten most runners. The treatment often is to get more sleep, cut back on caffeine or alcohol intake, or reduce the daily mileage. Overtraining can cause them.

Q. Do you have any advice about picking a doctor?

A. When you finally decide to see a physician about any heart irregularity, make sure the doctor understands runners. If he does not, he is sure to tell you to stop. A vivid example of this happened to one of our surgical residents.

He had begun a running program just a few months before. Like many beginners, he had enormous enthusiasm. Running had added "a new dimension" to his life. He felt fine, had lost weight, and seemed better able to survive his exhausting daily schedule. On days he didn't run, the world did not seem so bright.

Then one day he felt a few skips in his chest which were gone before he could check his pulse. The next day, midway through his run, the same thing happened. This time he was able to count the pulse; it was definitely irregular and remained irregular for several minutes. He hurried back to the hospital to attempt to document the type of skipped beats with a cardiogram. By the

177

time he returned, however, his heart action was regular, and his cardiogram was perfectly normal. He decided to ignore the skips—doctors are often the worst patients—and continue his running program. A week later the symptoms recurred, but this time the skips would not go away. Finally he mustered the courage to repeat the cardiogram, which documented an irregularity of the heartbeat called atrial fibrillation.

Thoroughly frightened now, and no longer willing or able to ignore the episodes, he sought medical advice. His cardiologist, to his credit, did not demand that the patient stop running, as many would have. After thoroughly examining him and performing an exercise ECG which was perfectly normal, the cardiologist told him it would probably be safe for him to run. However, he cautioned him to run "near the hospital," and smilingly suggested that it wouldn't be a bad idea if he ran with another doctor whenever he could.

Rather than cheering him, this verdict depressed our resident further. He grabbed me in the hospital corridor one day and asked my advice. I am usually reluctant to offer such advice without examining the patient myself, but he was quite agitated, and I was fairly certain that running would not be dangerous for him. I advised him to stop coffee for a while and reduce both the huge quantities of diet drinks he was consuming and the number of miles he was running each day. I assured him that the palpitations would then probably subside. I urged him not to run long and hard after sleepness nights, or when the physical stress of work left him very tired. Most importantly, I assured him that the presence of the atrial fibrillation did not imply any significant structural abnormality of his heart. He would not drop dead of a heart attack. Finally, if he was not better he should see me again for a more complete examination.

A few weeks later, I met him again in the corridor. He was running well, and noticed only an occasional palpitation which no longer disturbed him. The good feelings associated with running had returned, and the world looked brighter again.

Q. But aren't there some heart irregularities that may be dangerous?

A. There are indeed. The key is to find out whether there is any underlying heart problem. Irregularities frequently happen in people with normal hearts, like our surgical resident. In such cases they are not serious. However, if a known heart problem can be found, these irregularities may be important and require treatment.

On occasion we have found that a good exercise program is the best treatment for skipped beats. Running may thus cure rather than cause them in people with normal hearts.

Sudden Death

Q. Are these irregularities of the heartbeat the reason why joggers die suddenly?

A. This is a very thorny issue. There is absolutely no question that jogging is directly responsible for an occasional death. In such instances the mechanism for the sudden death is an acute breakdown in the heart's normal rhythmic pumping mechanism. Instead of an orderly contraction of the left ventricle, the heart's main pumping chamber, the contraction becomes totally disorganized, a condition we call ventricular fibrillation. Within minutes, if the fibrillation persists, irreversible damage occurs in the brain, followed a little later by damage to other vital organs.

Q. Is this what is meant by "cardiac arrest"?

A. Exactly. It means the heart has stopped pumping blood. Prompt emergency treatment can reverse the fibrillation. This is the concept behind the efforts we now call cardiopulmonary resuscitation, or CPR. If adequate CPR can be applied within the first few crucial minutes before brain damage occurs, then sudden death can be prevented.

That's why I demand that my heart patients, who are at higher risk than others for fibrillation and sudden death, exercise in a medically supervised group where CPR can be immediately instituted should this disaster occur (see Chapter 4).

Let me give you an example of how effective CPR can be. In a medically supervised exercise program in Seattle, Washington, involving several hundred subjects, 85 percent of whom were known to have heart disease, there have been twenty episodes of cardiac arrest. Each episode has been promptly terminated by adequate CPR, and there have been no deaths. Each of these twenty episodes would, of course, have been fatal had facilities not been immediately available to treat the emergency.

Q. Nevertheless, seemingly healthy people do drop dead suddenly while jogging. How do you account for these deaths? Could they have been prevented?

A. I am certain that many such deaths are predictable, that clues to a heart problem would have been present if looked for carefully. I am equally sure that no matter how careful we are, an occasional death will be caused by running. All the medical attention in the world is not going to prevent a runner from overdoing it at times, or running when he is sick. And despite their accurate diagnostic tools, doctors are still going to miss some potentially serious heart problems no matter how carefully they look.

Many seemingly well patients who die suddenly do not have normal hearts at all. They have significant, severe coronary disease which may have been "silent." By that I mean the individual had no symptoms from it. More commonly, I suspect, symptoms were present but ignored. But even the truly silent problems can sometimes be discovered during a thorough examination which includes an exercise ECG.

I believe we can fairly reliably predict who is most likely to have silent heart disease. Generally, the condition affects older people who possess one or more of the risk factors already discussed in Chapter 3. Such people deserve very thorough medical evaluation, and perhaps should begin their running programs in a supervised setting, even if their exams are normal.

Q. Some younger people also die suddenly. They seem too young to have serious coronary disease. Why do they die?

A. Coronary disease can occur at any age. I have seen it in teenagers. But you're right. In some younger persons there is a different mechanism that causes death.

Recently a group of investigators from the National Heart and Lung Institute in Bethesda, Maryland, studied precisely this question. They carefully examined the hearts of a group of young, otherwise apparently healthy people who died suddenly during exercise. A very high percentage of them had overdevelopment or thickening of the heart muscle, particularly the muscle of the left ventricle, the heart's strongest pumping chamber. The medical term for this is _hypertrophy_ of the heart. This thickening can be spread throughout the heart muscle or confined to a small area of the heart, and often obstructs flow from one chamber to another. Since heart murmurs or easily recognized abnormalities of the cardiogram are usually present, most of these patients have some clue to alert the physician.

An even more recent report, presented at the 1979 meeting of the American College of Cardiology, offers a clue to why some of the remainder, who have neither a heart murmur nor other signs of a heart problem, may have died suddenly. Post-mortem examinations of their hearts have shown that one of the coronary arteries may actually pass under small bridges of heart muscle. When the heart contracts, the muscle bridge may briefly constrict the artery and interfere with the flow of blood for a short period. At rest, or during moderate activity, this constriction is probably too brief to be important, but at very high heart rates produced by vigorous activity, the slight reduction of flow may still be great enough to provoke sudden death due to ventricular fibrillation.

About one person in two hundred is alleged to have these heart muscle bridges.

Q.   This obviously is a potentially serious problem. Is there any way to find out who may have them?

A.   This has not yet been studied carefully, but I suspect that a stress test might define most of the people who have them. Perhaps these muscle bridges may account for some of the supposedly false positive stress tests that are so common among younger, apparently healthy people.

THE CASE OF CONGRESSMAN BYRON

Before leaving the subject of sudden death, I feel obliged to comment briefly about the recent death of Congressman Goodloe Byron. His sudden death, while jogging, received widespread publicity. In fact, the publicity was so widespread that I can only conclude that someone seemed anxious to discredit running. If the

Congressman had died suddenly in his sleep, or mowing the lawn, it hardly would have rated a front page story in most of the nation's newspapers.

After his death I was deluged by worried patients and friends, some with, but most without, heart problems. They wanted to know how I could explain the death. How could it have been prevented? Could the same thing possibly happen to them?

A few days later more facts emerged in the newspapers. The family history was strong for coronary heart disease. Congressman Byron, although only 39, had considerable evidence of severe coronary disease. His exercise ECG was apparently strongly positive, and he evidently had symptoms suggesting angina. His cardiologist, although himself a champion of exercise for heart patients and a pioneer in the cardiac rehabilitation movement, was reported to have urged the Congressman to modify his exercise program, even though he had safely completed several marathons. The autopsy examination apparently confirmed the diagnosis of coronary artery disease.

His death might have been prevented had he run in a supervised program. The mechanism of his death was almost certainly ventricular fibrillation. CPR might have saved him. While we can probably attribute his sudden death to jogging, this incident should not imply necessarily that people with heart problems must stop jogging. Rather it suggests they must do it with adequate supervision.

Is it not fair also to ask a question: In this man with severe coronary artery disease, is it possible that jogging slowed the advance of the atherosclerosis? If he had not run, might he have died sooner? There are no definite answers to this intriguing question. But it certainly seems worth asking.

Q. Are you implying that once a diagnosis of a coronary heart problem is made all running should be supervised?

A. Ideally this should be the case. The longer the exercise is supervised after a heart attack, or if angina is present, the better. As I stated in Chapter 4 I am reluctant to let my coronary patients exercise alone, even if they have exercised without problems for years. I would feel better if they never left the group program.

Still I can understand Representative Byron's behavior. He must have believed that his superb physical condition, which allowed him to complete marathons, prevented the development of fatal heart problems. His death is tragic witness that this is not the case. A marathoner's life style does not confer complete immunity from heart disease.

Murmurs

Q. Earlier you mentioned heart murmurs as a clue to alert the physician to a potentially severe problem. We thought that murmurs were usually not significant. How can you distinguish between serious and harmless murmurs?

A. This can sometimes be very difficult, but the skilled cardiologist, using newer diagnostic techniques, can often sort out the serious murmurs from the innocuous ones.

Years ago doctors seemed overly cautious about murmurs, and unnecessarily restricted activity in many healthy people whose murmurs were really innocent. Now the pendulum seems to have swung the other way. Doctors tend to dismiss murmurs in young people as unimportant, as long as the patient feels all right and has no symptoms when he exercises. Such advice appears regularly in the running magazines. But I disagree. These murmurs should not be ignored. I believe they should be carefully evaluated because some of them are not entirely harmless.

Murmurs usually have a specific cause, and in the majority of patients it is possible to define the cause quite accurately. Therefore, my strong recommendation to anyone with a heart murmur, no matter how well he may feel, is to have the murmur checked by a competent cardiologist. If no significant abnormality is found, then the running program can safely be continued.

Q. What tests should be done?

A. Before any tests, a careful medical history and physical examination are important. A resting and exercise electrocardiogram should also be obtained. We now have available a relatively new, most useful diagnostic device, the echocardiogram. This medical application of sonar or ultrasound allows us to look inside the heart in a painless, totally safe way and enables us to measure heart structure and function quite precisely. In the study just discussed, most of the young people who dropped dead suddenly could probably have been diagnosed correctly if an echocardiogram had been performed.

Critics of this approach will counter that there are millions of joggers, and that very few of them drop dead. The procedures I recommend would, to be sure, be somewhat expensive and time consuming, and they would not uncover a large number of patients who might be seriously at risk. But I know that if I had a heart murmur, I would certainly want to know what was causing it, and whether exercise might help or harm me.

Other Important Signs and Symptoms

Q. What else might suggest a potentially serious medical problem?

A. *Breathlessness* should not be ignored. Most of you know the level of activity at which you ordinarily become breathless. If this changes much, medical advice should be sought. Sometimes breathlessness is an early sign of a heart problem. It may also be a result of a change in lung function, or the first symptom of anemia.

Other important symptoms, which demand medical attention, relate either to primary or secondary abnormalities of brain and nervous system function. Persistent severe *headaches*, frequent *dizzy spells, lightheadedness or incoordination, weakness of one side of the body or a single arm or leg, sudden loss or clumsiness of speech*, and actual *fainting* must be checked out immediately.

Diseases of Medical Progress

I would like to shift focus a little and discuss a whole new set of medical problems which are not really problems at all. (The best known of these, of course, is "athlete's heart," which we discussed in Chapter 4.) Perhaps the best name for them is "Diseases of Medical Progress." Some of them were never suspected until we started performing frequent medical tests on runners. Some produce rather frightening signs and symptoms but are not serious at all.

Let me give you an example of the latter type: Blood in the urine, the medical term is _hematuria_, can be extremely frightening. Some runners seem particularly prone to this, usually after long, exhausting runs. For years most experts thought the bleeding came from the prostate gland rather than the urinary bladder or kidneys. But this could hardly explain blood in the urine of women, who of course have no prostate gland. More recent evidence suggests that the blood comes from tearing or rupture of tiny veins on the inside of the bladder itself. In runners it probably is not caused by any serious medical problem, although recently some experts have suggested that recurrent hematuria may be a sign of serious dehydration. Of course, hematuria in nonathletes may be a warning of a serious problem, and should be checked immediately.

More common in runners, and equally benign, is the presence of albumin or protein in the urine after running. In nonathletes this may be a sign of a serious kidney disorder, but in runners it is innocuous. If it should occur, a few days of rest will make it disappear. Yet for years kidney specialists were uncertain whether exercise would eventually permanently damage the kidneys of people who developed albumin in the urine.

Recently a runner friend of mine came to me very distraught. During his routine yearly checkup, his physician had detected a mild anemia and also an abnormality of several substances in the blood called enzymes, which are tested for routinely because their blood levels often become abnormal early in the course of certain diseases of the liver and other organs. X-rays and other sophisticated tests had not revealed the source of his problem. His physicians were planning more rigorous testing, and even had considered the possibility of an exploratory operation.

I thought my friend had become a victim of medical progress, and that probably the abnormal findings were related to his running. However, he had been running for years and these changes had never been found in previous checkups. This was a bit unsettling, but a little further digging into his history provided a likely answer. In the last few months he had gradually increased his weekly running mileage because he had decided to run in a marathon.

I rarely urge a dedicated runner to stop completely unless there are overwhelming reasons for his doing so. But in this case we needed to prove that running, not something else more serious, had produced the abnormal blood tests. Reluctantly he took two weeks off and then the blood tests were repeated. As expected, they were normal.

Q. Why does running produce these changes? Earlier you said that one of the effects of training is to increase the number of red blood cells to improve the oxygen-carrying capacity of the blood. Wouldn't that make anemia very unlikely?

A. Your memory is good. But also remember that the blood is made up of two major parts, the blood cells and the plasma or liquid portion. Running causes an overall expansion of the total volume of blood, increasing both the number of cells and the amount of plasma. Our usual way of measuring red blood counts is to take a sample of the whole blood and check the relative proportions of blood cells to plasma. In some runners the plasma is increased even more than the cells so that a relative "anemia" or "pseudo anemia" occurs. Of course, this condition is not a real anemia at all.

The other blood test abnormalities, the elevated enzyme levels, occur because muscles also contain some of the same enzymes as liver cells. With vigorous exercise there may be mild damage to the muscle cells—after all, that's why your muscles are stiff and sore after vigorous exercise—and some of the content of the muscle cells, enzymes included, may leak into the bloodstream until healing occurs. This is also a perfectly benign finding and requires no treatment or reduction in mileage.

CHAPTER 9

Diet

PERHAPS NOTHING in the field of medicine generates more heat and less light than the subject of diet. No matter what recommendations are made, many readers will disagree with them. They are certain which diet is best for them. Many are probably right, because an agreeable diet is uniquely personal. It transcends the laws of physiology and biochemistry and must satisfy psychological needs and cultural habits as well.

A major problem about evaluating diets is that so many people, particularly athletes and their advisors, become evangelical about them, attempting to convince anyone who will listen that their diets offer unique advantages. The running magazines are filled with testimonials from successful runners and coaches describing diets and additives certain to improve performance. But even a cursory look discloses that these recommendations are so extraordinarily different that no single diet could possibly be defined as "the best."

The dietary idiosyncracies of runners are legendary. Some are strict vegetarians. Others stuff themselves with protein. Still others swallow huge amounts of vitamins and minerals. From vitamin A to zinc; you name it, and some runner is sure it helps his performance.

The top marathoners in the United States were recently polled about diet. Each had his favorite regular diet, as well as a special pre-race diet. Some had dietary "secrets" which they would not disclose. No wonder everyone, the physician included, disagrees.

Q. Aren't you still able to offer some general recommendations? Isn't there a good dietary program for both runners and nonrunners?

A. *There is growing evidence that a diet that is most likely to promote good health and longevity is one that is high in complex carbohydrates, low in fats, and contains only moderate amounts of proteins.*

Q. Before going further, will you define carbohydrate, fat, and protein?

A. Think of the three of them as the source of calories for energy and of most of the raw materials for the building, maintenance, and proper function of the body cells and tissues. They are three of the six major components of food. The others are *water*, *minerals*, and *vitamins*.

Carbohydrates

Carbohydrates are composed solely of three elements—carbon, hydrogen, and oxygen—arranged into molecules, each containing six carbon atoms, called sugars. Slight changes in the arrangement of the atoms of the sugar molecule produce a variety of different sugars. Among the common sugars are glucose, fructose, and galactose. Glucose is the sugar the body metabolizes directly as an energy source. Other sugars must be converted to glucose in the liver before the body can use them. Figure 32 shows the glucose molecule.

Carbohydrates are often divided into two main classes, *simple* and *complex*. Simple carbohydrates or sugars include the single sugar molecules like glucose or two sugar molecules hooked together, such as honey or table sugar. Nutritionists often say that these simple sugars provide "empty calories." They mean that our dietary sources of simple sugars contain no other important dietary constituents such as vitamins, minerals, or fiber.

Complex carbohydrates are formed when many sugar mole-

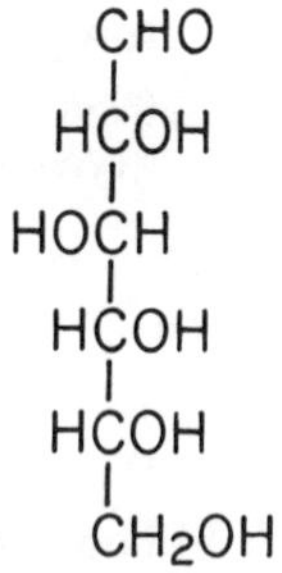

$$
\begin{array}{c}
\text{CHO} \\
| \\
\text{HCOH} \\
| \\
\text{HOCH} \\
| \\
\text{HCOH} \\
| \\
\text{HCOH} \\
| \\
\text{CH}_2\text{OH}
\end{array}
$$

FIGURE 32. _The glucose molecule._ _Glucose is the most important simple sugar molecule. Other simple sugars vary only slightly._

cules are joined together. Grains, fruits, and many vegetables are bountiful sources. Unlike simple carbohydrates, our food sources of complex carbohydrates are excellent sources of vitamins, minerals, and fiber; their calories are not "empty."

Q. Are there any other advantages in complex carbohydrates?

A. Simple carbohydrates are rapidly absorbed from the GI tract and induce vigorous production of insulin by the pancreas. If too much simple sugar is consumed, the finely tuned insulin mechanisms may be overwhelmed. High blood sugar levels, or even frank diabetes, may result. Sometimes the opposite happens; too much insulin is produced and the blood sugar falls too low, a condition called _hypoglycemia_. Complex carbohydrates, absorbed much more slowly, are better handled by the body.

Glycogen, the storage form of carbohydrate found in muscle and liver cells, is a series of glucose molecules hooked closely together. When glucose is needed, glycogen is broken down to supply it. Adequate stores of glycogen are thus vitally necessary for muscular activity and normal function of organs. During endurance activity such as long distance running, blood sugar levels would become dangerously low were there not a steady replacement supply coming from the breakdown of glycogen. When the glycogen stores themselves are depleted, sugar levels in the blood and muscle tissue fall. Brain and muscle function deteriorate rapidly.

An interesting, but fortunately rare, genetic disease of the muscles is characterized by absence of the enzyme necessary for the breakdown of muscle glycogen to glucose. Individuals so afflicted develop severe muscle cramps and pains when they at-

_189_

tempt even moderate physical activity because their muscle glucose level falls quickly and cannot be replenished by muscle glycogen breakdown.

Fats

Fats too are an important energy source. They will not dissolve in body fluids and, therefore, make excellent insulators for nerves and other parts of the nervous system. Fats form an important part of the wall of any cell. The two most important fats are cholesterol (Figure 33) and triglycerides (Figure 34).

In Chapter 3 we discussed the role of cholesterol as a risk factor in atherosclerosis. But cholesterol is also vital for normal cellular structure and function. Most cells have the ability to make their own cholesterol whenever they need it, so not much cholesterol, if any, is required in our diet.

Q. Isn't cholesterol a good source of calories?

A. This is a popular misconception. Cholesterol itself has no caloric value. The calories we obtain from fats come from triglycerides.

Each triglyceride molecule is composed of a backbone or framework of glycerol to which are attached three long, chainlike compounds called *fatty acids* (Figure 34). Metabolism or breakdown of the fatty acids provides the second important source

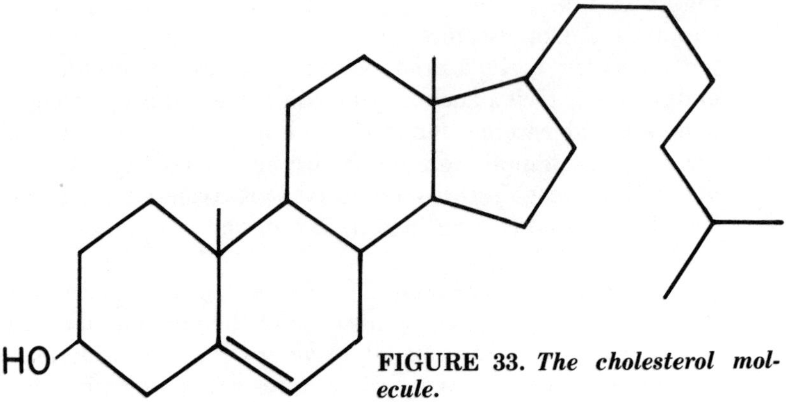

FIGURE 33. *The cholesterol molecule.*

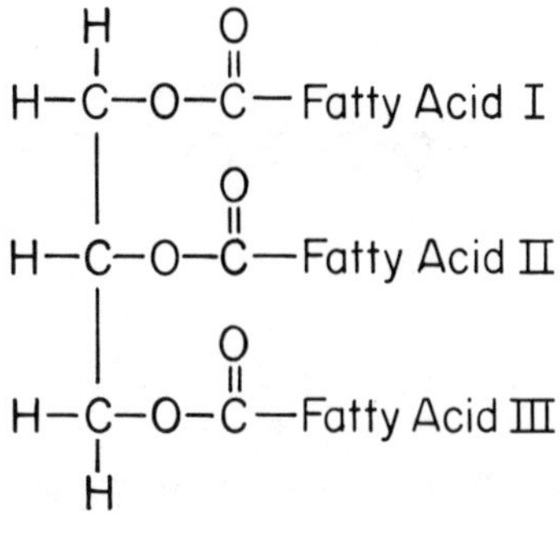

$$
\begin{array}{c}
\overset{\displaystyle H}{\underset{\displaystyle |}{}} \quad \overset{\displaystyle O}{\underset{\displaystyle \|}{}} \\
H-C-O-C-\text{Fatty Acid I} \\
| \\
\overset{\displaystyle O}{\underset{\displaystyle \|}{}} \\
H-C-O-C-\text{Fatty Acid II} \\
| \\
\overset{\displaystyle O}{\underset{\displaystyle \|}{}} \\
H-C-O-C-\text{Fatty Acid III} \\
| \\
H
\end{array}
$$

FIGURE 34. _The triglyceride molecule._ _Each triglyceride molecule is composed of three fatty acids attached to a framework of glycerol._

of energy for muscular work. Indeed, the fatty acids contained in triglycerides are by far our most important reserve energy supply for muscular work. Most of our extra calories, whether they come from carbohydrate, protein, or fat itself are converted to fatty acids and stored in triglycerides in fat tissue and muscle.

You have frequently seen the terms "saturated" and "unsaturated" fats. They refer to the kinds of fatty acids contained in the triglyceride. In Figure 35 examples of each are shown. Unsaturated fatty acids contain one or more of what the chemists call _double bonds_. In some poorly understood fashion, fats high in unsaturated fatty acids seem less likely to raise, and in fact may lower, the levels of cholesterol in the blood. Some diets recommend substituting foods high in unsaturated fatty acids, specially prepared salad oils and soft margarines for example, for butter and traditional dressings which contain saturated fatty acids.

Q. How much fat is required in a healthy diet?

A. Apparently very little, far less than we customarily consume even if we try to follow a fairly low fat diet. _Linoleic acid_ (Figure 35) is the only "essential" fatty acid which the body cannot make itself from other dietary sources, and only moderate amounts of this widely available and easily stored fatty acid are necessary. It has been estimated that if we stopped eating fat completely, most of us would be able to go six months without any measurable deficiency of linoleic acid.

Most authorities agree that our typical western diets contain far too much fat, and may well be the cause of atherosclerosis in many people. Now extremely low fat diets are being touted as the

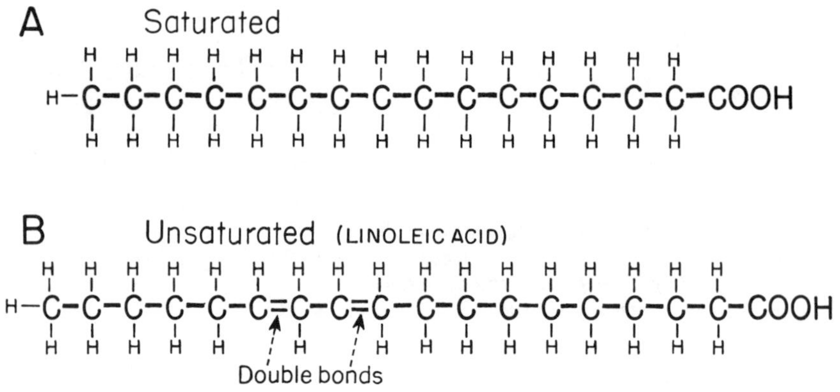

A   Saturated

H–C–C–C–C–C–C–C–C–C–C–C–C–C–C–C–COOH

B   Unsaturated (LINOLEIC ACID)

H–C–C–C–C–C–C=C–C≡C–C–C–C–C–C–C–C–C–COOH

Double bonds

FIGURE 35. *Saturated and unsaturated fatty acids.* *Unsaturated fatty acids have one or more double bonds between the carbon* (C) *atoms. The unsaturated fatty acid shown* (**B**) *is linoleic acid, the only "essential" fatty acid the body cannot make itself.*

most healthy for us. (A diet moderately low in fat is shown in Table 9; a very low fat diet in Table 10.) In general I agree with this theory, but I am a little uneasy about endorsing the very low fat diets completely, since we really don't know all the long-term effects of such severe fat restrictions.

THE PRITIKIN DIET

Q.   Is the Pritikin Diet one of this type?

A.   The Pritikin Diet is at this time the best-known of the very low fat diets. Pritikin is not a physician, but he apparently became interested in nutrition when he developed heart disease himself.

    His basic premises seem reasonable. He believes that high fat diets are dangerous, and that the less fat we eat the less likely we are to develop degenerative diseases (diseases of aging) such as atherosclerosis. He thinks that the low fat diets presently recommended by physicians and other members of the medical establishment are not nearly low enough in fat to be effective. He describes his diet as being quite similar to that consumed by a primitive Indian tribe from northern Mexico, the Tarahumaras, who regularly perform prodigious amounts of aerobic activity, and who are apparently free of atherosclerosis. Pritikin presumes this very low fat diet is safe for us because it seems to be safe for the Tarahumaras.

Up to this point I tend to agree with him. A very low fat diet makes sense to me, although, as I have just stated, I am a bit uneasy about how low it should be. But following such a diet is

TABLE 9. *Low Cholesterol-Low Saturated Fat Diet**

As a general rule you should:

1. Serve less beef, lamb, veal, pork, and ham. Substitute fish and poultry.
2. Use only very lean, well-trimmed meat. Remove skin from poultry.
3. Use only dairy products which have had the fat removed (skimmed).
4. Substitute polyunsaturated vegetable oils and margarine for butter and animal fats.
5. Use few egg yolks and other cholesterol-rich foods.
6. Limit your total calories if you are overweight.

ITEMS	YOU MAY INCLUDE	AVOID
Dairy products	Skim milk, buttermilk, cottage cheese or other cheese made from skim milk. Restrict egg yolks to three or less per week.	Whole milk, condensed milk, dried whole milk, chocolate milk, cream, non-dairy creamers, whipped topping, ice cream, ice milk, cheese (including cream cheese).
Meats Beef, lamb, veal, pork, ham	3 small servings of very lean meat per week. Bake, broil, or roast all meat, fish, and poultry.	All fatty meats, bacon, sausage, canned meat products, corned beef, duck, goose, fish roe, luncheon meats, cold cuts, frankfurters, meats canned or frozen in gravy or sauce, organ meat (liver, kidney, heart, brain), shrimp.
Chicken, turkey, Cornish hen	Remove skin of poultry after cooking.	
Fish	If canned, drain oil. Use shellfish other than shrimp.	

*In this diet, daily cholesterol is restricted to less than 300 milligrams. Saturated fat is also decreased. It is hoped that this diet will reduce the amount of fats (cholesterol and triglyceride) in the blood.
Data from the American Heart Association.

TABLE 9, cont.

ITEMS	YOU MAY INCLUDE	AVOID
Fats and oils[1]	Safflower and corn oil; soft margarine made from safflower, corn, sunflower, or cottonseed oil. The first ingredient on the label should be "liquid oil." Salad Dressing should be made from these oils.	Bacon and meat drippings, butter, regular margarine, coconut oil, olive oil, lard, salt pork, suet and chicken fat, solid vegetable shortening.
Breads and starches	All white and dark breads, cereals, bagels, hamburger and hot dog rolls, English muffins. Saltines and other non-oily crackers, pretzels (if salt restriction is not necessary). Rice, noodles, spaghetti, macaroni. Be careful about biscuits, corn bread, popcorn, etc. Eat them only if made at home with allowed fats.	Most commercial baked goods, including biscuits, muffins, corn bread, pancakes, waffles, cookies, crackers; mixes for biscuits, muffins, coffee cakes, cakes (except angel food), pies, sweet rolls, doughnuts, pastries.
Fruits and vegetables	All fruits and vegetables.	Vegetables frozen in butter sauce.
Desserts and sweets	Refined carbohydrates (sugar, honey, soft drinks) contain no fat, but they contribute to excess calories and weight gain.	Cookies, cakes, pastries, regular pudding and ice cream, whipped cream desserts, cheese cake, chocolate, coconut, candy made with chocolate, butter, cream, or coconut. All of these contain too much fat.
Alcoholic beverages	Usually acceptable in moderate amounts, but they too are a source of extra calories.	

[1]The recommended amounts will vary. If you have a severe fat problem, you will want to use very little.

194

TABLE 10. *Very Low Fat Diet**

1. As a general rule, you should consume no more than 3–4 ounces of lean meat, fish, or poultry daily, less if possible.
2. Replace the protein usually provided by meat products by increasing the intake of dried beans, peas, and lentils. Consume 2 glasses of skim milk daily. You may also consume small amounts of cheese with less than 2 percent butterfat.
3. Fruits, vegetables, and complex carbohydrates (breads, cereals, pasta, potatoes, and rice) should form the basis of your diet.
4. If you are overweight, your total calories may also be limited.

ITEM	YOU MAY INCLUDE	AVOID
Dairy products	Skim milk, buttermilk, low-fat cottage cheese. Cheese with less than 2 percent butterfat. Egg whites.	Whole milk, condensed milk, dried whole milk, evaporated whole milk, milk shakes or frappes, chocolate milk, cream, non-dairy creamers, commercial whipped topping.
Meats Beef, veal, lamb, pork	Limit to 3–4 ounces of very lean meat per day. Trim all fat. Bake, broil, or roast all meat, fish, and poultry.	Any fatty meats, bacon, sausage, canned meat products, corned beef, duck, goose, fish roe, fried meats or fish, frozen and packaged dinners, luncheon meats, cold cuts, frankfurters, meats canned or frozen in gravy or sauce, organ meats, (liver, kidney, heart, brain), shrimp.
Chicken, turkey, Cornish hen	Remove skin of poultry after cooking.	
Fish	Use lean fish; if canned, drain oil. Shellfish other than shrimp.	
Fats and oils	None.	Bacon and meat drippings, butter, margarine, coconut oil, salad oil, mayonnaise, lard, salt pork, suet and chicken fat, solid vegetable shortening.

*The total dietary fat is reduced to less than 10 percent of the daily calorie intake. Dietary cholesterol is less than 100 milligrams.
Data from the American Heart Association.

TABLE 10, cont.

ITEM	YOU MAY INCLUDE	AVOID
Breads and starches	All white and dark breads, cereals, bagels, hamburger and hot dog rolls, English muffins. Saltines and other non-oily crackers and pretzels are satisfactory if salt restriction is not necessary.	Most baked goods including muffins, corn bread, pancakes, waffles, cookies, crackers. Mixes for biscuits, muffins, coffee cakes, cakes (except angel food), pies, sweet rolls, doughnuts, pastries.
Fruits and vegetables	All fruits and vegetables.	Vegetables frozen in butter sauce.
Desserts and sweets	Refined carbohydrates (sugar, honey, soft drinks) contain no fat, but they contribute to excess calories and weight gain.	Cookies, cakes, pastries, regular pudding and ice cream, whipped cream desserts, cheesecake, chocolate, coconut, candy made with chocolate, butter, cream, or coconut. All of these contain too much fat.
Alcoholic beverages	Usually acceptable in moderate amounts, but they too are a source of extra calories.	

difficult; you must be very well motivated to maintain it. Several of my patients, with my complete endorsement, have attended the diet centers Pritikin has established. There, in a very structured, supervised environment, using skillful methods of food preparation, palatable low fat diets are strictly followed. My patients return enthusiastic. Most have lost weight and feel better, and equally important they are proud of their will power and discipline. They feel that the rather large sums charged for this service are worth it. But after a while, most have difficulty maintaining the diet. Previous bad dietary habits return along with the lost pounds.

Not only is the Pritikin Diet hard to follow, but also it is not much fun. Many favorite foods, and all types of alcohol, are banned. While such long-term austerity may benefit an occasional, severely ill heart patient, I believe a somewhat more liberal approach to diet will probably best serve most of us in the long run.

Q. What is the evidence that the Pritikin Diet reduces atherosclerosis or slows its development?

A. Surprisingly little. This is where Pritikin and I part company. In many respects, so far as the scientific community is concerned, he is his own worst enemy. He has a reasonable theory, but he destroys his credibility by making unsupported claims about the results of his diet. It will lower cholesterol, but this does not mean that it will reduce atherosclerosis or lengthen lives. Not enough time has elapsed to allow any firm conclusions. Moreover, Pritikin's public pronouncements about diet and nutrition are vastly oversimplified and often incorrect. In his evangelical fervor, he seems to have tossed caution, and science, to the wind.

I would recommend to all of you, as I do to my patients, that the Pritikin Diet is worth investigating if you are so inclined. His most recent book contains many interesting and enticing recipes that will make any low fat diet more palatable. I would also recommend, though, that you take his claims with the proverbial "grain of salt" and cheat often enough to make eating fun.

Proteins

Proteins are the third group of nutrients which supply calories. Proteins, however, are not a good energy source. We utilize proteins for calories only when our stores of carbohydrate and fat are seriously depleted, for example during long fasts or starvation. Proteins are much more important as a source of structural materials for cells, tissues, enzymes, hormones, and a variety of other substances.

Proteins are often large molecules composed of varying combinations of smaller, nitrogen-containing molecules called _amino acids_. Twenty-three different amino acids have so far been described. The body can make only fourteen of these itself. The other nine, described as "essential" dietary amino acids, must come from the diet. High protein foods include meat, some dairy products and grains, and a few vegetables and fruits. Strict vegetarians, unless they eat enough corn and beans, may develop amino acid deficiencies.

Foods which are good sources of carbohydrates, fats, and proteins are listed in Table 11.

Water

We can survive without food for a long time because we have ample reserve energy stores. We cannot survive without water for more than a few days. Our water reserves are small, and a certain amount of water is required each day to help the body excrete the toxic waste products of metabolism in the urine.

Water, of course, is the primary constituent of virtually all body tissues except the bones and parts of the nervous system. Some of our foods, particularly fruits and vegetables, contain a high percentage of water. A small amount of water is also pro-

TABLE 11. *Common Food Sources of Carbohydrates, Fats, and Proteins*

CARBOHYDRATES	FATS	PROTEINS
Complex carbohydrates	Dairy products (made	Dairy products
Bread	with whole milk)	Eggs
Cereals	Fatty meats	Cereals
Pasta	Vegetable oils	Meat
Rice	Chocolate	Poultry
Fruits	Peanut butter	Fish
Some vegetables	Nuts	Some vegetables
(dried beans,		(legumes)
potatoes, corn)		Peanut butter
Grains		Nuts
Simple carbohydrates		Grains
Sugar		
Syrup		
Honey		
Jellies		
Candy		

duced during the normal metabolism of some foods. But by far the most important source of water is the fluid we drink. It is almost impossible for a normal person to drink too much fluid. We have marvelously efficient ways for excreting extra water. We are far more vulnerable to excessive fluid loss.

Minerals

Minerals are a group of many chemical elements necessary for normal body structure and function. They are not a source of calories. Important minerals include sodium, calcium, phosphorus, magnesium, potassium, and iron. These are present in the body in relatively large amounts. A number of other minerals are required in much smaller or "trace" amounts. Some nutrition experts suggest that we have not paid sufficient attention to these trace minerals, zinc for example, and that our diets may be deficient in some of them. The evidence for this theory is as yet not very convincing, one of the problems being that the tiny amounts present in the body are very difficult to measure. This technical problem is gradually being solved, and we should soon know much more about the role of trace minerals in our bodies. At present I still believe that adequate supplies of necessary minerals are probably supplied by a balanced diet, and that mineral supplements are generally not necessary.

Vitamins

Vitamins are organic substances required in the diet in small amounts to allow the body to perform a number of important functions, such as the metabolism of food sources for energy and the production of hormones, blood cells, and many important body chemicals. Vitamins influence the rate at which many of the body's enzymes, substances which control important chemical reactions, operate. Without adequate supplies of vitamins, many of these enzyme-controlled reactions slow down or actually stop.

Vitamins are divided into two main types, _fat soluble_ and _water soluble_. The fat soluble vitamins, A, D, E, and K, can be

199

stored in relatively large amounts in the fat tissues, and are re-
leased when needed by the rest of the body. Daily intake is not
necessary. There may be some risk in consuming excessive
amounts of these vitamins, exceeding our capacity to store them.

Water soluble vitamins include the various B vitamins,
vitamin C, folic acid, and a number of other substances not yet
firmly designated by scientists as vitamins. Because they are soluble in water, the body has trouble storing them. Extra amounts
are excreted in the urine. Regular daily intake of most water
soluble vitamins is recommended.

Good dietary sources of the necessary vitamins are listed in
Table 12.

TABLE 12. *Major Dietary Sources of Vitamins*

VITAMIN	SOURCE
Fat soluble	
A	Liver, dairy products including fortified milk, egg yolk, fruits (deep yellow), vegetables (deep yellow and dark green leafy)
D	Fish liver oils, vitamin D fortified dairy products, liver, egg yolk
E	Vegetable oils, fruits, vegetables (lettuce)
K	Liver, eggs, fruits, vegetables, vegetable oils
Water soluble	
B-1 (thiamine)	Grains, enriched breads and cereals, organ meats, pork, peas and beans
B-2 (riboflavin)	Milk, cheese, green vegetables, beans, meat, en-riched bread, cereals
Niacin	Meat, whole grains, legumes, nuts, fish, poultry, en-riched breads, cereals
B-6 (pyridoxine)	Meat, chicken, whole grains, nuts, bananas
B-12	Meat, eggs, dairy products
Folic acid	Green vegetables, oranges, legumes, liver
Pantothenic acid	Meat (particularly liver), egg yolk
Biotin	Vegetables (particularly legumes), meats
C	Citrus fruits and juices, strawberries, melons, many vegetables

The "Well-Balanced" Diet

Q. Can you give us a diet which will ensure an adequate supply of all the essential nutrients?

A. By definition this is called a "well-balanced" diet. This diet should contain adequate amounts of the four main types of foods:

1. Fruits and vegetables.
2. Cereals and grains.
3. High protein foods: meat, poultry, fish, beans, and some nuts.
4. Milk and milk products.

A diet which includes at least four daily servings of grain and cereal products, four or more of fruits and vegetables, two servings of dairy products, and two of the high protein foods, plus enough water, will provide adequate amounts of the essential nutrients.

Critics of our current nutritional policies challenge this statement. They claim that growing food with artificial instead of natural fertilizers and processing, preserving, and cooking food by our present methods rob it of much of its nutritional value. They believe, therefore, that present recommendations for vitamin and mineral intake grossly underestimate our real needs. They urge that we supplement our diets with a variety of substances. Their arguments, often well-intentioned, passionate, and persuasive, are unfortunately not based on much acceptable scientific data. However, these claims must not be totally dismissed by the scientific community. This is an area which deserves continued study by able scientists.

Dietary Supplements

VITAMINS

Q. Do you recommend any vitamin supplements?

A. Usually not, if the diet seems adequate. Exercise does not appear to increase our vitamin requirements substantially, except perhaps for vitamin B-1 or thiamine, which is necessary for normal carbohydrate metabolism. Thiamine is readily available in many foods, so the runner need not worry about developing thiamine deficiency.

I have no strong objection to your taking one or two multivitamin tablets as "insurance," to make certain that any hidden dietary deficiencies are remedied. I would recommend them if your diet is very low in calories, or unusual in any other way.

What does trouble me is the craze in athletic circles for ingesting huge amounts of vitamins. The purpose is not to maintain normal physiological stores of vitamins, but rather to use vitamins as drugs in hopes of enhancing athletic performance. There is no acceptable scientific evidence to support this practice, only numerous unproven individual testimonials. If there are any "benefits" to such a program, I believe they are psychological. Further, the practice may be dangerous. Don't do it.

Q. Are you also suggesting that the large doses of vitamin C, recommended for the prevention and treatment of colds, should not be taken?

A. As you probably know, this theory too is controversial. Some, but not all, studies do suggest that large doses of vitamin C may reduce the frequency and severity of the common cold. But even where such an effect has been demonstrated, it is modest at best. This continues to be an area of research interest, as is the worth of extra vitamin E, which so many people are taking. So far the evidence does not convince me that you should consume large amounts of either vitamin C or E. We have little idea what the long-term consequences of taking large amounts of these vitamins might be. Until we do, we should presume the risks might well outweigh the benefits.

Q. Do you take vitamins yourself?

A. Never, and I rarely prescribe them for my patients.

MINERAL SUPPLEMENTS

Iron   Iron deficiency is common in menstruating women. It is reasonable to correct this with small daily iron supplements. When a deficiency is present, iron is readily absorbed from the GI tract. Large doses can cause abdominal pain and constipation and are not generally necessary. Iron is better absorbed when the stomach is empty, and one tablet daily is enough if you can tolerate the iron this way. However, if you must take it with food, to avoid an upset stomach, take a couple of tablets each day. Don't become alarmed if your bowel habits change and your stools become black. Both are normal results of daily iron intake.

Salt   Fortunately the enthusiasm for salt tablets for athletes has waned. Our diets provide us with plenty of salt, and our bodies conserve it very efficiently if necessary. Much more important is our often excessive salt ingestion. Many of us consume a hundred times as much salt as we really need. This may cause high blood pressure in susceptible individuals.

I recommend that everyone use as little salt as possible. A balanced diet will supply all you need, except in the rare instance when you are performing endurance activity in hot weather when you are not yet acclimated. Even then your taste and thirst mechanisms will tell you when you need salt.

Most fresh foods are relatively low in salt content. Surprisingly, even salt water fish do not contain excessive amounts of salt. Large amounts of salt are present, however, in most processed, prepared, or "fast" foods. Avoid them.

Potassium   Potassium supplements are rarely necessary, and may be very dangerous.

Potassium is widely available in most foods, particularly fruits, vegetables, meat, and dairy products. A reasonable diet will always supply adequate amounts. However, the body cannot conserve potassium quite as efficiently as it does salt, and potassium deficits can occur, particularly if there are massive losses from the GI tract after diarrhea or vomiting.

Exercise of high intensity and long duration, regularly per-

203

formed, is said to produce chronic potassium deficiency, but I think the evidence for this is slim. Because the body has no good warning signs or symptoms to tell us when potassium is in short supply, some have recommended potassium supplements during or immediately after such exercise.

I strongly disagree. I feel you should *never take a potassium supplement during or immediately after exercise.* Potassium leaks out of muscle and blood cells into the blood plasma when you run. Very high, potentially dangerous levels of potassium in the blood can result. Simultaneously, the ability of the kidneys to excrete the potassium in the urine is reduced, because urine formation is markedly suppressed during exercise. To add a potassium supplement at this point, which would further raise blood levels of potassium, makes no sense to me at all. Instead, wait a few hours and replenish your body's potassium stores with a well-balanced meal.

Magnesium Metabolism of this important mineral has not been well studied. Magnesium deficiency probably occurs in most cases under the same conditions as potassium depletion. Like potassium, magnesium is widely available in foods. An adequate diet should correct any deficiency.

OTHER DIETARY SUPPLEMENTS

Q. Do you feel the same way about bee pollen, herbal teas, lecithin, and all the other supplements for runners that are so widely promoted?

A. Absolutely. In my opinion they are worthless. However, I suspect I must be mellowing a bit. I used to think that everyone who promoted and endorsed supplements was trying to "rip off" runners. Now I believe that many of them are just well-intentioned but grossly misinformed "believers."

The Mystique of the High Protein Diet

Q. Many coaches and trainers recommend high protein diets for their athletes. Do you disagree with this practice?

A. Most emphatically. There is no good, scientific reason why a high protein diet should be useful. Its alleged benefits are probably psychological, and in fact this diet may be harmful. I am pleased to see a growing tendency to replace not only the high protein diet, but the traditional pre-game steak, with more easily digested carbohydrates.

The body can't store extra protein. Instead, it is converted through a series of complex biochemical reactions to fat, and we derive no extra or special energy from it. The part of the protein which is not incorporated into fat must be transformed in the liver and excreted in the kidneys, a complex process which may tax the body's digestive and metabolic processes unnecessarily.

High protein diets have other disadvantages. They are often expensive, so if money is a factor, be assured that you will do better on a cheaper, high carbohydrate diet. Many high protein foods are also high in fat. Take a look at your next steak, and see how much fat it contains. High protein meals also take longer to digest, and many runners complain that they make them lethargic and interfere with normal bowel function.

Having made all these negative statements about protein, let me hasten to add that many athletes swear by their high protein diets, and are sure their strength and performance suffer grievously if they eat anything else. I would make no attempt to change them, even though I am certain their diet is not necessary for good running and fitness.

Q. How much protein do you recommend?

A. There is a growing tendency to keep protein about 25 or 30 percent of the total calorie intake. But we probably could do with considerably less. Even 50 grams daily, less than 2 ounces, of high quality protein, will supply us with the essential amino acids. Certainly 100 grams is more than enough.

Daily Caloric Intake for Runners

Q. How many calories should we eat?

A. There is, of course, no single answer to this. It will depend on your weight and the intensity of your daily exercise. If you are fat, you must reduce your calorie intake. If your weight is normal, and you are increasing your mileage, for example before a marathon, you may have to raise your calorie intake enormously, perhaps to 4000 or 5000 calories per day, to maintain your weight.

Tables 13 and 14 present two diets, one for 1500 calories, if you must lose weight with your running program, the other for 3500 calories if you are at your best weight and want to maintain

TABLE 13. *1500 Calorie Diet*

900 cal. carbohydrate = 225 gm (60% of calories)
375 cal. protein = 94 gm (25% of calories)
225 cal. fat = 24 gm (15% of calories)

BREAKFAST
1 serving of fruit or juice
2 servings of bread or cereal
1 cup skim milk
    coffee or tea if desired

LUNCH
3 ounce portion *very lean* meat, poultry without skin, or fish (water-packed if canned). Or substitute ¾ cup dry cottage cheese or 3 ounces low-fat cheese. (Read labels: Cheese should have 2 grams or less fat per ounce.)
2 servings bread or substitute
1 serving of vegetable
1 serving of fruit

MID-AFTERNOON
1 serving of fruit
1 serving of crackers or bread

DINNER
5 ounce portion *very lean* meat, skinless poultry, or fish. 1½ cups cooked dried beans or peas may be substituted
2 servings bread or "starchy" vegetables
2 servings of vegetable
1 serving of fruit

EVENING
1 cup skim milk
2 servings crackers, cereal, or bread
1 serving of fruit

TABLE 14. *3500 Calorie Diet*

2100 cal Carbohydrate = 525gm (60 percent of calories)
875 cal Protein = 218gm (25 percent of calories)
525 cal Fat = 58gm (15 percent of calories)

BREAKFAST

2 servings of fruit
2 ounces low-fat cheese (Read labels. Cheese should have 2 grams or less fat per ounce)
4 servings of bread, cereal, or bread substitute
coffee or tea, if desired

MID-MORNING

1 serving of fruit
3 servings of bread or substitute
1 cup skim milk

LUNCH

5 ounce portion of *very lean* meat, poultry without skin or fish (water-packed if canned). Or substitute 1¼ cup dry cottage cheese or 1½ cups cooked dried peas or beans
4 servings bread, "starchy vegetable," or substitute
2 servings vegetables
2 servings of fruit
1 cup skim milk

MID-AFTERNOON

2 ounce portion low fat cheese or ½ c. dry cottage cheese
4 servings bread or substitute
1 serving of fruit

DINNER

6 ounce portion of *very lean* meat, poultry without skin or fish
5 servings of bread, "starchy vegetable," or other substitute
3 servings of vegetables
2 servings of fruit
1 cup skim milk

EVENING

3 ounces very lean meat, poultry, fish or low fat cheese or ¾ cup cottage cheese
4 servings bread or substitute
1 serving fruit
1 cup skim milk

Portion sizes for fruit, bread, and "starchy vegetables" are listed below. The portion size listed is for one "serving."

FRUIT and FRUIT JUICES (fresh or canned without sugar)

Apple, 1 small	Grapefruit, ½	Raisins, 2 Tbsp.
Applesauce, ½ cup	Grapes, 12	Watermelon, 1 cup
Banana, ½ small	Honeydew melon, ⅛	

TABLE 14, cont.

Blackberries, ½ cup	Orange, 1	
Raspberries, ½ cup	Peach, 1	Grapefruit juice, ½ cup
Strawberries, ¾ cup	Pear, 1	Orange juice, ½ cup
Blueberries, ½ cup	Pineapple, ½ cup	Apple juice or cider, ⅓ cup
Cantaloupe, ¼	Plums, 2	Grape juice, ¼ cup
Cherries, 10	Prunes, 2	Prune juice, ¼ cup

BREADS, CEREALS, and STARCHY VEGETABLES

Bread, 1 slice	*Cereal, cooked ½ cup	Winter squash, ½ cup
English muffin, ½	*Cereal, dry, ¾ cup	Lima beans, cooked, ½ cup
Bagel, ½	Cooked rice, ½ cup	Baked beans, ¼ cup
Graham crackers, 2	Cooked spaghetti or	Corn, ⅓ cup
Saltines, 6	macaroni, ½ cup	Mashed potatoes, ½ cup
Soda crackers, 4	Peas, ½ cup	Sweet potatoes, ¼ cup
Round, thin crackers, 6		Whole potato, 1 small

*Avoid cereals processed with sugar

Avoid all added fats. These include butter, margarine, cream, salad oils, mayonnaise, and fats added during cooking. Eliminate egg yolks, cheese containing over 2% butterfat, and all medium fat and high fat meats. These included bacon, sausage, luncheon meats, frankfurters, duck, goose, liver, and meat canned or frozen in gravy or sauce.

Avoid refined carbohydrates (as in table sugar, honey, soft drinks, cookies, cake, candy, pastry, and ice cream) and alcoholic beverages which contribute to excess calories and to subsequent weight gain.

it despite a vigorous daily running program. These diets contain what I would consider a reasonable balance of carbohydrate (60 percent), protein (25 percent), and fat (15 percent).

If you want to lower your fat intake further, perhaps to 5 to 10 percent, you will be approaching the type of diet recommended by Pritikin.

Other Special Diets

HIGH FIBER

Q. Do you recommend a high fiber diet? We understand that this kind of diet may help prevent a number of medical problems.

A. A high fiber diet makes sense. The fiber, or roughage, is chiefly made up of complex carbohydrates which the intestine cannot metabolize, and which are not absorbed. This adds bulk to the stools and is a good way to prevent constipation. A high fiber diet is filling without excessive calories. Because it emphasizes grains, vegetables, and fruits, it is a healthy diet, low in fat and high in carbohydrate. Some recent reports suggest that high fiber diets may also confer other health benefits such as reduced chances of bowel cancer and diverticulitis.

There are also disadvantages. Remember that an important ingredient of a "good diet" is that you are comfortable with it. Many who try high fiber diets suffer terribly from cramps, gas, and diarrhea. If you switch to a high fiber diet, do so gradually, and never just before an important race.

LOW SALT

When severe high blood pressure is present, a low salt diet is often recommended. Strict adherence to this type of diet may considerably reduce the amount of drugs necessary to treat the high pressure. In Table 15 is a list of foods high in salt. It is probably a good idea for everyone to avoid them, not only those with high blood pressure.

DIABETIC

Most diabetics require a special diet. Once their caloric needs are carefully defined, including the estimated caloric cost of their running, the proper percentage of carbohydrate, protein, and fat can be estimated. The diabetic should not eat simple sugars, since he cannot produce the insulin required to metabolize the sugar properly. We used to believe that diabetics should not eat complex carbohydrates either, and placed them on diets which were relatively high in protein and fat, and low in all types of carbohydrates. This may have been a serious error. High fat intakes may be even more likely to cause hardening of the arteries in diabetics than in the normal population. Diabetics are better off with a diet fairly high in complex carbohydrates, and low in fat. They generally tolerate this diet very well.

TABLE 15. *Foods with High Salt Content*

Celery salt	Catsup	Meat tenderizers
Garlic salt	Chili sauce	Soy sauce
Onion salt	Meat and vegetable	Worcestershire sauce
Commercial bouillon	extracts	Olives, pickles, relish
Canned or packaged	Barbecue sauces	Cooking wine (salt has
soups	Meat sauces	been added)

Salty or smoked meat (bacon, bologna, chipped or corned beef, frankfurters, ham, meats koshered by salting, luncheon meats, salt pork, sausage, smoked tongue).

Salty or smoked fish (anchovies, caviar, salted cod, herring, sardines, etc.).

Processed cheese or cheese spreads unless low sodium dietetic; salty cheese such as Roquefort or blue cheese.

Regular peanut butter.

Sauerkraut, pickles, or other vegetables prepared in brine.

Bread and rolls with salt topping, salted popcorn, potato chips, corn chips, pretzels, etc. Salted nuts, party spreads, dips, and other heavily salted snack foods.

Alcohol

Q. Will alcohol affect our running program and fitness?

A. I discussed this briefly earlier (page 39). There is no good evidence that moderate amounts of any type of alcohol do much harm, and in fact, may favor the production of high density lipoproteins, which may protect against atherosclerosis (pp. 39–41). But also remember that alcohol, except for beer, is a source of empty calories. It is hard to lose much weight if you drink a lot of alcohol, and if it constitutes too high a percentage of your daily calorie intake, you may develop vitamin and mineral deficiencies.

Larger quantities of alcohol, beyond four or five ounces a day, may significantly impair the function of even the normal heart, or may cause irregularities of the heart's rhythm. I would strongly advise against exercise for several hours after you have ingested much alcohol of any type. Alcohol also blurs sensory perception and probably increases the chance of injury from running.

Q. Beer has been recommended as an ideal drink for runners. Do you agree?

A. Beer does contain some minerals and complex carbohydrates; it is thus not merely a source of empty calories. It seems to be a perfectly satisfactory way to replenish lost fluid, minerals, and calories after exercise. Whether it may be equally useful during exercise, as some have stated, is another question. Each time I try to drink some when I am running, I develop mild heartburn. I like beer, but save it for after I run.

Summary

Q. Will you summarize your dietary recommendations?

A. Your diet should be high in complex carbohydrate, relatively low in protein, and very low in fat.

Calorie intake must be adjusted to your weight and the intensity of your running program.

Salt intake should be low. Avoid the salt shaker and processed foods.

Menstruating women should take extra iron. Vitamin supplements are probably not necessary, but one or two multivitamin tablets will not do any harm, and may help if you are on a special diet. All other supplements are unnecessary.

Avoid additives, artificial sweeteners, for example. How dangerous they may be is uncertain, but until the evidence is clearer, it would seem prudent not to use them.

A little alcohol will probably not hurt you.

Consume a diet that is comfortable for you. Make it high in fiber if you can.

Be wary of most of what you read about nutrition and diets. These remain among the most controversial, least scientific areas of biology and medicine.

Q. Does that warning also apply to what you have just said in this chapter?

A. Absolutely.

Q. One final question. Do runners need a special diet?

A. No.

CHAPTER 10

Running Beyond Fitness

THIS CHAPTER is particularly for those of you who have been "hooked." Running is now an important part of your daily life; you miss it if you skip a day or two. You are already running enough, perhaps 18 or 20 miles each week, to derive major health benefits. Yet you are considering running more. Why?

For most runners, the answer is very simple. They enjoy the experience of running itself. It has become not just painful payment for a healthy body, but an important, enjoyable experience in its own right. I have watched a number of runners reach this stage almost unconsciously. In fact, I was one of them. It often happens when the runner breaks through the 3 or 4 mile daily barrier. The first couple of miles may still be drudgery, to be endured not enjoyed. But then the feelings change. The aches disappear, rhythm develops, and running becomes fun. I am not sure how this happens, but it seems so common that there must be some important physiological mechanism behind it.

Running as a Positive Addiction

When you reach this point be careful. You may become addicted. Running has been described as a "positive addiction". Runners jokingly refer to their daily run as getting their "fix." If they don't run, they develop "withdrawal" symptoms. They become grouchy, tense, and restless. They often feel fat and sloppy even if they have not gained an ounce. They must run longer and harder to develop the "good feelings" running regularly gives them. At this point there is a great temptation to increase mileage too fast. Injuries are common. Be careful. Run enough to enjoy it, but don't push too hard.

There are other good reasons for going "beyond fitness." You may want to run in races. You may not be consumed by the need to win, but you certainly don't want to embarrass yourself by not finishing or running slower than you need to. So you intensify your training as you approach the race. I have found that pointing to a race every few months is the best way to sustain a high intensity running program.

Better health is another reason some runners increase their mileage.

Q. But you said earlier (page 42) that running 18 to 21 miles each week seemed to confer maximum health benefits. Why run further?

A. Because a lot of runners firmly believe that a marathoner's training program confers even more protection, if not complete immunity, from heart attacks and other disease caused by atherosclerosis.

Q. Do you?

A. I think so. Certainly the immunity is not complete. Enough carefully documented cases of heart attacks, and deaths caused by heart attacks, have been described in marathoners to disprove that part of the theory. But I suspect that more intensive training, provided you are healthy to begin with, does provide further health benefits.

I have a final, personal reason for regularly running long weekly mileage. I love to eat, and my intensive running program lets me eat virtually anything I want, at times in rather gluttonous quantities.

But enough of the reasons for running "beyond fitness." We should find out how to do it.

General Guidelines

Q. What are your general recommendations for training beyond fitness?

A. The key is to proceed slowly, and define your goals very early. Make certain your timetable allows enough leeway for slowing down if you are injured. *You must not feel rushed.* You are certain to hurt yourself if you push too hard.

The details of your program will depend on your particular goal. Soon we will discuss how to prepare for a marathon, but before that there are some general rules to follow if you want to go beyond your steady 18 to 20 miles each week and prepare for a road race.

1. *The older you are, the more gradually you must increase your mileage base, and the longer it will take you to prepare for a race.* I have watched youngsters finish a marathon, wobbly and agonized to be sure, who prepared by running just a few miles weekly for a month or two. This would be impossible for most of us. Don't even consider it.
2. *For several weeks before the race, your daily mileage should average at least one-third the race distance.* For example, if you are preparing for a 10-mile race, you should run at least 3 or 4 miles daily if you want to finish. If you are preparing for a marathon, you should average about 9 miles a day for several weeks. Of course, if you are seeking peak performance, your training should be much more intense.
3. *As your mileage increases, you must also increase your stretching–strengthening program.* Be sure to do it at least twice daily.
4. *Don't run if you are hurt.* Cut back or even stop for a day or two. If you don't, you risk making the injury much worse, and disrupting your whole training program.

Q. Do you recommend varying the amount you run each day, or should it be kept constant?

A. If you are preparing for a race, it is probably better to alternate hard and easy days, while also taking one long run each week.

But if you feel more comfortable with steady daily mileage, do it that way. The fastest marathon I ever ran came after a training program based on constant daily mileage. Later I switched to a hard–easy program, but I am not sure this change has really helped.

Training for a Marathon: The Six-Month Program

Perhaps it will be easier to understand a race training program if we discuss preparing for a marathon. Whole books have been devoted to this subject, but it really isn't very complicated.

First, give yourself enough time. If this is your first marathon, and if you are starting from a base of 15 to 20 miles per week, you will probably need six months for adequate preparation. Take even longer if you are older. I'm sure that some of you might get away with a shorter training period, but six months leaves plenty of time to recover from minor injuries, and to increase your weekly mileage slowly and safely.

Second, clearly define your personal goals. Do you just want to finish? Then perhaps 30 to 50 miles a week for two or three months before the race is enough, provided you run slowly and don't push yourself. On the other hand, if you really want to do your best, you should aim for 80 to 100 miles per week or more. Good marathoners regularly average well over 100 miles per week during peak training.

As a compromise, let's devise a program aiming for peak training mileage of 60 miles per week. This program should allow you to finish with a respectable time, but it is not so intense that you are likely to hurt yourself.

Divide the six-month program into two three-month periods. The first three months should be devoted to advancing slowly to your maximum training mileage. The second three months are devoted to maintaining this mileage base, adding speed work, and tapering toward the end of the program.

THE FIRST THREE MONTHS: REACHING YOUR MILEAGE GOALS

Assuming you start from a base of 20 miles per week, you have three months (thirteen weeks) to add 40 miles, so that you will

reach your weekly mileage goal of 60 miles. This means that you must add about 3 miles per week.

Q. Does it matter how we add the 3 miles each week?

A. Yes it does. Do not add the 3 miles to one day's program. Instead, spread them out, preferably by adding 1 mile to each of three separate days.

Q. Should we include a long weekly run?

A. In most cases, *yes.* A weekly long run is very helpful psychologically because it provides a concrete example of real progress. You will also probably do better if you take at least one day off each week, generally after your long run.

   At the end of your first four weeks of training, you should be running 32 miles weekly (20 miles base, plus 3 added miles each week for four weeks). This might be divided conveniently in the following way:

Sunday	rest
Monday	6 miles
Tuesday	4 miles
Wednesday	6 miles
Thursday	4 miles
Friday	4 miles
Saturday	8 miles at slower pace

   At the conclusion of the second month of training, or about nine weeks after you started, you should be up to about 47 miles per week, perhaps divided as follows:

Sunday	rest
Monday	9 miles
Tuesday	6 miles at a faster pace
Wednesday	9 miles
Thursday	6 miles at a faster pace
Friday	5 miles
Saturday	12 miles at a slower pace

   At this point the average time you spend running is more than an hour. You should be in excellent condition, and if you have no injuries, you might consider beginning an interval or speed program. Such a program may significantly help your over-all speed during the race. Equally important, it will help to break the monotony of your daily one-speed workouts. But remember that speed work must not interfere with the regular increase in your mileage base, which at this stage is still more important than speed.

After three months, you will have reached your peak of 60 miles each week, perhaps divided as follows:

Sunday	rest
Monday	12 miles
Tuesday	8 miles with some speed work
Wednesday	12 miles
Thursday	8 miles with some speed work
Friday	5 miles with speed work
Saturday	15 miles

THE SECOND THREE MONTHS: MAINTAINING YOUR FITNESS AND TAPERING

You should continue this intensity of training for the next two months. If you are comfortable, you might want to increase your speed a little, or even increase your mileage. But try to curb your enthusiasm. Distance is still more important for you than speed.

During the fifth month, try to make one change. Gradually increase the length of your weekly long run. If this is your first marathon, I would strongly recommend at least two 20-mile runs before the race. If you know you can run 20 miles without collaps-ing, you will be much more confident on the day of the race that you can run 26 miles. You will also be better able to pace yourself.

During the sixth month, there is a tendency among novice runners to push too hard. They are not confident that they have achieved satisfactory conditioning. Although better runners usu-ally sustain high mileage nearly to the end, the rest of us should cut down our weekly mileage by perhaps 20 to 30 percent. Con-tinue the long weekly run, but take more days off if you want to. Place more emphasis on alternating hard and easy days. You may want to split your daily mileage into two shorter sessions, but don't split your weekly long runs.

The Week Before the Race   Now it's time to make some changes. High intensity training is no longer necessary; your muscles are now well conditioned and are not going to be changed much by frantic last-minute training. Rest and let your minor injuries heal. You should ready yourself psychologically. Individual needs determine what you should do. I have found the following program helpful.

Most races take place on Sundays. About a week before, the Saturday or Sunday before the race, take your last weekly long run. Rest on Monday. Run a few easy miles on Tuesday, Wednesday, and Thursday. Just how far depends on how you feel. But don't do any speed work. Friday and Saturday it is probably best not to run at all. If you must run, keep the mileage short and easy. Stretch twice each day whether you run or not.

I find that this reduced program the last week restores me psychologically as well as physically, and I begin to look forward to the race.

Figure 36 summarizes in graphic form the weekly mileage to be attained during the six-month training program.

Q.   Several authorities have stated that gradually increasing the time you run, rather than your absolute mileage, is a better way to prepare. They say this technique reduces the emphasis on speed, and permits you to run as slowly as you like. What do you think?

A.   I have tried training both ways and asked many beginning runners which method they preferred. The great majority feel they do better by increasing their mileage rather than their time. Most could not give a specific reason for their choice, but they felt more comfortable training this way. If you choose to use time as your guide, settle on an average speed, 9 or 10 miles per minute for example, and convert my mileage recommendations per day to minutes per run.

CARBOHYDRATE LOADING

Q.   We have heard a lot about dietary changes before a race, particularly carbohydrate loading. What do you recommend?

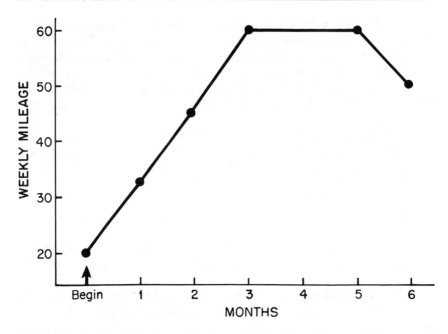

FIGURE 36. *Weekly mileage during a six-month training period.*

A.   There is some scientific evidence to support carbohydrate loading. The total amount of aerobic work that could be performed by trained athletes seemed to increase if diets high in carbohydrates were consumed for a few days prior to their testing. The total amount of glycogen crammed into the exercising muscles could be doubled or tripled by carbohydrate loading. This added muscle glycogen is probably the reason for the enhanced performance.

   Most, but by no means all, of our best marathoners practice some type of carbohydrate loading. I think it works, and urge each of you to try it. But don't decide to do it for the first time the week before your first marathon. Try it at least once during training to make sure you can tolerate the fairly radical change in diet.

   There is certainly no agreement about the best way to carbohydrate load. There is room for considerable variation. Many runners simply increase their daily carbohydrate intake without making other dietary changes. Others embark on a more complex program.

220

The program begins a week before the race with the last long run on Sunday. This is called the _depletion run_ because it uses all the carbohydrates stored in the exercising muscles. For the next three days—Monday, Tuesday, and Wednesday—muscle glycogen concentration is kept low by consuming a high protein, low carbohydrate diet. This diet is thought to increase the avidity of the muscle cells for carbohydrate. During the next three days—Thursday, Friday, and Saturday—the diet is changed radically. Protein is reduced as low as possible, and huge amounts of complex carbohydrates are consumed to pack the carbohydrate-starved muscle cells with glycogen. Some runners carbohydrate load right through breakfast on the day of the race. Others stop the night before, and consume a very light breakfast.

I tried this method a couple of times and did not like it at all. During the three days of the high protein, low carbohydrate intake I became lethargic, and lost a couple of pounds. When I then carbohydrate loaded for the next three days, I quickly gained back the lost pounds plus five more, and my bowels rebelled.

Q. Why did you gain so much weight?

A. My family is certain it was due to sheer gluttony, but I doubt this. When you increase your glycogen stores, you must store large quantities of water also. The extra fluid is responsible for much of the weight gain. This is just the reverse of what happens when you start a low carbohydrate diet to lose weight. Most of the early weight loss is due to fluid loss as glycogen is depleted, not to loss of fat.

I prefer a less radical change in diet before a race. During the week before, I try to cut my protein intake in half, and replace these calories with added complex carbohydrate. A couple of days before the race I indulge all my fancies and eat as much carbohydrate as I like.

Q. Has this program helped you run better?

A. I think it has, but so many other factors are involved in determining performance that it is hard to be sure. The most important factor, of course, is the quality of the training, but carbohydrate loading probably does help a little. The extra muscle glycogen it provides also may reduce chances of developing the severe muscle pain and weakness which so commonly afflict marathoners in later stages of a race.

THE WALL

Q. Is this what is meant by "the wall"?

A. Precisely. We now believe that "hitting the wall" occurs when muscles are depleted of glycogen. Even though adequate supplies of fatty acids are available, the glycogen-depleted muscle cells cannot use them. The "wall" is most commonly encountered at 15 to 20 miles.

   The well-trained runner is also less likely to "hit the wall," because he uses fatty acids for muscular work better throughout the race, leaving more muscle glycogen for the last few miles.

THE DAY OF THE RACE

Q. What should we eat the day of the race?

A. Here again there is tremendous variation. Each of you will have to find out what suits you best. Some runners don't eat at all, and only drink fluids. I prefer a modest breakfast of easily digested carbohydrates at least three or four hours before the race. Bread and jelly with some fruit suits me fine. I finish with a couple of cups of black coffee, and eat no more until after the race. If it is hot, I continue to drink water up to an hour before the race. This still leaves time to urinate before the start.

   You should eat no sugar or simple carbohydrate during the last couple of hours. There is some evidence that the surge of insulin production that sugar causes interferes with the muscle's ability to use fatty acids. However, simple sugar consumed a few minutes before the race may improve performance. By the time this sugar is absorbed from the intestine into the bloodstream, you will already be running. Exercise shuts down insulin production somewhat, keeping the blood sugar levels higher and making more available for the muscles and brain. But I would again caution you not to try this trick for the first time just before an important race. The sugar may upset your stomach and ruin rather than help your performance. You should try it at least once before one of your weekly long runs.

If it's hot, drink a couple of cups of water just before the race begins. Once you start running, as we have seen, blood flow to the kidneys falls precipitously, and the amount of urine produced is much reduced. This water taken just before you start will not be lost in the urine, but will serve to replenish the water you lose in your sweat.

Q. What kind of warm-up program do you recommend before the race?

A. This depends on how fast you plan to run. Better runners warm up extensively. In addition to vigorous stretching, which we all should do, many of them run a couple of miles very slowly. This helps loosen their muscles and prevent muscle pulls which might occur during the early fast pace. Also a period of slow running seems to prime the circulatory system. Blood flow to the exercising muscles is increased and oxygen transport is enhanced. Warmed up muscles seem to utilize fatty acids more efficiently, and are better prepared for a fast early pace.

However, I do not recommend this program for most of you. I do stretch extensively before the race, but I do not run at all. This would only place an unnecessary, extra burden on my musculoskeletal system. Instead I use the first couple of miles of the race as my warm-up period. I'm not concerned about muscle pulls because I am not starting at a fast pace.

Q. Does coffee before the race help?

A. Many runners think that one or two cups an hour or two before the race improves performance. This opinion is based on some recent evidence that caffeine in coffee stimulates epinephrine (adrenalin) production by the nervous system, which in turn speeds the breakdown of fats into fatty acids. This is supposed to supply an extra fuel source for the muscles.

Even if this is true, I'm not sure it's necessary. Most runners are so excited before the race they already are producing large amounts of epinephrine, all they can possibly need. I drink coffee several hours before a race because I like it, not because I think it will do much for my performance.

Q. What other recommendations do you have for us before the race?

A. Safety pins to attach your number aren't always supplied, so I pin four of them to my shirt when I dress for the race. If you can, bring extras, since you will almost certainly find runners who have forgotten theirs.

I also bring some petroleum jelly along. Just before the race begins I apply it to areas which may get irritated, for example the inner thighs and nipples. Some runners also apply it generously to their toes and feet to prevent blisters.

I also carry a small face towel and a plastic straw. I cannot drink comfortably from a cup while I am moving. I either gag or swallow too much air with it. The straw lets me sip water slowly without stopping. The face cloth serves a dual purpose. While it's dry it keeps my glasses clean and my eyes free from irritating sweat. Once it gets wet, I use it to soak up water to cool myself with.

I also pack at least one towel and some warm clothing and make certain they are readily available after the race.

DURING THE RACE

Q. What should we drink during the race itself?

A. This depends on the temperature and humidity. The hotter the temperature and more humid the air, the more water you should drink. Take a couple of cups every 2 or 3 miles. Drink early, before you are thirsty. Your thirst sensation lags well behind your fluid needs. By the time you feel thirsty you may be seriously dry. Water consumed late in the race is not as important. Much of it will probably not be absorbed while you are still running.

Water has never caused me any trouble during a race. It is the only fluid I drink. Some runners prefer one of the various commercial sugar and electrolyte drinks. But I don't like their taste, and I doubt they help much during the race anyway. The sugar concentration of most of them is too high, and this may slow their absorption from the intestine into the blood, and also may upset the stomach, as I have mentioned. So if you do try them, dilute them with equal parts of water, and never use them for the first time during a race. Experiment during one of your long training runs. Some runners swear by them, but I think water is the only fluid a well-conditioned runner requires during a race.

Q. Any other suggestions?

A. Don't give in to the temptation to start the race too fast. Your epinephrine is flowing and you are anxious to get going. But the combination of a fast early pace and an inadequate warm-up can be disastrous. I have witnessed this problem in several of my friends who are not experienced runners. Even though they have run 20 miles or more comfortably just a week or two before, after 5 or 10 miles of the race, they are aching and tired. Some have to drop out; at best they finish with a disappointing time. This happens because their fast early pace reduces their capacity to use fatty acids as energy, or they may actually exceed their aerobic capacity and begin to accumulate lactic acid.

If this is your first marathon, forget about your time. Don't let anything lessen your chances of finishing. Start at the back of the crowd with the other slower runners, and make certain you run the first 2 or 3 miles slowly, certainly no faster than your planned average pace per mile for the whole race. At the 3 or 4 mile mark, the crowd of runners will have thinned and you will be able to establish your own rhythm and pace. Run with a friend or find someone whose pace is the same as yours. Good runners may be able to concentrate on race tactics, but the rest of us need companionship to help us cope with the enormous demands we are making on our bodies and our minds.

Each of you will have unique problems during the race. For me, the first 10 miles are easy. I am used to that distance and am pumped up by the excitement of the race and the crowds. But I always have problems between 10 and 15 miles. I am tired and the finish seems far away. My legs are so heavy I am certain I will soon be forced to drop out. I must really push myself at this point. At about 15 miles, the load lightens a bit. I am more than half way there, and it's almost as if I can see the finish line. I have never really "hit the wall," but at 18 or 19 miles, I do get a little low, and once more must push myself to keep moving. Once I get beyond 20 miles, the end is really in sight. I know by then I will finish even if I must walk the last few miles.

AFTER THE RACE

Q. Are there any special precautions to take after the race?

A. Make sure warm clothing is available. Unless it is very hot, you are likely to feel chilled once you stop running. Most good marathons have adequate medical facilities at the finish. If you don't feel well, don't be bashful. Ask for medical help. Unfortunately, unless you are a very early finisher, the medical facilities are likely to be jammed. It will help to have a family member or friend waiting for you to make sure that you are physically and psychologically intact. It is also important to start drinking again. Water is still the best drink, but some prefer beer, tea, or soda.

Some authorities recommend lying down with your legs elevated immediately after you finish. This may reduce your postrace muscle stiffness and soreness by draining away the toxic substances that build up in your muscles during the race. I prefer to head for a hot shower instead.

Most runners aren't ready to eat heavily for at least an hour or two after the race. If you must travel a long distance by car, have someone else drive. If you are staying overnight in the area, pack some aspirin or stronger painkiller to help you sleep. Even a sleeping pill may be necessary the first night.

Don't schedule yourself too heavily for the following few days. You will very likely be stiff and sore, and have to move slowly. You also should have a brief respite during which you can fully savor your accomplishment.

What Next? Keeping in Shape

Q. How soon can we begin to run again after the race?

A. It's distressing how quickly fitness can be lost after a marathon if you stop running. I understand why many of you do not want to lose it. If you have done well, you will probably be so "high" that you will immediately plan for your next race. But even if you are not too stiff and sore, rest a couple of days. Then if you feel like running, do what pleases you.

Some runners keep in marathon shape year round. They may compete as often as once a month. Their secret is not to push hard in every race. Some of the marathons are run as training races. You might consider doing the same. After all, if you can handle a weekly training run of 20 miles during your peak training, you should be able to run 26 miles every few weeks if you don't push too hard.

This was vividly demonstrated to me after my second marathon. My training had been inadequate, and I feared that I might not be able to finish. At the starting line, I silently vowed that my only goal would be to finish, no matter how long it took me. Four hours later, when I finally crossed the finish line, still running easily, I felt quite well. After my first marathon, when I had pushed myself very hard, I walked uncomfortably for several days. The day after the second marathon I felt nearly normal. I resisted the urge to run then, but the next day I jogged an easy 7 miles and was ready to go again. I am sure I could have run another slow-paced marathon a couple of weeks later. In the fall of 1979 I proved it by running two marathons only two weeks apart. The key was that I did not push too hard in either of them.

However, most of you, I suspect, will want to lower your training intensity, for a while at least, after your first marathon. How can you do this and still maintain a reasonable level of fitness?

I have found that this is most easily accomplished by taking at least one long run each week. Now, between marathons, no matter how little I have run the rest of the week, I make certain that I run at least 10 miles once each week. With this regimen, I find it much easier to increase my mileage when I resume vigorous training again.

Once you have finished your first marathon, the major physical and psychological hurdles have been leaped. You have learned an enormous amount about your body and are probably surprised how much work it can tolerate. If you are planning to run in another marathon, prepare to take some chances. Add more speed work during your training and decide early on a time to aim for. Try not only to finish, but to do it in your best time. You may be surprised how fast you really are.

CHAPTER 11

Does Gender Make a Difference?

Q. WHOLE BOOKS have been devoted to women's running. Are the problems of women runners really so different?

A. The similarities are far greater than the differences, and virtually everything I have said thus far applies equally to women and men. But there are some differences which are worth discussing. Many of these are caused by the sex hormones, estrogens and progesterone in women, testosterone in men. Muscle strength and bone density, pelvic and hip structure, and the menstrual cycle are examples of important characteristics that can effect women's running.

Testosterone is required for the development of muscle bulk and strength. Because they have minimal amounts of testosterone, women will never perform as well as men in athletics that depend on strength, such as weight lifting. But strength is less important for endurance activities. In fact, some authorities believe that properly trained women are uniquely suited for endurance activities such as long distance running. They point to the fact that women's performances have improved far more rapidly than those of men in the last decade. Women marathoners, for example, are now running faster than the best men did 20 years ago. These writers feel that the major reason women have not performed even better is chiefly cultural. Young girls have not received the support of family and friends, and the help of competent trainers and coaches that is readily available to talented young men. Now that these cultural barriers are crumbling, they predict parity and perhaps even superiority for women.

Q. Why would they predict that women might perform endurance activity better than men?

A. Because of differences in body composition. Women have a higher proportion of body fat, about 25 percent at normal body weight, compared to 12 to 15 percent for men. Even very lean, world class female distance runners have significantly more fat than male runners.

Much of this fat is deposited under the skin, and may act as insulation to prevent heat loss when it is cold. Perhaps this explains why women tolerate long periods of swimming in cold water so well.

Some have theorized that this extra fat tissue also provides women with a better energy source for endurance exercise. But this is controversial. Recent evidence suggests that even the thinnest of us have plenty of fat available as a potential source of energy for muscular work (see page 11). However, muscles depleted of glycogen cannot use this fat for energy no matter how much is available. Thus, extra fat may be a liability rather than an asset in distance running. If it can't be burned, the fat becomes merely weight that must be carried around.

One reason that men have a relatively lower percentage of body fat is that their bones and muscles are much heavier than those of women and hence comprise a larger part of their total body weight. This may help in activities requiring strength, but much of it also becomes excess baggage when they run.

Q. What are the other differences between men and women that may affect their running?

A. Women have relatively smaller hearts, but I doubt that this has much physiological significance.

Women also appear to sweat less, and yet they do not seem more prone to developing problems during hot weather running. Perhaps they have better heat control mechanisms, or possibly their smaller muscles generate less heat.

Many younger women are anemic, often due to blood loss

during normal menstruation. Anemia or low red blood cell counts reduce the oxygen-carrying capacity of the blood, and hence the amount of oxygen that can go to the muscles. Even when there is ample replacement of iron and the other substances necessary for red blood cell production, women's blood counts tend to remain on the low side.

Q.   Earlier you recommended iron supplements for women who are still menstruating (page 211). Do women require any other dietary supplements?

A.   Not if they are consuming a reasonably well balanced diet. However, women seem to diet more than men, so it is hard to be certain they are obtaining the proper nutrients. To be sure about this, vitamin supplements seem reasonable.

Another important difference, whether they run or not, is that women live longer, chiefly because they are less susceptible to atherosclerosis, as mentioned in Chapter 3. Unlike many men who begin to run to prevent heart attacks and preserve their health, women have less compelling need to run purely for health reasons.

Special Recommendations for Women

Q.   Do you have any special advice for the woman who is just beginning?

A.   Older women who are not accustomed to exercise must be particularly careful in beginning a running program. Years of relative inactivity may have weakened their musculo-skeletal systems. Women's bones are less dense, and hence more likely to develop stress fractures. To avoid these, they must wear a very well-cushioned training shoe. Their Achilles tendons may be shortened by years of wearing high heels. To prevent injury, women should pay special attention to the stretching exercises to lengthen the Achilles tendon (page 100). An extra heel lift may also help. Women are said to be less susceptible to heel injuries, however, because they have extra fat tissue in the heel pads. They also seem to be less prone to muscle pulls.

The Hips and Pelvis

Women's hips and pelvis are generally broader than men's—excellent for child bearing, but not so good for running. They are particularly susceptible to knee injuries for this reason.

Q. Why should broad hips cause knee injuries?

A. The knee joint is designed to move the lower leg back and forth. It functions best when the femur, the large, strong bone which forms part of both the hip and knee joints, makes a fairly straight line with the joint itself (Figure 37A). If the hips are wide, the femur joins the knee joint at an angle, and joint motion can be altered significantly (Figure 37B). The patella or kneecap also

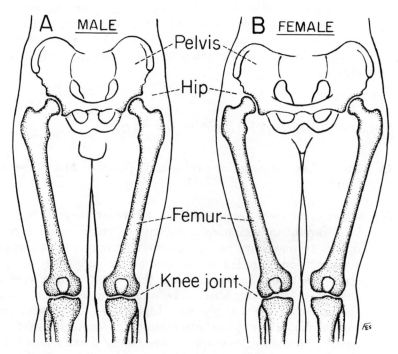

FIGURE 37. *The hip.* *The female pelvis is wider and broader, causing the femur to join the knee joint at a greater angle, interfering with normal knee joint motion and kneecap function.*

may be pulled to one side and stops gliding smoothly in its groove over the joint. Its under surface may become roughened and irritated, causing pain and even swelling of the knee. This is probably the most common of the various causes of "runner's knee" (page 157) in women.

Women runners can help prevent this problem by a vigorous strengthening program for the quadriceps (page 106), the large muscle which runs over the front of the patella and inserts just below it. Equally important, they may need an insert or orthotic under the inner arch of their foot (page 149) to reduce the angulation, in turn reducing the stress on the knee each time the foot strikes the ground.

Health Benefits

VARICOSE VEINS

In addition to the development of cardiovascular fitness, as described in Chapter 2, women may derive other benefits from running. If running is started early enough in life, it may retard the development of varicose veins, for example.

Q. How does running do this?

A. We really aren't certain, but we do know that physical inactivity seems to be related to their appearance. They are a curse of women in affluent western societies. Men seem less commonly afflicted.

Perhaps running works simply because runners lose weight. Or the reason may be more complicated, related to a unique situation present only in the leg veins.

The leg veins' function, like that of veins everywhere else, is to return blood to the heart. But, unlike veins elsewhere, the leg veins must perform this function much of the time against the pull of gravity. To accomplish this task requires the help of the leg muscles. Each time these muscles contract, they squeeze or constrict the veins and pump the blood upwards toward the heart. The leg veins contain a series of valves which prevent the blood from dropping back each time the muscles relax. Varicose veins occur when the valves of the main veins of the legs become incompetent and leaky and the veins themselves enlarge. This process is probably retarded by an effective muscle pumping action. Age and inactivity weaken the pumping effect. Running almost certainly strengthens it considerably and may in this way slow the formation of varicose veins.

In addition to the aesthetic benefits, there is a real health benefit to avoiding varicose veins. Women with varicose veins are more likely to develop phlebitis or inflammation of the veins, as well as ankle swelling and ulcers of the leg.

MUSCLES

Q.   Can running cause bulging leg muscles?

A.   On the contrary, just the opposite happens. Bulging muscles are usually the result of isometric activity and high testosterone levels. Women's legs, like the rest of the body, tend to become trimmer due to exercise and weight loss.

Running and the Menstrual Cycle

Q.   How does running affect the menstrual cycle?

A.   This seems to vary tremendously. Some women note no change. Others develop irregular or scanty periods. In some, periods stop completely for months. Early in training, these changes seem related to weight loss. A similar phenomenon frequently happens in women who start very stringent diets. Later, high intensity training, even without further weight loss, may provoke these changes. Why this happens is unclear. Perhaps cessation of periods is related to reduction in the proportion of body fat below a critical level.

Q.   Is this something to worry about?

A.   Apparently not. When training intensity is reduced, or weight loss stops, normal periods usually return. Patients who remain understandably concerned about normal menstrual function should cut back their training until their periods begin. Ordinarily this is convincing evidence that they are again functioning normally, and that this is not a serious problem.

Q. Can you become pregnant if your periods have stopped during your running program?

A. It is possible, but probably much less likely. If you want to avoid pregnancy, however, I would not rely on this as your sole method of prevention. On the other hand, if you want to become pregnant, you will probably improve your chances by reducing your exercise until your periods return.

Q. How else are the menstrual periods changed?

A. Many women find they are less bothered by the annoying symptoms which sometimes occur just prior to and during the first couple of days of their periods. They may have fewer cramps and backaches, accumulate less fluid, and feel less bloated. Some just "feel better" in a general way. But these changes are hardly universal. Many women feel no different. Others remain so uncomfortable that they must stop running completely for a few days.

Q. Is it safe to run during days you bleed heavily?

A. Absolutely. You may need extra protection, but there is certainly no danger to your health.

Q. If you run while you are menstruating, will your performance suffer?

A. World records have allegedly been set by women running while they are menstruating. However, most of the women I have questioned about this do not feel quite so fit or strong for a couple of days after their period begins. Many reduce their running pace a little during this time.

Pregnancy

Q. Is it safe to run when you are pregnant?

A. Apparently it is, if you have been running regularly before you became pregnant. *However, it might be risky to begin or intensify your running program once you are pregnant.*

Because this is such an individual matter, you must consult your obstetrician. Many obstetricians now tend to be less reluctant to permit intensive exercise, like running, during pregnancy, and they may even enthusiastically encourage it, if there is no obvious contra-indication such as a history of miscarriage or bleeding. They realize that exercise during pregnancy helps prevent excessive weight gain and makes many of their patients feel better. Others, however, remain unalterably opposed to running because they think it increases the chances of miscarriage.

Q. If you are running during pregnancy, when should you stop?

A. Some women have continued right up to the day of delivery. Most stop or markedly restrict their running during the last two or three months of the pregnancy.

Other Health Benefits

Q. Are there other potential health benefits for women who run?

A. There are at least two others.

First, running frequently cures constipation, a problem which often plagues otherwise healthy women. Constipation seems invariably to be the result of physical inactivity and improper diet. Running improves intestinal activity, and runners also usually consume a relatively high carbohydrate, high roughage diet which is less constipating.

Second, running may also slow the development of a common bone disorder called osteoporosis, which is characterized by a loss of bone density and size. Women after the menopause seem particularly likely to develop osteoporosis, which may be caused by a combination of physical inactivity plus hormonal and nutritional deficiencies. The stress of running on the bones of the legs, pelvis, and hips seems to strengthen them and, while it is still too early to be certain about this, may slow the development of osteoporosis.

CHAPTER 12

Running for Children

Q. IN THE Introduction you stated that this book was primarily aimed toward people over 30 who wanted to begin to run and to those who had potential or real heart problems. Why then a chapter devoted to children?

A. Because increasing numbers of young children are running, and most seem to come from families in which the parents also run. Many of your children may already be running with you. Or you may wonder if it is safe to persuade them to begin. Since many parents have asked me about this, I will try to summarize the scanty evidence.

I had been relatively oblivious to the fact that many children were running long distances. My first real encounter, a rather dramatic one, came at about the fifteenth mile of my first marathon, in 1977 in New York. Marathons were still a bit strange to New Yorkers then, and they were much more reserved than the Boston Marathon crowds. I was beginning to tire a little, feeling a bit low and wondering how I could possibly struggle through the next 11 miles, when suddenly the crowd began to roar. I looked back, but I saw nothing particularly unusual, just a pack of plodding, middle-aged runners like myself, none likely to evoke such a response. Yet the roar persisted. Only several minutes later did I find the reason. There, slowly coming up behind us, was a little blonde boy, reaching barely to our waists, who could have been no older than 5 or 6. He was running with an adult, his father I presumed. He slowly passed our pack.

During long races one looks for any possible incentive to stir one's sagging psyche and weakening muscles. The sight of this mere child passing me provided the stimulation I needed to quicken my pace. We passed each other at least a dozen times during the rest of the race. To this day I do not remember who won our personal duel.

I was much too tired to talk to the child or his father during the race, but I had plenty of time to think about the wisdom of a child that young running a marathon. My immediate reaction, like many of our reactions to strange, somewhat unexpected encounters, was totally negative. "This is clearly wrong. This kid is too young. He is going to hurt himself. He will do irreversible damage to his bones and joints." I silently chastised his father for pushing him to do it.

Yet I had to admit that the child actually seemed to be enjoying himself. Obviously, he must have liked to run or he never would have been able to train hard enough to finish a marathon. Perhaps it wasn't so crazy.

At the finish line I looked around. A few young children had already finished. More gradually arrived. I decided then to see if there was any evidence that long distance running could harm them.

Is It Safe?

The comments that follow apply to all children before the time of puberty, but clearly the potential physical and psychological risks of running seem greater the younger the child.

My own brief search of the literature, as well as direct questioning of orthopedic surgeons and podiatrists, produced no clear facts. Almost nothing had previously been written about running for children. Yet everyone I asked had his own opinions. Many believed that the thinner, weaker bones of youngsters might be damaged. They were particularly concerned about the epiphyses,

those areas near the ends of the long bones that control the growth rate of the bone. They were also worried that the joints themselves might be injured by the repetitive stress of running before they were fully developed. Since there simply were no data, the consensus seemed to be that it would be silly to take any chances, and that long distance running probably should be discouraged. Yet a vocal minority felt just the opposite. They had not seen any harm done by running and were inclined to let children go ahead if they wanted to.

There are other reasons for being concerned about the safety of long distance running. Children are less able to withstand the extremes of temperature. They may be particularly susceptible to dehydration in hot weather, since they usually can't be persuaded to drink before they are thirsty. Also their skin surface area, which helps define the rate of water loss, is high compared to their body mass, making them more prone to excessive water loss during hot weather. In cold weather, the opposite seems true. Their relatively large surface area, through which they lose heat, makes it more difficult for them to maintain normal body temperature.

I also asked several psychiatrists about the psychological aspects of running. Were the kids who ran the victims of ambitious parents, the runners' counterpart of the Little League father? While many kids ran because they wanted to, the psychiatrists agreed that some of the children undoubtedly were unduly influenced by their families. Children saw their parents running and wanted to join them. Conscious or unconscious encouragement followed, so they continued to run.

The psychiatrists felt that most children were not psychologically constituted to continue the high intensity of training necessary to run long distances. For those who could, however, there seemed to be no real psychological danger from running itself. What they did fear was that the intense competition which might evolve during races might not be healthy for most children. Moreover, it might produce a bunch of kids who were heroes at age 10 and burnt out and bored 15. Still, there were certainly many children for whom racing and competition might have salutary benefits. Running might be for them a way to reduce aggression and increase self-esteem. In general, the psychiatrists recommended that if children did run, age-group competition and striving for records should definitely be deemphasized.

Will Early Training Help Later Performance?

Another fascinating, but as yet unanswered question, is whether training begun at such an early age can significantly improve adult performance. We have always thought that the decade between ages 25 and 35 was the best for distance runners. Is this really true physiologically? Or is it just because most runners begin intensive distance training rather late? Will kids who run 5 to 10 miles a day at age 5, provided they have the right genes to begin with, be better distance runners when they are in their later twenties? Or will they peak and wear out early, like many swimmers?

As long as no injuries occur, it makes physiological sense to me that training bones, joints, and muscles still in their growth or formative period might well produce better running performance later. Why should distance running be different from other sports, or even from playing the piano or violin? We should soon learn the answers to these questions. Enough children have been running long enough to provide the needed information within the next several years.

Suggestions For Parents

Q.   What is your advice to parents?

A.   Let your kids run if they really want to. Most will probably stop after a few weeks because they will be bored. But if they continue, don't push them to run more than a few miles each day. If they want to go further, the initiative must be theirs entirely.

One of my children has recently begun to run with me, and it has been fun for both of us. I look forward to our runs because it's a regular opportunity to be alone together. Talking and expressing deeper feelings seem easier during this time. Indeed, I have become so fond of these interludes that I must continually curb my desire to prolong them by pushing her, consciously or unconsciously, to run longer distances with me. Don't let yourself fall into this trap, either. Your child will probably get bored and stop, or hurt himself by too much running.

241

Also always remember that rapidly growing children may be very vulnerable to any underlying orthopedic abnormalities. These must be looked for and corrected. A child's feet will grow with dismaying rapidity. Be prepared to buy new shoes regularly and always be sure the shoes fit well. Most kids are also certain not to take care of their shoes. You must check their heels regularly.

Make sure that your child drinks plenty of water in hot weather, or is warmly dressed in layers if he runs in the cold. Finally, prepare yourself for that time when your child, instead of plodding alongside or behind you, will become impatient with your slow pace and run on, leaving you behind. Then both of you may have to look elsewhere for companionship.

CHAPTER 13

The Social Side of Running

RUNNING CAN unite or disrupt a family. It has become a new way to meet friends. It often helps provide useful group therapy. It can change your self-image and even your major interests. In short, its social effects can be enormous.

The Family

Q. How does running change the family?

A. If both wife and husband run, the possible benefits are obvious. If the kids join them, so much the better. But if one of the couple runs much farther or faster, problems may arise. Men particularly may have trouble adjusting to wives who are better runners. One husband I know refers rather sneeringly to his marathon-running spouse as "my wife, the jock." Perhaps his metaphor is a bit mixed, but his feelings seem clear. He ran for several months, and actually was beginning to enjoy it. But he never was able to come close to his wife's ability, so he stopped.

His was probably not the best solution. The problems are undoubtedly worse when only one of the couple runs, particularly if he or she is really addicted. I speak from experience. My long-suffering family shudders quietly each time I announce plans to enter another marathon. They are all too aware how much my intensified training program will alter their daily routine. Dinner will invariably be late. Household repairs and chores never seem to be done. The grass will grow menacingly high. Even bills will not be paid on time. It would be easier for everyone if I ran in the morning before the day really begins for them. That is the time I would recommend if your family gets restless. But my creaking bones and muscles rebel, so I must wait until later.

Even if your family somehow adjusts to these demands, they may not survive the change running may make in you. If you are not careful, much of your conversation, indeed an increasing part of your social interaction, will revolve around running, to the increasing consternation and boredom of nonrunners. For your family's sake, I urge you to avoid other runners off the road or track as much as you can.

There are a couple of other important considerations. Many runners loudly proclaim the marvelous change running has made in their sex lives. They have once more become proud of and in tune with their bodies, and these feelings are often associated with more rewarding sexual activity. But the opposite can also happen. If your training program is intense, and running consumes much of your leisure time, you may be too tired or busy for a rewarding sex life. Moreover, a newly sleek spouse may prove very threatening to an overweight partner.

Runners as Social Bores

I have probably attended my last "carbohydrate-loading" party, at least if I plan to take my wife.

The Saturday night before the last Boston Marathon we were invited to such a party. I had a fine time. At least one, but often both, members of the couples were runners. We talked about running all evening, stuffed ourselves with carefree abandon, and quenched our thirsts, certain not only that what we were doing was fun, but that it would surely enhance our performance 36 hours later. My wife, on the other hand, had a miserable time. She is reasonably tolerant of my fondness for running, but her idea of a stimulating evening does not include listening to a bunch of runners discussing nothing else. She swears that she has no real prejudices against runners, and I tend to believe her. She would feel the same way about groups of engineers, surgeons, businessmen, or college professors who talked only about their jobs.

At your next party, watch the runners. They swoop together to corners, swapping tall stories about new training techniques, marvelous new shoes, and particularly about their real or imagined injuries. (Runners love to talk about their injuries to other runners.) Or they will socialize with nonrunners, which is worse, since they bore them with tales of how marvelous they feel and how much newly found energy they have acquired. (Note that runners rarely mention their injuries to nonrunners.) They pontificate at great length about how much one is missing if one does not run. It is your responsibility as a runner, if you see someone behaving this way, to lead him gently, but forcefully, back to the runners' corner, where at least he will bore only other runners.

Q. Do people at social gatherings bother you with questions about running?

A. I would hardly call it a bother. They used to ask me about their rheumatism or gall bladders once they found out I was a doctor. Now it's running, and I am often only too eager to respond at great length, again much to the consternation of my wife, family, and nonrunning friends. But I am improving. With great effort, I can sometimes restrain myself and change the subject, or at least direct my questioner to the runners' corner.

Improving Our Social Image

To improve our social image and keep the party invitations coming, I propose that we runners resolve the following:

1. Absolutely never introduce the subject of running in social situations when nonrunners are present. If someone else is unwise enough to bring it up, change the subject to politics, the weather, or sex.

245

2. When asked if you run, smile modestly with downcast eyes, and answer "A little." Avoid further questions. If this tactic is unsuccessful, above all be modest!
3. If you cannot possibly avoid talking about running, do so in a distant corner with no more than one or two runners. If more of you gather together, the hostess may think you are ruining her party. Even worse, she may come to join the discussion herself.
4. Never wear running shoes to parties or other social events. It is gauche, and something only a nonrunner might do.
5. Stop feeling so important. No matter what your speed and distance, there are thousands of people who are still much better than you are.

Effective Community Action

Instead of boring your friends and relatives, channel your enthusiasm for running in more productive directions. If you believe that running is important, an effective way to make people feel and look better, and to promote good health, then consider taking responsibility for promoting it in your community and place of employment. Lobby for safe, interesting running trails and tracks. Encourage schools to include running in their physical education programs. Seek sponsorship for running clinics and fun runs by business, professional, and civic groups. Promote the establishing of supervised running programs for those who need them.

If all of us, physicians and laymen alike, work together, I believe we have the potential to do more to improve our health and the quality of our lives than wonder drugs and scientific breakthroughs can possibly accomplish. We should all, therefore, be responsible for providing an environment which promotes and supports running as well as other types of aerobic activity for all age groups and classes of our society.

Glossary

ACCLIMATIZE. To adapt to a new or different climate or temperature.

ADRENALINE (*see* Epinephrine).

AEROBIC. Requiring oxygen.

AEROBIC ACTIVITY OR EXERCISE. (*Also* dynamic, isotonic.) Exercise performed, using large muscle groups, at an intensity low enough so that all the energy (ATP) required for muscular work is produced from the complete metabolism of glucose and fatty acids with oxygen.

AEROBIC CAPACITY. (*Also* peak or maximal aerobic capacity or maximal aerobic power.) The amount of oxygen required or used by the body during peak or maximal muscular work. It is a measure of cardiovascular fitness.

ALBUMEN. One of the important proteins of the body. Most of it circulates in the bloodstream.

AMINO ACIDS. Nitrogen-containing compounds from which all proteins are formed.

ANAEROBIC. Not requiring oxygen.

ANAEROBIC EXERCISE OR ACTIVITY. Muscular activity of an intensity so high that the exercising muscle's energy requirements (ATP) cannot be met aerobically. The extra energy is obtained by the metabolism of glucose without oxygen to lactic acid (lactate), which is toxic to the muscles.

ANDROGENS. A group of male sex hormones, the most important of which is testosterone.

ANEMIA. Reduction in the volume of red blood cells by a decrease in their number or size or both.

ANGINA. (*Also* angina pectoris.) Pressure, discomfort, or actual pain in the front of the chest, arms, or jaw, usually provoked by effort or tension. Angina occurs because of an inadequate supply of blood to the heart muscle. Almost all cases of angina are caused by narrowing or blockage of the coronary arteries by atherosclerosis.

ANGIOGRAM. A test performed to define the structure of various parts of the circulatory system by injecting special x-ray dyes and taking a series of x-ray pictures as the dye passes through the circulatory system.

AORTA. The main and largest artery of the body, connected directly to the left ventricle of the heart, which then branches carrying blood to all parts of the body.

ARRHYTHMIA. Irregularity of the pulse; too slow or rapid beating of the heart; or abnormality in the conduction of the heart's impulse to the different parts of the heart.

ARTERY. A blood vessel which carries blood away from the heart to the rest of the body. All arteries, except those in the lungs, carry oxygen-rich red blood for use by the tissues.

ARTERIOSCLEROSIS. (*see* Atherosclerosis).

ATHEROSCLEROSIS. Aging, damage, degeneration, and often thickening and infiltration by fatty substances of the inner layers of the arteries. If this process is severe enough, partial or complete block of blood flow through the arteries may occur. Although the terms "hardening of the arteries" and "arteriosclerosis" do not have precisely the same meaning as atherosclerosis, most people, including physicians, use the terms interchangeably.

ATHLETE'S HEART. A term describing the changes that a regular high level of physical activity will produce in the normal heart. Once thought to be an abnormal condition, these changes are now known to be a normal, indeed desirable, response of the heart to exercise.

ATRIAL FIBRILLATION (*see* Fibrillation).

AUTONOMIC NERVOUS SYSTEM. The part of the nervous system that is not under our voluntary control. Its two major components, the sympathetic and parasympathetic nervous systems, control such important functions as breathing, heart rate and function, blood pressure, and intestinal activity.

ATRIAL FIBRILLATION. An arrhythmia of the heart characterized by irregular, disordered beating of the atria (storage chambers) of the heart.

ATP (adenosine triphosphate; high energy phosphate bonds). The chemical compounds produced by the breakdown of energy sources (chiefly glucose and fatty acids), which provide the energy necessary for muscle contraction and other cellular function.

BALL OF THE FOOT. The prominent part of the bottom of the front of the foot, just behind the toes. It is composed of the ends or "heads" of the five metatarsal bones and forms the front part of the arch of the foot.

BLISTER. A collection of fluid in the outer layers of the skin, usually caused by irritation of the skin, but also sometimes caused by exposure to excessive heat or cold.

BLOOD PRESSURE. The pressure exerted in the arteries by the rhythmic pumping of blood in the arteries by the heart. It can readily be measured in the arms or legs with a blood pressure cuff. The blood pressure has two major phases: SYSTOLIC BLOOD PRESSURE: The peak or highest pressure in the arteries, which is achieved during systole when the heart contracts and expels a large quantity of blood into the arteries. DIASTOLIC BLOOD PRESSURE: The lowest recorded pressure during the period after contraction when the heart is relaxed (diastole). The blood pressure is usually described as "systolic over diastolic," or written as systolic/diastolic. For example: If the systolic pressure is 120 and the diastolic pressure is 80, it will be written as 120/80.

BURSA. Fluid-filled sacs generally located where tendons (the ends of muscles) run over bony prominences near the joints. They are designed to cushion the tendons and prevent irritation and damage.

BURSITIS. Inflammation of a bursa.

CALCIUM. One of the body's important elements, necessary for normal cell and tissue function as well as bone structure. Ample amounts are required in our diets, particularly during periods of growth.

CALLOUS (callus). (1) Thickening or overgrowth of the skin due to chronic friction or irritation. (2) The hard, bone-like substance produced at the fracture line early in the healing phase of a fracture.

CALORIE (calory). Actually, a unit of heat. When the term is used to describe the human body it defines the heat produced by the metabolism or burning of energy sources—carbohydrates, fats, and proteins—in food or body tissues.

CAPILLARIES. Tiny, thin-walled structures between arteries and veins, across which substances are transferred from the arterial blood to the cells or from the cells to be carried away in the venous blood.

CARBOHYDRATE LOADING OR PACKING. A method of increasing the muscle's glycogen (sugar) content by a major increase in the amount of carbohydrate eaten for several days before a race or long run.

CARBOHYDRATES. Substances containing only the elements carbon, hydrogen, and oxygen arranged to form compounds called sugars, which in turn may be joined together in various combinations. SIMPLE CARBOHYDRATES: substances containing only one or two sugar molecules (e.g., table sugar or honey). COMPLEX CARBOHYDRATES: Substances composed of many sugars linked together (e.g., starches and grains).

CARBON DIOXIDE (CO_2). A gas which is one of the end products of all metabolism. It is excreted or exhaled through the lungs.

CARBON MONOXIDE (CO). A toxic, potentially lethal, gas produced by a variety of industrial processes and the burning of gasoline.

CARDIAC. Referring to the heart.

CARDIAC ARREST. Absence of effective beating of the heart.

249

CARDIAC ARRHYTHMIA (*see* Arrhythmia).

CARDIAC OUTPUT. The amount of blood pumped by the heart each minute.

CARDIOVASCULAR. Referring to the heart and the blood vessels which carry blood to the tissues (arteries) and from the tissues back to the heart (veins).

CARDIOVASCULAR FITNESS. The capacity of the body to perform aerobic muscular exercise. Its level is defined by VO_2 Max, the amount of oxygen consumed by the body at peak exercise. Cardiovascular fitness can be improved by the regular performance of aerobic exercise.

CATECHOLAMINES. Hormones and transmitter substances formed in the cells of the sympathetic nervous system and the adrenal gland, necessary for the function of the sympathetic nervous system. The two most important are epinephrine (adrenaline) and nor-epinephrine (nor-adrenaline).

CHARLEY HORSE. Pain usually caused by a pull, tear, or inflammation of muscle fibers.

CHLORIDE. An important element often present in combination with sodium to form common table salt or sodium chloride (NaCl).

CHOLESTEROL. One of the major fats or lipids contained in both food and the body's cells and fluids. Its level can be measured in the blood. High levels of cholesterol are associated with an increased risk of atherosclerosis.

CHONDROMALACCIA. Literally, "softening of the cartilage." In this book, the term is used to describe the disease of the cartilaginous, inner surface of the patella commonly referred to as "runner's knee."

COLLATERAL BLOOD VESSELS. Small blood vessels formed in the body in response to blockage of arteries, which bypass or divert blood around the blockage and deliver it to the tissues ordinarily supplied by the blocked artery.

CORE TEMPERATURE (central temperature). The temperature inside the body itself, usually estimated accurately by obtaining the rectal temperature. Oral or mouth temperatures are often falsely low as a measure of core temperature.

CORONARY (coronary occlusion, coronary thrombosis). (*See also* Myocardial infarction.) A term used to describe damage to the heart muscle. A more accurate term is "myocardial infarction."

CORONARY ANGIOGRAM. A test which involves direct injection of x-ray due into the coronary arteries.

CORONARY ARTERIES. The arteries which bring oxygen-rich blood to heart muscles.

CORONARY DISEASE. Abnormalities of the coronary arteries. Most coronary disease is caused by atherosclerosis, which narrows or blocks one or more of the coronary arteries.

CPR (cardiopulmonary resuscitation). The method of restoring effective function of the heart and lungs after cardiac arrest.

CRAMP. Severe, painful, sustained muscle contraction.

DEHYDRATION. Reduction in the amount of water in the body.

DIABETES MELLITUS (diabetes). An abnormality of carbohydrate (sugar) metabolism characterized by abnormally high blood sugar levels and often by the appearance of sugar in the urine. Most cases of diabetes are caused by an absolute or relative lack of insulin, the hormone made by the pancreas which is necessary for the entrance of sugar (glucose) into the cells of the body.

DIAPHRAGM. The large muscle which separates the chest and abdominal cavities.

DIAPHRAGMATIC BREATHING. Breathing caused by contraction and relaxation of the diaphragm. As the diaphragm contracts during inhalation, it moves toward the abdomen, enlarging the lung cavity and drawing air into the lungs. The abdominal contents are simultaneously pushed outward and down. As the diaphragm relaxes, it moves upward, reducing the volume of the lungs and expelled air from them (exhalation).

DIASTOLE. The period between heart contractions when the heart is relaxed and able to fill with blood.

DIASTOLIC BLOOD PRESSURE (see Blood pressure).

DIETARY FIBER. Constituents of foods which cannot be digested (absorbed) by the body and are excreted largely unchanged in the stools. High fiber diets provide bulk for adequate stool production, often produce a satisfied or full feeling without excessive calorie intake, and are high in complex carbohydrates and low in fat.

DYNAMIC EXERCISE (see Aerobic exercise).

ELECTROCARDIOGRAM (ECG, EKG). The electrical activity of the heart, usually recorded at rest on special paper.

EMPHYSEMA. Chronic lung disease characterized by stretching, loss of elasticity, and overinflation of the lung tissue with breakdown and disruption of the alveoli or tiny air sacs where gas exchange in the lungs takes place (oxygen from the lungs into the bloodstream and carbon dioxide from the bloodstream to the lungs). Emphysema has many possible causes. By far the most common is a combination of smoking and aging of the lung tissue.

EMPTY CALORIES. Food and drink generally containing simple sugars which offer no other nutritional benefit such as minerals, vitamins, fiber, etc. Examples are hard candy, alcohol, and table sugar.

ENDOTHELIUM. The inner lining of the heart and blood vessels (arteries and veins).

ENZYMES. Substances in the cells and body fluids which control the speed at which all biochemical reactions take place within the body.

EPINEPHRINE. (See also Autonomic nervous system, Catecholamines, and Sympathetic nervous system.) One of the important hormones, made chiefly in the adrenal gland, required for function of the sympathetic nervous system.

EPIPHYSES. The parts of bone in which growth occurs. In long bones they are usually located toward the ends of the bones near the joints.

ESTROGENS. Female sex hormones manufactured chiefly by the ovaries.

EXERCISE TEST (exercise ECG, stress test). Measurement of the electrocardiogram and other cardiovascular functions during exercise. It is usually performed on a treadmill or bicycle with gradual increase in the level of exercise performed.

EXTRA SYSTOLE (see Premature beat).

FASCIA. Specialized, fibrous tissue, usually extremely tough and strong, which supports body structures and separates muscle groups.

FATS (lipids). Chemical compounds which share a common property, the inability to dissolve in water or various body fluids. They are an important source of food and energy and also are important parts of all body cells and tissues. Cholesterol and triglycerides are the most important fats.

FATTY ACIDS. Compounds composed of long chains of carbon atoms which serve as an important source of energy for the body. Fatty acids are part of the triglyceride molecule and are stored in fat tissue in this form. Fatty acids are "saturated" when all the bonds between the carbon atoms are filled and "unsaturated" when the bonds are incomplete.

FEMUR. The single large bone of the upper leg which forms part of both the knee and hip joints.

FIBER (see Dietary fiber).

FIBRILLATION. Random, ineffective, disordered contractions of the heart muscle. ATRIAL FIBRILLATION: Fibrillation present in the upper heart chambers or atria. VENTRICULAR FIBRILLATION: Fibrillation present in the lower or pumping chambers. Unless immediately reversed, ventricular fibrillation is fatal.

FITNESS (see Cardiovascular fitness).

FROSTBITE. The local freezing or injury resulting from the exposure of the skin to cold temperatures. In some instances underlying structures are also injured.

FUELS. Substances used by the muscles for energy production, chiefly carbohydrates and fatty acids.

GASTROINTESTINAL (GI). Literally, referring to the stomach and intestines. Now the term is used to describe all the parts of the body required for the ingestion, absorption, and excretion of foods.

GLUCOSE. The most important of the many different simple sugars present in the body. It is present as well as in many foods.

GLUTEN. A protein contained in wheat and some other grains. Many individuals are sensitive or allergic to foods containing gluten.

GLYCOGEN. The storage form of sugar, primarily in muscles and the liver. It is broken down to glucose to meet the body's energy needs.

HAMSTRINGS. The group of muscles in the back of the thigh involved in movement of both the hip and knee joints.

HEART ATTACK (*see* Myocardial infarction). A very imprecise term, with different meanings to different people. Some use it to describe any severe heart symptom, but it is generally used to describe a myocardial infarction.

HEART MURMURS. Sounds heard through the stethoscope when listening to the heart. In most cases produced by increasing turbulence of the blood as it passes through the heart chambers. Some murmurs are benign or functional. (There is no underlying structural abnormality of the heart to account for them.) Other murmurs are organic and are caused by structural abnormalities within the heart.

HEART VALVES. Four structures which separate the four heart chambers, alternately opening and closing to aid the passage of blood through the heart. The four valves include: (1) The TRICUSPID, between the right atrium and right ventricle; (2) the PULMONIC, separating the right ventricle from the pulmonary artery; (3) the MITRAL, between the left atrium and left ventricle; (4) the AORTIC, separating the left ventricle from the aorta.

HEAT STROKE. An acute, potentially lethal condition which results from excessive fluid loss and marked increase in body temperature, usually caused by intense exercise performed in hot weather without adequate fluid replacement.

HEMATURIA. Blood in the urine.

HEMOGLOBIN. The specialized pigment in the red blood cells which avidly combines with oxygen and carries it to the tissues.

HIGH BLOOD PRESSURE (*see* Hypertension).

HIGH DENSITY LIPOPROTEINS (HDL). (*See also* Lipoprotein.) The lipoprotein which carries cholesterol away from tissues for removal by the liver.

HIGH ENERGY PHOSPHATE BONDS (*see* ATP).

HORMONES. Substances produced by some of the glands in the body which then are carried by the blood to influence the activity of cells and tissues elsewhere. For example, the pancreas produces insulin, a hormone which regulates sugar metabolism in cells throughout the body.

HYPERGLYCEMIA. High blood sugar.

HYPERTENSION. High blood pressure.

HYPOGLYCEMIA. Low blood sugar.

INFARCT OR INFARCTION (*see* Myocardial infarction).

INSULIN. The hormone made by the pancreas which controls a variety of important body processes, including the uptake of glucose into the body's cells.

IRON. An important element required for many body processes, including normal production and function of red blood cells and hemoglobin.

ISOMETRIC EXERCISE. Exercise which requires isometric muscle contraction.

ISOMETRIC MUSCLE CONTRACTION. Contraction or tensing of the muscle without shortening.

ISOTONIC EXERCISE. Aerobic exercise.

ISOTONIC MUSCLE CONTRACTION. Contraction of the muscle which produces shortening.

LABILE HYPERTENSION. Blood pressure that varies, often very rapidly, from normal to elevated levels.

LACTIC ACID (lactate). The end product of the anaerobic metabolism of glucose. High levels of lactic acid which may quickly accumulate during high-intensity anaerobic exercise cause pain and fatigue and interfere with normal muscle function.

LACTASE. A sugar-splitting enzyme in the small intestine which splits lactose (milk sugar) into glucose and galactose.

LACTASE DEFICIENCY. Reduced levels of lactase activity, interfering with lactose breakdown and absorption. Often suggested by abdominal cramps and diarrhea after ingestion of milk or milk products.

LEFT VENTRICLE (see Ventricle). The major pumping chamber of the heart, which pumps blood to the tissues.

LIGAMENT. A band or sheet of fibrous tissues which connects two or more bones, usually within a joint.

LIPIDS (see Fats).

LOW DENSITY LIPOPROTEIN (LDL). The lipoprotein chiefly responsible for transporting cholesterol in the blood.

LIPOPROTEINS. Chemical compounds formed between lipids and proteins to allow transport of the otherwise insoluble lipids in body fluids and blood.

MAGNESIUM. An important element required for normal body function. Regular dietary intake is required for good health. Magnesium is widely present in food.

MAXIMUM AEROBIC POWER (capacity) (see Aerobic capacity).

MAXIMUM EXPECTED HEART RATE. The fastest heart rate for any age group. It tends to fall with age, and is independent of fitness. It can be calculated approximately by subtracting the age from 220.

MAXIMUM OXYGEN CONSUMPTION (see VO_2 and Aerobic activity).

MET (Metabolic equivalent). A term describing, in terms of oxygen consumption and corrected for differences in body weight, the oxygen requirement of physical activity. One MET, the oxygen requirement at rest, equals approximately the consumption of 3.5 milliliters of oxygen per kilogram of body weight per minute.

METABOLISM. All the chemical processes: (1) which contribute to the buildup (anabolism) or breakdown (catabolism) of cells and tissues; (2) in living cells the processes by which energy and the materials needed for continued normal cellular function are produced, utilized, and excreted.

MINERALS. Inorganic substances necessary for normal body function. The body cannot make minerals. They are necessary in our diet and

254

widely present in many foods. Some nutritionists loosely use this term to describe all the chemical elements—e.g., sodium, iron, magnesium, and calcium—which do not appear in elemental form in nature, but rather are combined with other elements to form compounds; e.g. Sodium chloride.

MORTON'S SYNDROME (Morton's toe). A combination of abnormalities of the fore foot, the most obvious of which is a first toe which is shorter than the second, which often causes excessive pronation of the foot during running. A variety of related injuries may be produced by this excessive foot pronation.

MURMUR (*see* heart murmur).

MYOCARDIAL. Referring to heart muscle.

MYOCARDIAL INFARCTION (heart attack). Damage and death of heart muscle (myocardium) caused by inadequate blood supply. It is almost always due to disease (atherosclerosis) of the coronary arteries. Other terms often used (sometimes inaccurately) to describe this same process include coronary, coronary occlusion, coronary thrombosis, heart attack, and MI.

MYOCARDIUM. The heart muscle.

NOR-EPINEPHRINE (nor-adrenaline). A hormone-transmitter substance produced in the nerve endings of the sympathetic nervous system required for the production of most of the important effects of the sympathetic nervous system.

OBESITY. Greater than normal body weight caused by an increased percentage of body fat.

ORTHOTICS. Devices or supports inserted into shoes to correct a variety of musculo-skeletal deformities.

OSTEOPOROSIS. Disease of bone, occurring chiefly in older people, characterized by loss of calcium and supporting tissues and resulting in loss of bone strength, density, and mass.

OXYGEN. A gas present in the air which is vitally necessary for most normal body processes.

OXYGEN CONSUMPTION. (*See also* VO_2 and Aerobic activity.) The quantity of oxygen consumed or required by the body to function at any given time. The amount of oxygen required by a given activity is a method of estimating the intensity of the activity.

OXYGEN DEBT. The amount of oxygen required by the body to metabolize the lactic acid produced by previous anaerobic activity.

PALPITATIONS. (*See also* Premature beats.) A feeling of irregularity, skipping, or jumping of the heartbeat or pulse.

PARASYMPATHETIC NERVOUS SYSTEM (*see* Autonomic nervous system).

PATELLA. The kneecap, the front part of the knee joint.

PELVIS. The large bony structure at the lower end of the spine which forms the low back, part of the hips, and bony area in the groin.

PERISTALSIS. Rhythmic contraction and relaxation of the stomach and intestines which help to digest food and propel it down the intestinal tract.

PHOSPHAGENIC EXERCISE (activity). High-intensity exercise performed for a brief period which uses ATP already stored in the exercising muscles.

PHOSPHORUS. An important element widely abundant in nature and required in the diet. Often combined with oxygen to form phosphates.

PLANTAR FASCIA. The fascia that supports the arch and bottom of the foot.

PODIATRIST. A non-physician specialist trained in the diagnosis and treatment of abnormalities of the feet and related conditions.

POTASSIUM. An important element, in particularly high concentration inside cells. It is widely available in many foods.

PREMATURE BEATS (extra systoles). Heartbeats which come earlier than expected, causing an irregularity of the heartbeat or pulse which may be felt as palpitations. Premature beats may be single or repetitive, occasional or very frequent. They may arise from many parts of the heart and often may be accurately diagnosed by electrocardiography.

PROGESTERONE. A female hormone produced chiefly in the ovaries.

PRONATE. To rotate inward.

PROTEIN. Large chemical molecules made up of various amino acids. Adequate protein intake in the diet is necessary to allow the body to produce the cell and tissue proteins necessary for normal body function.

PULMONARY. Relating to the lungs.

PULSE. The expansion of blood vessels, felt as an impulse or beat, caused by each contraction of the heart. *Arterial pulse*, commonly called "the pulse": The pulse felt when an artery is lightly palpated or touched.

PULSE RATE. The number of pulse beats felt per minute. In most cases this accurately reflects the number of heartbeats per minute.

QUADRICEPS MUSCLE. The four muscles in the front of the thigh. They attach to the lower leg below the knee and extend (straighten) the lower leg.

RED BLOOD CELLS. The cells in the blood whose main function is to carry oxygen to the tissues. These cells give blood its color. When they contain oxygen (in the arteries) they are bright red. After they lose oxygen in the tissues they become darker and bluer (in the veins).

RIGHT VENTRICLE (*see* Ventricles).

RISK FACTORS. In this book, those factors which increase the risk of developing atherosclerosis.

RUNNER'S KNEE. Commonly used to describe any of several overuse injuries in runners involving the knee joint and nearby structures. Some also use this term to refer specifically to chondromalaccia of the patella.

SACROILIAC. Part of the low back and pelvis. The area formed by the sacral and iliac bones on either side of the lower spine.

SALT (NaCl, sodium). (1) Generally referring to common table salt or sodium chloride (NaCl). (2) Sometimes referring only to sodium. (3) A chemical term describing any compound formed by the action of an acid and a base.

SATURATED FATTY ACID (*see* Fatty acid).

SCIATICA. A term referring to symptoms, usually pain, caused by irritation or damage to the sciatic nerve which runs from the lower back and pelvic area down the back of the leg.

SHIN SPLINTS. Generally, a pain in the shin near the bone, caused by injury to structures in that area. Specifically, tears in the shin muscle fibers where they attach to the prominent bone in the front, inner part of the shin.

SODIUM. (*See also* Salt.) An important element, widely present in nature.

SODIUM CHLORIDE (NaCl). Salt.

SPRAIN. Injury to a joint usually involving the ligaments or tendons without fracture or dislocation of the bones that form the joints.

SPUR. A hard, bony projection; for example, heel spurs.

STARCHES. In nutrition, certain types of complex carbohydrates found, for example, in grains and potatoes.

STROKE. Abnormal function in one or more parts of the brain due to interference with its blood supply. Symptoms may include paralysis, altered sensation, inability to speak, or many others. The blood supply may be reduced by narrowing or blockage of the arteries by atherosclerosis, rupture of the artery (ruptured aneurysm), or a blood clot formed in the heart or large arteries and carried to the brain in the bloodstream (embolus).

SUGAR. (*See also* Carbohydrates.) (1) Generally, a chemical term referring to any of a variety of somewhat similar compounds which all contain six carbon atoms plus hydrogen and oxygen arranged in a particular way. (2) Table sugar. (3) Specifically, glucose.

SYMPATHETIC NERVOUS SYSTEM (*see* Autonomic nervous system).

SYSTOLE. The period during the heart cycle when the heart contracts and expels blood into the arteries.

SYSTOLIC BLOOD PRESSURE. (*See also* Blood pressure.) The pressure measured in the arteries when the heart contracts during systole.

TACHYCARDIA. Rapid heartbeat.

TARGET HEART RATE. (1) Generally, that heart rate which defines aerobic activity intense enough to produce a training effect (increase in VO_2 Max). (2) Specifically, between 70 and 85 percent of the age-corrected maximum expected heart rate.

TESTOSTERONE. The major male sex hormone, produced in the testicles.

TRACE MINERALS OR ELEMENTS. Minerals (elements) present in the body in very small amounts.

TRAINING EFFECT. In this book, defined as the increase in maximal oxygen consumption (VO_2 Max) produced by regular performance of aerobic exercise.

TREADMILL TEST (see Exercise test).

TRIGLYCERIDES. Important fats (lipids) which constitute a major source and storage form of energy. Each triglyceride molecule is made up of three fatty acid molecules attached to a compound called glycerol.

TYPE A PERSONALITY. Competitive, ambitious, time-oriented. Individuals with this personality are felt to have an increased risk for developing atherosclerosis.

UNSATURATED FATTY ACIDS (see Fatty acids).

VALVES (see Heart valves).

VARICOSE VEINS. Dilated, tortuous veins, usually in the legs, whose valves are incompetent or damaged.

VASCULAR. Referring to the blood vessels, arteries, capillaries, and veins.

VEINS. Thin-walled blood vessels which return blood to the heart.

VENTRICLES. The lower, muscular pumping chambers of the heart. There are two ventricles: (1) The LEFT VENTRICLE pumps blood rich in oxygen to the rest of the body tissue. (2) The RIGHT VENTRICLE pumps blood poor in oxygen to the lungs.

VENTRICULAR FIBRILLATION (see Fibrillation).

VITAMINS. Chemical substances necessary for normal metabolism. Most vitamins work by acting as necessary co-factors for specific chemical or physiological reactions.

VO_2 Max (maximal oxygen consumption). The maximum amount of oxygen the body can use; that is, the amount of oxygen consumed during maximal physical activity. Also called maximal aerobic power or capacity.

"THE WALL." That point during endurance or aerobic activity, more specifically long distance running, when muscle function is impaired and symptoms occur, presumably because all the muscle's glycogen stores have been used.

ZINC. An element required by the body in trace amounts.

Sources

ASTRAND, P.O. and K. RODAHL. *Textbook of Work Physiology*. 2nd ed. New York: McGraw-Hill, 1970.

BONDY, P.K., and P. FELIG, eds. *Duncan's Diseases of Metabolism*. 7th ed. Philadelphia: W.B. Saunders, 1974.

CLARKSON, O.A., and A.O. MALMBERG, eds. *Coronary Heart Disease and Physical Fitness*. Baltimore: University Park Press, 1971.

FLETCHER, G.F., and J.D. CANTWELL, *Exercise and Coronary Heart Disease*. Springfield, Ill.: Charles C. Thomas, 1974.

HOWALD, H., and J.R. POORTMANS, eds. *Metabolic Adaptation to Prolonged Physical Exercise*. Basil, Switzerland: Birkhauser Verlag, 1975.

HURST, J. WILLIS, ed. *The Heart*. 4th ed. New York: McGraw-Hill, 1978.

KANNEL, W. *The Framingham Heart Study: Habits and Coronary Heart Disease*. Public Health Service Publication No. 1515. Washington, D.C.: U.S. Government Printing Office, 1966.

LEVY; RIFKIND; DENNIS; and ERNST. *Nutrition, Lipids and Coronary Heart Disease*. New York: Raven Press, 1979.

MILVY, PAUL, ed. *The Marathon: Physiological, Medical, Epidemiological and Psychological Studies*. New York: Academy of Sciences, 1977.

NAUGHTON, J.P., and H. K. HELLERSTERN, eds. *Exercise Testing and Exercise Training in Coronary Heart Disease*. New York: Academic Press, 1973.

Nutritive Value of American Foods, Agricultural Handbook No. 456. Washington, D.C.: U.S. Department of Agriculture, 1975.

O'DONOGHUE, DON H., M.D. *Treatment of Injuries to Athletes.* Philadelphia: W.B. Saunders, 1976.

Smoking and Health: A Report of the Surgeon General. Publication No. 79-50066. Washington, D.C.: U.S. Department of Health, Education, and Welfare, 1979.

WATT, B.K., and A.C. MERRILL. *Composition of Foods—Raw, Processed, and Prepared.* Washington, D.C.: U.S. Department of Agriculture, 1963.

WHITE; HANDLER; SMITH; HILL; and LEHMAN. *Principles of Biochemistry.* 6th ed. New York: McGraw-Hill, 1978.

Annotated Bibliography

If you want to read more about running and fitness, the following may help you. I have included only books and periodicals that I personally have found informative. This is by no means a complete list.

ON THE SCIENCE OF RUNNING

ASTRAND, P.O., and K. RODAHL. *Textbook of Work Physiology.* 2nd ed. New York: McGraw-Hill, 1976.
>   For years the bible of exercise physiologists. Make sure to get the second edition, which is more up to date.

JENSEN, C.R., and A.G. FISHER. *Scientific Basis of Athletic Conditioning.* Philadelphia: Lea and Febiger, 1977.
>   Written for the coach, teacher, and graduate student of physical education. The interested layman with some scientific training will find much useful information here.

MILVY, PAUL, ed. *The Marathon: Physiological, Medical and Epidemiological Studies.* Annals of the New York Academy of Sciences, *301,* 1977. *Also* New York: The New York Academy of Sciences, 1977.
>   This huge volume is a gold mine of information about exercise physiology, the medical aspects of running, and the history of the marathon. It is a compendium of papers presented at a conference

held after the New York Marathon, in October 1976. It is strongly recommended, but difficult to find. If it is not available otherwise, you might write directly to the New York Academy of Sciences.

ON CARDIAC REHABILITATION

FLETCHER, G.F., and J.D. CANTWELL. *Exercise and Coronary Heart Disease.* 2nd ed. Springfield, Il.: Charles C. Thomas, 1979.
I have found this the best single volume devoted to cardiac rehabilitation. It is up to date and prudent in its claims and recommendations. The book summarizes the authors' considerable personal experience in this field.

FOR WOMEN

COOPER, MILDRED, and KENNETH COOPER. *Aerobics for Women.* New York: Bantam Books, 1973.
I recommend reading *Aerobics* first. Some women may be sufficiently inspired to go on to this helpful book.

ULLYOT, JOAN. *Women's Running.* Mountain View, Ca.: World Publications, 1976.
The author is a marathoner and scientist. Even though its tone is a bit strident at times, both women and men will find this book helpful and perhaps even inspiring. By far the best book devoted solely to women's running.

FOR HEART PATIENTS

COHN, KEITH; D. DUKE; and J.A. MADRID. *Coming Back: A Guide to Recovering from Heart Attacks and Living Comfortably with Coronary Disease.* Reading, Ma.: Addison Wesley, 1979.
All patients who have heart disease will find this book helpful. It takes a very positive approach to living with a heart problem and discusses the role of exercise intelligently.

GENERAL READING

BENSON, HERBERT. *The Relaxation Response.* New York: William Morrow, 1975.
A scholarly review of meditation techniques, with a description of how these can benefit you.

CALDWELL, JOHN. *Cross-Country Skiing Today*. Brattleboro, Vt.: The Stephen Greene Press, 1977.
>   Must reading for anyone who plans to begin cross-country skiing.

COOPER, KENNETH. *Aerobics*. New York: Bantam Books, 1968.
>   The first "best-seller" by a pioneer in the fitness and running movement. Although published in 1968, it is still reasonably current, and considerably more useful than the author's more recent *The New Aerobics*. Some of you may find his point system appealing.

FIXX, JAMES F. *The Complete Book of Running*. New York: Random House, 1977.
>   Many of you may have already read this book; it was on the best-seller lists for months. It is well written and contains much useful information. The chapter on the Boston Marathon is gem. A little short on the medical aspects of running, and at times a bit inaccurate in some of its scientific discussion.

FRIEDMAN, M., and R. ROSENMAN. *Type A Behavior and Your Heart*. New York: Knopf. 1974.
>   The authors carefully describe the evidence that this personality type is a serious cardiac risk factor. They then describe how this risk can be modified.

MANZI, R.; P. JOKL; and O.W. DAYTON. *The Runner's Complete Medical Guide*. New York: Summit Books, 1979.
>   Fairly detailed advice about running injuries which may save a trip to the doctor. Clearly written for the layman.

MERKIN, G., and M. HOFFMAN. *The Sports Medicine Book*. Boston: Little, Brown, 1978.
>   A useful "how to" book. The chapters on diet and injuries are excellent. At times it is a little too "rah-rah" for my taste.

POLLOCK, M.L.; J.H. WILMONT; and S.M. FOX, II. *Health and Fitness through Physical Activity*. New York: Wiley, 1978.
>   If you are scientifically oriented and prepared to put up with some rather dry writing, you will find much interesting information in this book. It is written by three acknowledged experts in the field of exercise, and is a fairly comprehensive work. Physicians also may find it helpful.

PRITIKIN, N., and P.M. McGrady. *The Pritikin Program for Diet and Exercise*. New York: Grosset & Dunlap, 1979.
>   Buy this book for the recipes. They are excellent and can make a very low fat diet palatable and even interesting. Much of the rest of the book seems based on enthusiastic endorsement, rather than on scientific verification of the alleged benefits of the program.

SHEEHAN, GEORGE. *Medical Advice for Runners*. Mountain View, Ca.: World Publications, 1978.

———. *Running and Being*. New York: Simon and Schuster, 1978.
>   George Sheehan, M.D., is widely regarded as the poet, philosopher, even guru, of the running scene. But there was a time when he

was better known for his knowledge about the medical problems of runners. This is usefully summarized in his first book. The second is devoted to more philosophical matters and consists largely of reprints of articles previously published elsewhere; I found it much less satisfying than the first and at times a bit emotional. Whether you agree with the author's philosophy or not, you will certainly be charmed by his style.

ZOHMAN, LEONORE R. *Exercise Your Way to Fitness and Health.* CPC International, 1974.

I give this small booklet, written by a cardiologist with considerable experience in cardiac rehabilitation, to patients and friends who want to start an exercise program safely. It is not readily available through the usual channels, however.

PERIODICALS

Runner's World.

This magazine has become rather too slick and glossy, but it remains by far the best of the periodicals for the novice. Some experts may prefer *Track and Field News*, but if you have a limited budget, this is the monthly magazine to buy.

The Runner.

Occasional superb articles and an overall excellent layout and photography at times make this newer monthly magazine appealing. Generally it is a pale imitation of *Runner's World*. After all, how much is there to say about running?

TABLE 16. *Metric Equivalents*

VOLUME

1 cubic centimeter (cc) or milliliter (ml) = 1 gram of water
1 liter (L) = 1000 cc or ml, slightly more than a quart
1 ounce = approximately 30 cc or ml
1 pint = a few ml less than half a liter (500 ml)

WEIGHT

1 gram (g) = the weight of 1 ml or 1 cc of water
1 kilogram (kg) = 1000 g, or 2.2 pounds
1 milligram (mg) = 1/1000 of a gram
1 pound = 455 grams

LENGTH

1 meter (m) = 39.37 inches
1 kilometer (km) = 1000 m, or .62 miles
1 mile = 1.6 km
1 centimeter (cm) = 1/100 of a meter
2.54 cm = 1 inch
1 millimeter (mm) = 1/1000 of an inch
10 mm = 1 cm
25.4 mm = 1 inch

TABLE 17. *Metric Conversions*

MILES TO KILOMETERS		KILOMETERS TO MILES	
1	1.6	1	.62
¼	.4	2	1.25
½	.8	4	2.5
2	3.2	6	3.7
4	6.4	10	6.2
6	9.6	16	10
10	16		
26.2	42.2		

Index